SACRED SOUND

SACRED SOUND

Experiencing music in world religions

Guy L. Beck, editor

Wilfrid Laurier University Press

We acknowledge the financial support of the Government of Canada through the Book Publishing Industry Development Program for our publishing activities.

Library and Archives Canada Cataloguing in Publication

Sacred sound : experiencing music in world religions / Guy L. Beck, editor.

Accompanied by a compact disc.
Includes bibliographical references and index.

ISBN-10: 0-88920-421-7
ISBN-13: 978-0-88920-421-8

1. Music—Religious aspects. 2. Music—Philosophy and aesthetics.
I. Beck, Guy L., 1948– II. Title.

ML3921.S123 2006   781.7   C2006-903526-1

Front cover painting by Guru Nanak and Bhai Mardana, from a nineteenth-century manuscript, MSS Panj. D4 (Folio 8v), at the British Library, London; back cover painting by Kajal Beck, "King David Playing His Harp" (from medieval manuscripts). Cover and text design by Pam Woodland.

This book is printed on Ancient Forest Friendly paper (100% post-consumer recycled).

Printed in Canada

CONTENTS

ACKNOWLEDGMENTS

When Dr. Harold Coward and I discussed the idea for a book project on religion and music one evening during the annual meeting of the American Academy of Religion in New Orleans in 1996, we were both aware that it would break new ground. Yet it is largely due to his initiative that the project actually began to take shape by March 2000, when we met again at Louisiana State University in Baton Rouge. After details were worked out, an innovative concept was under way that combined written chapters with author-performances as part of the 2001 Distinguished Lecture Series at the University of Victoria (BC). For his steadfastness and tireless encouragement at every step I wish to sincerely thank Prof. Coward, then director, as well as his staff at the Centre for Studies in Religion and Society at the University of Victoria (BC), including Peggy Faulds of the Division of Continuing Education for her work in coordinating the series.

I also wish to thank each of the contributors for lending their considerable expertise, both as scholars and performers, to this pioneering project. My sincere appreciation goes to Prof. Sanford Hinderlie, College of Music, Loyola University New Orleans, for providing the necessary recording and engineering skills to create the accompanying CD. In addition, my earnest thanks to Brian Henderson and the staff of Wilfrid Laurier University Press for their continued interest in and support for this project that made the final product possible. Lastly, thanks to Kajal, my artist wife, for contributing her illustrations and helping to sustain my efforts through constant encouragement.

Guy L. Beck
Tulane University
New Orleans, 2006

INTRODUCTION

Guy L. Beck

efore embarking on this project, I spent many years observing a wide variety of religious traditions and noting the use of chant and music in each as part of public and private religious practice. Throughout America and Europe, I attended services at Christian churches and cathedrals, Jewish temples and synagogues, Islamic mosques, Sufi centres, meeting places of new religious movements, and many different kinds of retreat centres. In all cases there were tonal recitations, chants, hymns, sacred songs, or other musical numbers that seemed to generate spiritual elation, social cohesion, and empowerment within identifiable communities. Extended excursions to India and Nepal provided similar evidence of how music and chant pervade myriad types of religious worship in the East. Besides visiting traditional Hindu, Buddhist, Jain, and Sikh gatherings, my itinerary included many modern religious organizations. At the end of the day, I determined that there were almost no communities or groups within the major world religions in which chant and music did not play a vital role.

As a trained musician and a historian of religions, I was astonished at the seemingly intrinsic connection between religious ritual and musical activity, despite often radical differences in theological orientation—monotheism, polytheism, pantheism, monism, goddess worship, atheism, animism, spiritualism, and others all have this connection. It was apparent to me that group performances of sacred songs or hymns consolidated various human communities into a religious world of their own, reinforcing identities and boundaries as if by some mysterious thread. In each

1

case, music was the "glue" in the ritual that bound together word and action and also reinforced static social and religious hierarchies, as sociologist Emile Durkheim believed it would. Music and chant were also creative and fluid, helping to bring about newer and more expressive forms of *communitas*, as anthropologist Victor Turner explained in his theory of ritual process. Upon further study and reflection, I formed the opinion that a basic understanding of the role of music and chant in the cultic life of religious communities was desirable—in fact, indispensable—for scholars and students of comparative religion to reach the most accurate and authentic portrait possible of the nature of religious experience. However, an initial survey of the field of religious studies revealed that little attention has been given to this otherwise important dimension of religion.

Similar concerns about the lack of study on the topic of religion and music had been voiced over thirty years ago by S.G.F. Brandon in *A Dictionary of Comparative Religion* (1970): "The connection between music and religion is so generally recognized that it is surprising to find how little work has been done, particularly from the side of comparative religion, in relating the phenomenology of the two." Attempting to peruse the work of anthropologists and musicologists for work on music in religious contexts was equally disconcerting, as Brandon also affirmed: "Musicologists, ethnomusicologists and anthropologists have assembled details of instruments, scales, rhythm, harmony (if any) and performance from many ethnic and religious areas. But, although so much is known about the practical function of music in various contexts, little attention has been paid to its significance as an aspect of religious action." Even historians who examined the development of music seem to have sidestepped the enormous importance of religion in music-making: "Histories of music, which normally cover more or less the same ground, beginning with 'primitive' music and proceeding, via the ancient civilizations, to music in the Orient and the West, frequently tend to overlook the religious significance of their material."[1]

Since the situation highlighted by Brandon has not been sufficiently remedied to date, I continue to share his apprehension that, despite a kind of commonsensical acceptance of the connection between religion and music, there has been a systemic lack of academic attention to this important subject among religious studies teachers and scholars over the past fifty years, with two splendid exceptions. *Sacred Sound: Music in Religious Thought and Practice* (1983), edited by Joyce Irwin, is a very substantial anthology that was both published in a limited edition, and not designed to be a "textbook" of religion and music in world religions, while still exploring some of the theoretical aspects of the intersection of music and religion in specific cases. *Enchanting Powers: Music in the World's Religions*

(1997), a more recently published volume of essays edited by Lawrence Sullivan, also provides the student and reader with expert, in-depth articles on music in a few world religions, but is not well-rounded enough in scope for use as a general textbook. In my own case, I have been teaching courses on religion and music at several institutions over the past decade, yet have not found a satisfactory textbook or anthology of recordings for use in the classroom.

Sacred Sound: Experiencing Music in World Religions is partially designed to fill my immediate need for a textbook and audio anthology for the classroom, by providing an introductory guide for students and scholars in the field, including an accompanying CD of selected examples. While there are numerous instances of purely instrumental music in religion, the focus of the current book and CD is on vocal music, especially chants, hymns, and sacred songs of different varieties that have been memorized and passed down in more-or-less fixed form through succeeding generations to the present, and that continue to renew, invigorate, and transform the lives of religious communities. The essays in this collection are primarily concerned with the role of chant and musical performance of sacred texts in six of the traditional major world religions: Judaism, Christianity, Islam, Hinduism, Sikhism, and Buddhism. In some ways, it is a practical sequel to Irwin and Sullivan, and is designed also to help close the widening gap between religious studies and music. At this point, it is appropriate to sketch some useful guidelines for study and directions for further inquiry, including tips where, and where not, to look.

One of the principal axioms in the academic field of religious studies has been that religion is a universal part of human culture and civilization. Scholars strive to collect data in order to validate the presence of religion in many forms, and then proceed to interpret that data in a variety of ways. A particular religion, including its cultic and social dimensions, is ideally perceived as a kind of "artistic creation" in total human response to the presence of the sacred or the divine, which can be conceived in a variety of ways. As a "work of art," religion then elicits interpretation through the hermeneutical methods of the humanities, rather than through the purely logical explanations employed in the social and natural sciences. Using the terms the phenomenology of religion or the history of religions, scholars in the field of religious studies stress that other religions can be understood or apprehended by outsiders without the necessity of faith, commitment, or cultic participation. Such "empathetic understanding" is without regard to race, gender, nationality, social standing, or religious affiliation.

A common tenet of musicologists and ethnomusicologists is that music is a universal aspect of culture which includes religion as one of its principal components. The field of ethnomusicology has been designed to encompass the wide variety of folk and non-Western musical traditions. Thus, while religion and music are both acknowledged as universal features of human culture and society, it is their special coincidence and association that has been largely overlooked and which beckons our immediate attention.

In Rudolf Otto's classic work in religious studies, *The Idea of the Holy*, there is the view that the feelings associated with music are very similar to feelings of the holy itself, the numinous, which is something "wholly other": "Music, in short, arouses in us an experience and vibrations of mood that are quite specific in kind.... The resultant complex mood is, as it were, a fabric, in which the general human feelings and emotional states constitute the warp, and the non-rational music-feelings the woof.... The real content of music is not drawn from the ordinary human emotions at all, and ... is in no way merely a second language, alongside the usual one, by which these emotions find expression. Musical feeling is rather (like numinous feeling) something 'wholly other.'"[2] Consequently, the human response to music is composed of similar feelings and experiences as toward the numinous, such as *mysterium tremendum* (mystery and awe) and *fascinans* (attraction).

Phenomenologist of religion Gerardus van der Leeuw, in his famous work *Religion in Essence and Manifestation* (1938), stated that "musical expression of the holy occupies an extensive domain in worship. There is hardly any worship without music."[3] In his other major work, *Sacred and Profane Beauty: The Holy in Art* (1963), there is an entire section devoted to "Music and Religion" (part 6, 211–62) that includes subsections entitled "Holy Sound," and the "Theological Aesthetics of Music." Here, he clearly affirms again that "almost all worship uses music ... religion can no more do without singing that it can without the word.... Music represents the great struggle of reaching the wholly other, which it can never express."[4]

After further exploration, however, one discovers that further studies of the connection between religion and music along the lines of Otto and Van der Leeuw's earlier insights are comparatively few. The detailed study of sacred music and chant seems to have played a relatively minor role in the overall development of the phenomenology of religion, comparative religion, or the history of religions. Consequently, discussions of music and chant are conspicuously absent in the foundational works of these fields, by pioneer scholars such as Joachim Wach (1958), Mircea Eliade (1958, 1959, 1978, 1982, 1985), Joseph M. Kitagawa (1966, 1967, 1987), Raffaele Pettazzoni (1967), Ninian Smart (1973), and Jacques Waardenburg (1973). Moreover, music is almost completely neglected in discussions regarding current theories and methods in religious studies, such as those found in the work of Thomas Ryba (1991), Robert A. Segal (1992), Daniel L. Pals (1996), Mark C. Taylor (1998), Willi Braun and Russell T. McCutcheon (2000), and Carl Olson (2003).

The coverage given by general reference and teaching materials makes the need for this collection even more apparent. Many of the basic reference dictionaries and encyclopedias on religion and world religions avoid treatment of music and chant. For example, *The Perennial Dictionary of World Religions* (1989), edited by Keith Crim et al., *The HarperCollins Dictionary of Religion* (1995), edited by Jonathan Z. Smith, and *Merriam-Webster's Encyclopedia of World Religions* (1999), edited by Wendy Doniger, carry no entries on music. The first edition of R.C. Zaehner's otherwise balanced treatment of the major faiths in the world, *Concise Encyclopaedia of Living Faiths* (1959), is also silent on the role of chant or music. The exception among major reference works is, of course, the multi-volume *Encyclopedia of Religion* (1987), edited by Mircea Eliade, of which volume 10 (163–215), contains several articles that discuss the role of music in important religious traditions. The new second edition (2005) of this work, edited by Lindsay Jones, contains updated revisions of these articles, along with new entries on music and religion. A decade after Eliade's original work, the *Oxford Dictionary of World Religions* (1997), edited by John Bowker, reaffirmed the importance of music by stating that "music...has been a major part of all religions. It has powers to alter and match moods, to sustain and evoke emotion, to induce trance or 'ecstasy' states, to express worship, and to entertain."[5]

In reference works on religion for popular consumption, there are mixed tidings. Gregg Stebben's *Everything You Need to Know about Religion* (1999) does not mention sacred music at all, yet John Renard's *The Handy Religion Answer Book* (2002) has useful subsections within each chapter "Are Music and Dance Important in Religious Ritual?"

In education, most of the standard college textbooks on world religions currently available do not discuss the subject of music and chant in religion: see, for example, Huston Smith (1958, revised 1991), Geoffrey Parrinder (1971), John Fenton (1993, 2001), Niels C. Nielson, Jr. (1993), Lewis M. Hopfe and Mark R. Woodward (2001), Mary Pat Fisher (2002), David S. Noss (2003), Robert S. Ellwood and Barbara A. McGraw (2005), and William A. Young (2005). An exception can be found in Theodore Ludwig's text, *Sacred Paths of the East* (2001):

> The art of music has been found to be a powerful presenter of the sacred in almost all religions. The beautiful sounds of music—gripping rhythm, haunting melody, special qualities of different instruments—reach to deep levels of aesthetic sensibility and express many different aspects of

the experience of the sacred. It is particularly powerful when words are wedded to music in sacred chants, mantras, hymns, and the like. The art of music, whether a solitary flute or the ringing "Hallelujah Chorus" of Handel's *Messiah*, gathers and directs spiritual emotions and evokes the sacred presence as no other art does.[6]

Reflecting Rudolf Otto's early assessment, Gary E. Kessler's *Studying Religion: An Introduction through Cases* (2003) states simply that "Music, like religion, has the power to transform human life and to transport us into another time and place."[7]

Paralleling the present textbook situation, current university programs in religious studies and musicology have tended not only to be mutually exclusive but often to proceed in entirely separate directions. Unless musically trained, religion and theology professors have hesitated to bring music into their classes, and music instructors who have trained only in musicology often avoid questions of religious meaning as well as theological issues. Religious studies courses have all too often concentrated mostly on the study of texts, doctrines, and beliefs, coupled with discussion of the social history of religious communities. Inquiries into the actual experiences of believers in the embodied context of worship have been conspicuously lacking, experiences that invariably involve tonal or musical activity. Sharing this view, Vivian-Lee Nyitray, a professor of religion, recalled that "in the classroom, apart from music punctuating the occasional documentary, religion was a surprisingly quiet field of study."[8] In classes on ethnomusicology and music history, instructors normally give considerable attention to the scale and rhythm systems of various world cultures, along with surveys of musical instruments. While useful in themselves, students are often left to draw their own connections between the musical traditions discussed and the actual religious rituals and cultic life that are almost always relevant to them. Moreover, the subcategory "sacred music" in music department curricula is misleading, usually referring to choral art music of the Christian tradition which is then studied independently of its liturgical and theological context.

Some hints of pedagogical change are appearing, however. A team of scholars associated with the American Academy of Religion contributed to a recent *Religious Studies News* issue (Spring 2001) devoted to teaching religion and music. In this feature, several authors, including myself, argued that since chant and music are intrinsically related to religion, and since sacred vocal utterances are well-nigh universal, the topic of music belongs within any classroom presentation of religion. In their articles, Stephen Marini of Wellesley College observed that "sacred music is an intrinsic element of virtually every religious culture," and Carol M. Babiracki of Syracuse University stated that "music and dance performances are intrinsic to the practice of religion throughout the world."[9]

As Brandon also suggested, the study of religion by musicologists and ethnomusicologists presents another imbalance. While the *New Harvard Dictionary of Music* (1986), edited by Don Michael Randel, does not have an entry on religion, the multi-volume *Garland Encyclopedia of World Music* (2000), edited by Bruno Nettl and Ruth M. Stone, contains numerous articles that describe and explain music in various religious contexts. The reader is also well-rewarded by consulting the articles on various religions in the second edition of the multi-volume *New Grove Dictionary of Music and Musicians* (2001), edited by Stanley Sadie, and some specific forms of religious music are discussed in textbooks by Jeff Titon (1984) and Kay Shelemay (2001). Fortunately, the renowned ethnomusicologist Bruno Nettl has, for now, more or less settled the issue of the role of music in religion with this broadly conceived statement in his popular textbook, *Excursions in World Music* (2001): "In all societies, music is found in religious ritual—it is almost everywhere a mainstay of sacred ceremonies—leading some scholars to suggest that perhaps music was actually invented for humans to have a special way of communicating with the supernatural."[10]

The academic distance between the study of religion and the study of music in the West, however, is not due to any apparently conscious decision on the part of scholars. In an attempt to diagnose the problem, I suggest that at least two major reasons for this neglect lie in European approaches to the ideas of religion and music. First, much confusion resides in the misguided understanding that "religion" is merely a set of beliefs and doctrines incorporated in scripture and sacred texts. The extreme stress on "silent textual study" in modern academic religious studies, to the detriment of oral traditions, betrays certain Protestant attitudes towards scripture as being primarily a written document that is read quietly in private space. In this tradition, direct access to the meaning of a sacred text is thought to be available to the devout regardless of the original language, as exemplified by the English King James Bible (1611). This notion may have worked well within Protestant circles, but does not faithfully or accurately represent other religious world views. The overall shift from hearing scripture recited aloud in liturgical languages by priests in churches or temples to the reading of the vernacular printed word in churches and private homes has opened the way to the modern Western academic attachment to written language as the primary carrier of religious meaning.

To redress this imbalance, we need to recall that prior to the Western Renaissance and Reformation and the invention of the printing press, sacred texts in virtually all religious traditions, including Judaism and Christianity, were recited orally, sung, or somehow intoned musically.

From the beginnings of their respective traditions, devout prophets, chazzans, cantors, priests, friars, ministers, mullahs, imams, pundits, gurus, swamis, *rāgīs*, *bhikkhus*, roshis, monks, and others have chanted and sung Jewish psalms, Christian hymns, Qur'ānic verses and Islamic calls to prayer, Vedic verses, Hindu *ślokas* and *bhajans*, Sikh *shabads*, and Buddhist sūtras. Oral practice was often upheld as statutory, and formally sustained within the traditions themselves. As Hebrew scholar Joshua R. Jacobson notes, "Jewish law requires that ritual texts be chanted."[11] The Qur'ān in Islam is not considered authentic when it is studied in translation or read silently, with the highest accolades given to those who memorize the entire text in Arabic, demonstrating their skills in unaided oral recitation. Buddhist sūtras and mantras are almost always chanted or intoned aloud, as are the important Sikh prayers and songs. For thousands of years Hindu dharma (law) forbade the writing or reproducing of certain holy texts, with serious penalties for violation. The Vedas are believed to have been passed down orally for over three thousand years, and the chanting and hearing of sacred verses and mantras, often regardless of the comprehension of meaning, still constitutes the most common form of access to scripture for the pious multitude of Hindus.

Consequently, the purely silent approach to religious studies easily forgets to treat "Holy Scripture" as a "living text." And while anthropologists and sociologists often consider texts in terms of their authoritative function within a community, the holy text is not merely a living text in that sense. It is also a "breathing" text, which is accessible to millions of believers primarily by hearing it chanted or sung. Whether or not the semantic meaning of the text is understood, and there is a body of evidence that supports it is not in many traditions, it is really the power of the oral form of the scriptural text that truly invokes emotional, intuitive, and memory-laden processes in the majority of religious practitioners.[12]

Drawing on a comparison from history may help to illustrate this point. The philosopher and historian R.G. Collingwood once remarked that understanding history is best achieved if historical events are re-enacted in the human mind. To understand religion, then, one may mentally re-enact religious situations of worship or liturgy. But, unlike historical situations, religious situations are incomplete in silence, and inaccessible through the silent study of texts. Description may lead to critical reflection, but we argue that both of these silent techniques are ineffective for a complete understanding of religion. Encountering and incorporating sacred sound enhances the ability to understand religion at its deepest levels. Less involved with mere musical analysis (musicology), the purpose of this book is to assist in achieving the goal of a more authentic and accurate understanding of the ritual context of music in religious life. In this way, we discover that music and chant are most often located at the core of religious life in any culture, tied in with ritual and liturgical action. Just as it is unthinkable to approach or understand a religious liturgy without the oral dimension, it is just as impossible to effectively penetrate a religious tradition without the musical dimension.

A second reason for the divide between the studies of religion and music is that a persistent dichotomy between religion and culture has tended to separate academic studies of religion and music in the West. When the German philosopher Immanuel Kant postulated a realm of aesthetics separate from religious experience in the late eighteenth century, he forged a distinction that endured into the early twentieth century. According to his reasoning, religion and music should be viewed as separate aspects of the human enterprise that were each associated, in the fashion of German theologians Friedrich Schleiermacher and Albrecht Ritschl, with a single psychic function. In practical terms, this meant that the temple and the concert stage were considered venues for separate genres of musical performance: one for religious experience, and the other for aesthetic or secular amusement. Rudolf Otto challenged this Kantian distinction in 1917, by bringing the aesthetic dimension of music into closer proximity to religious experience, or what he called the "numinous."

Many recent theologians have begun to reject this strict separation of music and religion, since religion, more broadly defined, is now believed to permeate culture and society more thoroughly than previously thought. This dichotomy has been circumvented most visibly by progressive theologians and historians of religion who assert that the sacred is to be found in all dimensions of culture, including the secular. In Protestant theology, Paul Tillich (1959) and David Harned (1966) have maintained that religion is the substance of culture and that culture is the form of religion, whereby no irreligious art is, ultimately, possible. In Russian Orthodox thought, Nicolas Berdyaev has pondered how art is essentially a religious phenomenon. Moreover, current works by Andrew Greeley (1989) and Richard Viladesau (2000) within the Roman Catholic tradition affirm the legitimate place of the theological analysis of culture in all its forms of expression. In the field of natural theology, Anthony Monti (2003) has recently affirmed that the arts are theological by their very nature and not simply when they are explicitly religious, arguing that works of art convey the real presence of God, even when not labelled as such.

By seriously considering music and demonstrating its central role in a number of world religions, this book also serves to reject the Kantian dichotomy. Music and chant can no longer be viewed as marginal to religious experience or as gratuitous to some kind of theoretical religious enterprise, but must be seen as integrated into deep primary levels of religious meaning throughout world history. The former dichotomous situation may be the case in certain contexts both east and west, in much the same way as "classical" music has gained a separate and privileged status as a form of elite entertainment. Yet, from a newer global perspective, religion is much more than stated doctrine and belief, since it is woven throughout the fabric of all cultures and societies. Accordingly, religious music often unveils the core or mystery of a faith tradition in ways that elude theology, philosophy, linguistics, historiography, literary criticism, or the social sciences. Enlarging upon Rudolf Otto's notion of the holy or "numinous" as beyond the scope of reason and morality, the findings in this collection demonstrate that the holy or "sacred," as a category of practical human experience, does not truly exist in a vacuum, nor solely in the intellect or merely in silence, but as consistently bound up with vocal and musical expression.

Thus, the overall importance of chant and music for the study of religion can be seen to be inestimable: there is virtually no religious tradition in the course of history that has not given primacy to oral articulation and transmission through sacred chant or music. For most religions throughout history, myths and sacred stories seem to have been embodied not only in written literature but, more importantly, in musical performance, combining vocal and instrumental music and, often, dance. Both vocal and instrumental music have functioned together in very significant ways to bridge the gap between the realms of myth and ritual. Musical instruments, whether played solo or in ensembles, are frequently a vital part of religious observances, though there are instances where only vocalization has been considered proper for religious worship, such as in medieval Judaism, Islam, and Theravāda Buddhism. In almost every culture worldwide music and musical instruments are believed to have divine origin. We may easily forget that, in Western culture, music is the only art or craft that is actually named after a divinity or divinities: the Greek Muses. In India, as in ancient Greece, the gods themselves play musical instruments, and even though the Bible holds that music was "invented" by the human Jubal, this occurred in the earliest period of the patriarchs. In the Islamic record, the instruments of the Arabs, such as the ud, also are attributed to the same patriarchs.

The successful pursuit of the comparative study of sacred song or religious music therefore requires a refined approach within the discipline of religious studies, drawing upon several related disciplines like linguistics, psychology, theology, musicology, ritual studies, and liturgical studies. While religion itself may be studied from a variety of approaches, many scholars affirm that the most effective method of integrating these different disciplines and maintaining religion or the sacred as an autonomous category at the same time is that of the phenomenology of religion, sometimes referred to as the history of religions. This method does not evaluate a particular religion, much less try to prove or disprove the truth of its claims or practices. Phenomenology of religion aims to understand religion as a human phenomenon, both in a broad sense and in its specialized expressions, as an accepted fact of history and experience. A basic premise of this approach, one that distinguishes it from other disciplines, is the awareness that understanding a religion, especially one that is foreign to the student or scholar, is only possible when there is the recognition of its absolute value for the believers. While the existence and true nature of God—the divine, Supreme Being, and so on—is debated in disciplines such as theology and philosophy of religion, the goal of the phenomenologist or historian of religions is to understand and interpret the various religions of the world in ways that are intelligible to the larger human community. This necessarily involves developing a distinct symbolic language with which to describe, classify, and reflect upon the multitude of religious expressions found around the world. Technical terms such as the sacred, profane, numinous, hierophany, *axis mundi*, *illo tempore*, rites of passage, and eschatology, for example, tend to have a more-or-less stable meaning throughout the discipline, in addition to more generally accepted categories like myth, ritual, scripture, deity, community, initiation, priesthood, and liturgy. None of these terms are limited to a specific religion or context, and so serve to enhance the universality of the discipline, which, by its very nature, is comparative.

There are some theoretical approaches found in scholarship in related disciplines such as linguistics and psychology that may initially help us understand why sound and orality are primary in the transmission of religious texts and traditions. In his important work *The Presence of the Word* (1967), Walter Ong explains how the sonic dimension of reality functions in special ways that are different from the other sense experiences. For him, sound conveys or reveals presence more than the tactile or the visual senses. Since sound expresses the interiority of people more than other sense experience, including movement and gesture, it best serves to bind people together in a religious community. David Burrows, in his *Sound, Speech, and Music* (1990), builds upon this premise by arguing that since song originates deeper in the human body than speech, and as there is less semantic intention in singing as opposed to speaking, it is the musical or tonal dimension of sound, rather than mere speech, that more fully unites people instead of dividing them. In terms of religion, the goal of uniting believers of any persuasion into a unified community is more readily achieved when there is a commonly understood frame of reference shared by all members. Within the context of a sacred text or teaching, the tonal dimension of language serves to bring that text or teaching more effectively into a common symbolic realm. Accordingly, key religious texts in all the world's religious traditions are almost always sung or chanted in some form of tonal performance rather than merely read aloud. Characterized by scholars like Rudolf Otto as symbolizing or expressing the "wholly other" of religious experience, sacred music transcends language and forms a bridge between myth and ritual in cultic life. As such, the text of sacred songs can be said to form part of the domain of mythos, the intuitive realm of timeless truths and narratives of the gods, goddesses, and spiritual beings. Often classified as separate from but complementary to reason (*logos*) and temporality, mythos is generally better communicated through symbolic language than through everyday language, and belongs to the imagination and the unconscious mind as distinct from the rational conscious mind. The psychology of music in relation to symbol and myth took a refreshing turn in the fascinating work of Victor Zuckerkandl (1956, 1973). The work of Gilbert Rouget (1986) is also important here in relation to the psychological states of musical trance and possession.

Within Black theology, Jon Michael Spencer has formed a new discipline devoted to the study of music in theological terms. Called theomusicology, it seeks to interpret music theologically, and looks particularly towards locating expressions of ultimate—that is, of transcendent meaning and value—in all forms of music. In his work, which has spread in myriad directions that include gospel, jazz, and blues, he has also developed a methodology to study the general human musical experience and analyze it theologically. While Spencer's special area of expertise is African American culture, theomusicology as an academic discipline may be expanded within a broader framework that can also be effective in examining many other forms of religious music. According to Spencer, the theomusicologist alone is qualified to identify and interpret all types of music from the theological perspective, and not the ordinary ethnomusicologist who does not have, or at least has not demonstrated, the capability of interpreting the sacred in music in its varying, and often concealed, forms and guises. As he explains, "I believe theomusicology has begun ... to find an appropriate musicological language that discloses and discourses with the theology in all forms of music—sacred, secular, and profane; popular, folk, and classical; vocal, instrumental and 'archetypal.' This is something ethnomusicology has not done."[13]

While this volume is not an exercise in theomusicology, essays within it touch upon similar patterns of inquiry and analysis, and serve to broaden the terrain. I have done this in my own work on "sonic theology," which was originally applied to Hinduism in its discussion of sacred sound (see Guy L. Beck, *Sonic Theology: Hinduism and Sacred Sound*, 1993). The more refined alternative, "tonal theology," found in my current work in progress, serves to explicate many of the concepts and issues surrounding musical tone and its relation to the sacred in religious traditions. The problematic issue with Spencer's term and approach is its apparent application to only theistic traditions. But the term theology may also be used with caution when referring to the "sacred" rather than strictly to a personal or theistic deity. In this way, non-theistic traditions like Buddhism and Jainism may be accommodated as they certainly recognize the realm of the sacred, though in non-theistic terms. There is an aspect of Spencer's theomusicology, however, that is quite relevant to the phenomenological approach of our book. It involves the acceptance of traditional or mythic descriptions regarding the divine origin of music and the arts, and necessitates the "bracketing out" (*epoché*) of overly rational and skeptical attitudes stemming from the Enlightenment, such as the view of nineteenth-century musicologists that music literally "evolved" from elementary and savage notions into that which is "mastered by learned skills." As Spencer describes it, "the theomusicologist proceeds under the assumption that the mythologies and theologies of the culture(s) being studied make up the authoritative or normative sources for understanding."[14] This parallels the accepted view within the history of religions, which corrects the misleading notion of many social scientists that the sacred world views of humankind somehow simply emerged out of primitive profane existence as futile attempts to explain the inexplicable. In fact, scholars and students who follow the lead of Mircea Eliade generally posit that primitive or archaic man viewed the cosmos as entirely sacred, and that profane existence gradually encroached itself upon society as it plunged into history. Music, in terms of this approach, would then be seen as a vital means of returning to primordial sacrality, through its inclusion in repetitive ritual activities that re-enact cosmogonic events.

The systematic study of music apart from practical theory and performance is normally referred to as musicology, or music history. This includes analysis of performance genres and styles, the evolution of harmony and rhythm, and the history and cultural context of the great composers. Until recently, these studies were limited primarily to Western art music, which was believed to represent the zenith of musical achievement. The relatively new discipline of ethnomusicology, often associated with anthropology, studies mainly the music of non-Western cultures and has made great strides over the past five decades in bringing world music to prominence. Developed and established within this field are a number of flexible, meta-cultural systems of classification of diverse types of instruments, scale systems, rhythmic patterns, and performance styles that are helpful in the study of the music of various world traditions. Ethnomusi-

cology is affiliated with the social sciences, but, as religion is more generally viewed by ethnomusicologists as just one among many aspects of culture, special provenance is seldom given to religious music.

The pairing of religion and music in our book may initially create the
impression of just another coupling, like the series of courses that many
institutions offer linking religion with a wide range of topics. While religion is in fact related tangentially with, for example, the environment,
marriage, health care, politics, racial issues, and so on, it has a much more
integral relationship with music. The authors in this book posit that religion is tied to music and chant on a very basic level of practice and experience, even if not proclaimed as such in theology or doctrine. This complex
interlacing of music and religion is succinctly explained by Robin Sylvan
in his book, *Traces of the Spirit: The Religious Dimensions of Popular Music*
(2002): "Music is capable of functioning simultaneously at many different
levels (physiological, psychological, sociocultural, semiological, virtual,
ritual, and spiritual) and integrating them into a coherent whole. So for a
complex multidimensional phenomenon like religion, which also functions simultaneously at multiple levels, the fact that music is capable of con-
veying all these levels of complexity in a compelling and integrated
package makes it a vehicle par excellence to carry the religious impulse."[15]

The academic study of ritual and liturgy has begun to receive more
proper attention, and is one of the more promising venues for the study of
religion and music. Pioneers in the field of ritual studies like Victor Turner,
Catherine Bell, and Ronald Grimes, while not dealing directly with music
in their research, have provided a firm academic foundation upon which
studies in religion and music can fit together very well. The most reward-
ing subfield for religion and music in terms of the work that has accumulated is liturgical studies. In this domain, normally the nest of specialists,
there is a vast corpus of material dealing with music and chant, mainly in
Jewish and Christian liturgies. Liturgy (from the Greek words *laos*, "people," and *ergos*, "work" or "action") means a series of rites that combine
word, music, action, symbol, and/or object that is performed on behalf of
a group. This usually refers to the public ritual or worship of a religious
community that is performed by priests or other functionaries. We also
invoke the term "paraliturgical" to denote private or individual rituals
that are nonetheless tied symbolically to larger public liturgies. Documents of the Second Vatican Council on sacred music explicate the close
and necessary connection between the divine word and musical expression
as directives for all types of liturgical activity within Roman Catholicism,
including the sacraments: "Liturgical worship is given a more noble form
when it is celebrated in song.... The unity of hearts is more commonly
achieved by the union of voice.... One cannot find anything more reli-

gious and more joyful in sacred celebrations than a whole congregation expressing its faith and devotion in song."[16]

Current academic work in liturgical studies confirms the centrality of music in all religious worship: "Instead of being treated as decoration and extraneous to the 'real business' of worship, music is integral to the expression of liturgical content and bodily engagement. Text and music together—musical liturgy or sung prayer—are appreciated for their power to illumine the mind and move the heart."[17] While the serious study of liturgy has been often confined to Christianity, especially Roman Catholicism and Eastern Orthodoxy, the obvious presence of "liturgy" in many other religious traditions expands the possibilities for critical study of the presence of music in religious rites worldwide. An indication of the widening of the liturgical lens is found in the number of non-Christian entries found in *The New Westminster Dictionary of Liturgy and Worship* (2002), ed. Paul Bradshaw: Jewish worship, Islamic worship, Hindu worship, Buddhist worship, Sikh worship, and Shinto worship. In each case, the presence of music and chant is woven into the description of the ritual and liturgical dimensions by the individual authors.

Liturgist Edward Foley has outlined some of the basic properties of music as it relates to the Jewish and Christian liturgies, and which may helpfully provoke broader insights into other traditions. He states, "As one of the 'languages' of the rite, liturgical music is considered integral or necessary to worship according to the official teaching of the church.... The irreplaceable nature of music's contribution to worship is a function of its special acoustical properties. These enable music to engage the assembly, reveal the divine and enable the communion between assembly and God in ways unique to this art form." Accordingly, he enumerates four acoustic properties which allow music to accomplish these things: "music is time bound, music is the indicator of personal presence, music is dynamic, and music is intangible." Regarding the latter property and in line with Otto's perspective, he explains that "music has symbolized the mysterious and wholly other since the dawn of creation.... This elusiveness in form and content is part of the reason why music is so often used for communicating with the spirit world. In the Judeo-Christian tradition music is an effective means for communicating with a God who is both present and hidden."[18] For ritual worship to sustain that necessary element of mystery within religious life, he finds sacred music must continue to act as a link and balancing factor between word and action in all religious rituals, public and private, that prevents their decline into the extremes of either verbal pedagogy or mindless ritualistic action.

In order to extend the subject of religion and music beyond the West, and to provide a broader framework for analysis, I will consider some of the themes that have appeared in Western liturgical studies further. Since the role of music often parallels the role of worship in religion, it is helpful to classify some of the standard functions of religious music in relation to worship situations. If, indeed, music is understood as sacred or "religious," then the contributors intend that it serves or functions in some kind of relationship to what is of absolute value to believers, such as the sacred or a transcendent reality. Sometimes expressed in terms of myth and ritual, liturgy invariably involves music and chant. Earlier scholars had speculated on the question of which came first, myth or ritual. Today the consensus is that both are contiguous at very primal levels, in antiquity and among tribal religions today. Historian of religion William E. Paden has stated, "As myth expresses world foundations in terms of word and image, ritual dramatizes world foundations in terms of performance. The two concepts, myth and ritual, are equally important in understanding religion. Indeed, the Roman term *religio* meant something very close to ritual observance. Worlds are formed not only through representations but also through actions, and a religious system is simultaneously a system of mythic language and a system of observances."[19] Liturgical studies scholar Louis Bouyer has even affirmed that word and rite, myth and ritual, have a kind of primordial connection: "Sacred words and sacred actions are as a matter of fact always found joined together … their constant connection must mean a natural relationship."[20] These statements support the general notion in this volume that myth and ritual constitute the "language" of the sacred, which is bound together with music and chant as well, at very basic levels.

To help provide some new perspectives for approaching diverse types of religious music and chant as they form part of sacred rituals in all of the worlds religions, it would be useful to present some basic vocabulary terms that, hopefully, will more fully define some of the different types or styles of music and chant that are too often simply, and naively, lumped together under the term "religious music." Some of these functional types may seem to be determined solely by the semantic meaning of the text, but it is the context which more truly illuminates the overall sense and purpose. For example, the concept of sacrifice is often divided into two types: propitiation (seeking favour or blessing) and expiation (asking forgiveness of sin). As such, one may examine the role of music in terms of one of these approaches to the divine. Another important approach to the worship of the divine is doxological. This means that humans, in response to receiving the gift of life from their Creator, offer praise. Ethically speaking, humans are thus under a kind of obligation to make music for the glory of God and not for their own amusement. This function is termed doxological (Greek *doxa*, "glory") because music is used to glorify or praise the divine. Music as doxology is also fully present in other theistic traditions like Hinduism, Islam, and Sikhism, but not in Buddhism, which does not recognize a Creator.

Buddhism uses music for other purposes, however, such as *apotropaia*, in which unwanted spirits or demons are literally "chased away" through the chanting of specific texts or the playing of loud and brash instruments. This effect is similarly obtained in many tribal religions. In the Roman Catholic Mass or Eucharist, as well as in the Orthodox Divine Liturgy, the term *epiclesis*, borrowed from classical pagan vocabulary, is often used to depict the priestly action of inviting the Holy Spirit into the sacramental bread and wine. In a broader sense, chant or music as *epiclesis* denotes the tonal invitation of any deity or spirit to a sacrifice or worship occasion, which was precisely the function of many Vedic chants in India and in other parts of the ancient world. Music here serves a distinct purpose apart from mere praise or expiation, and may also be part of a ritual that re-enacts a creation myth, such as the music of New Year festivals and ritual combat. If music is meant to assist in remembering a past historical or mythical event, it then functions as anamnesis, as in music during Passover or Easter. Music or chant also may function as petitionary prayer, or *litaneia*, such as in the Catholic *Kyrie eleison* ("Lord Have Mercy"), or in many of the Sikh *shabads*. When the aim of music is to create a mood of contrition, it functions as *katanyxis*. When it purifies us from sin or defilement, it is catharsis. Music that is eschatological represents or expresses a future state of being, such as found in the biblical books of Isaiah (6:3) and Revelation (5:8–10). This type may also be found in certain Jewish messianic songs, Christian hymns, Hindu *bhajans*, or Sikh *shabads*. When music or chant is utilized to bring about a communion between the human and divine world, it functions as *koinonia*. The notion of musical unity among human beings, martyrs, and saints, is found in the Catholic Church, but also in archaic and Asian religions where music celebrates a communal meal among humans and the gods, as practiced in ancient Vedic India. When musical texts teach doctrine, they are didactic, as found in Jewish lessons and the chanting of the Buddhist Pali Canon. When they give thanks for blessings already received, they are eucharistic, as in some Sikh and Jewish songs. In religious mysticism, such as Sufism, Hasidism, Hindu Bhakti, and some Buddhist sects, we find that music is employed to achieve particular states of ecstasy and bliss, termed exstasis in the texts of ancient mystery religions.

According to Theodore H. Gaster in his book *Thespis* (1961), the seasonal rituals of all societies followed patterns of *kenosis* (emptying) and *plerosis* (fulfilling). Within this rubric of the ritual process, he elaborated upon four basic types. *Kenosis* included rites of mortification and rites of purgation, whereas *plerosis* included rites of invigoration and rites of jubilation. *Plerosis* also includes initiation rites, communal meal festivals, and communion with the departed ancestors. Since almost all myths are portrayed through chant and music, and as myths are coupled with these rites, chant and music may also function in many ways that parallel the ritual practices associated with renunciation and replenishment, with purgation and revitalization.

At this point I offer some clarification in terms of musicology and poetics. What is often meant by the term "recitation" in religious traditions is not simply an audible reading, as in certain Protestant denominations and in the craft of narrative story-telling, but essentially a tonal recitation that includes the use of musical notes. Even a strict monotone qualifies here. The best term that encompasses the use of either a monotone or a few (two to four) additional tones in the recitation of a text is cantillation. While the term "chant" may include cantillation, it is a much broader category that sometimes comprises complete musical scales, as in Gregorian and Qur'ānic chant. Cantillation has been most commonly associated with the tonal recitation of parts of the Hebrew Bible, yet may be expanded to include other traditions. A useful distinction in this regard will be made between non-metrical cantillation and metrical cantillation, which often parallels the difference between prose and poetry. These both fall within the broader categories of non-metrical chant and metrical chant, respectively. Non-metrical means that the rhythm of the recitation is governed by the patterns of the words and accents rather than by a fixed-time duration. There is generally more scope for individual interpretation in performance when there is no metre. Non-metrical texts such as the Psalms from the Hebrew Bible, much of the Buddhist Pali Canon, and some Sikh prayers are not rendered according to fixed-time durations. Recitations of these may be understood as non-metrical cantillation, since they involve only a few musical notes. Although the Qur'ān in Islam is written in poetic prose and is non-metrical, the recitation of it involves many notes of the scale, and so is best classified as non-metrical chant. The Hindu *Rig-Veda* is in metrical verse, but as its recitation involves the use of roughly three notes, it may be classified as metrical cantillation. Sacred songs labelled as hymns ("praise songs") are most often metrical texts set with many notes, in either classical or vernacular languages, as in classical Greek hymns, Protestant hymns and chorales, and Hindu *dhrupads*. This type would also include many Hindu *bhajans* and Sikh *shabads*. Examples of non-metrical texts with many notes are Sufi songs, qawwālī *ḥamd*, and some Jewish liturgical and paraliturgical songs.

All of these functional types or styles of religious music or chant are still found within the six religious traditions discussed in this book, sometimes within the same text or rite. By extracting terms and concepts from various specific contexts, whether classical, pagan, Jewish, or Christian, and applying them to other traditions in a non-partisan manner, a new symbolic language may thus be created that enhances our understanding of the various roles that music and chant have played, and continue to play, within religious ritual and experience. And, since many otherwise distinct religions and cultures employ similar musical systems and instruments in their worship and ritual and, conversely, numerous styles and performance practices of sacred music prevail within each of the so-called world religions, a vocabulary that is neutral and not culturally-specific is all the more necessary and effective. From a global viewpoint, the category of sacred music covers an exceedingly wide spectrum when we include the millions of believers in the world who belong to what is termed "indigenous religions." As such, we are just beginning to understand the overall significance of music in religion—at the tip of the tonal iceberg, so to speak. A new collection of readings entitled *Indigenous Religious Musics*, edited by Karen Ralls-MacLeod and Graham Harvey (2000), has helped to begin the exploration of this important field.

Part of what makes this new collection of essays significant is that it attempts to bridge the now outdated dichotomy between scholarship and performance. In the Western social sciences and humanities, there has been a long-standing wall of separation between the so-called "objective scholar" as subject, and the object of his or her inquiry. Referred to as the "old paradigm" by more progressive thinkers, this dichotomy of insider/outsider or musician/scholar, also known to anthropologists as emic/etic, has continued to inform attitudes for well over a century. Within the field of ethnomusicology, the old paradigm appeared in the work of early ethnomusicologists who laid the foundation of the "science" of ethnic music studies and archiving. Alan P. Merriam, in his very influential *The Anthropology of Music* (1964), stressed that maintaining a rigid distinction between the outside observer and the "native" musician or informant was the best method to achieve successful research work in the field. At that time, over forty years ago, very few Western scholars had achieved competency in ethnic music performance, and the question of their expertise was not viewed as relevant for the study of ethnic (non-Western) music. There also remained some reservations in the field of ethnomusicology about the importance of the effect of "native" music on the scholar, and thus an entire source of musical experiences went largely untapped. A professor or scholar might attempt to play an exotic instrument or sing songs of a certain culture, but his or her expertise was usually not considered as "representing" that tradition in any serious manner.

In recent years, a shift in the social sciences and ethnomusicology has changed the focus from "culture" to "people." Instead of the "neutral ground" of objective observation (by the researcher) of the object of "culture" (the researched), both parties are subject to investigation, since both are "people." The interactions among all types of people, insiders and outsiders, have sparked a degree of attention resulting in a new hermeneutical paradigm, in which the impact of the researcher on the researched and vice versa is considered worthy of exploration and analysis. Accordingly, the "new ethnomusicology" is much more reflexive and dialogical for the study of world music, and is more interested in the lived musical experiences of all parties concerned, including recognizing both the possibility and real legitimacy of a scholar who is, simultaneously, a "native" musician.

In the case of this book, all of the authors presenting material on music and religion have drawn upon their own skills and experiences as both scholars and performers of these sacred music traditions, and so fall into this new category, whereby their principal sources are not solely and necessarily other native musicians.

Attempting to reveal and reinforce the vital interconnection between religious studies and music, this book—the first of its kind—aims to provide an introductory survey on the important role of music and chant in six of the world's great religions: Judaism, Christianity, Islam, Hinduism, Sikhism, and Buddhism. Scholar-performers in these six traditions present here the foundational themes and issues regarding their music. Besides introducing historical themes and textual sources, including hymnals and songbooks, the authors discuss the role of chant in the early communities, music in public liturgy and in private devotions, and music and chant as a spiritual discipline or means of release. They then conclude with some comments regarding the future role of music within their particular tradition. What makes this presentation particularly unique is that each of the authors is also a performer of religious music and chant of his or her tradition.

Within each chapter, there are examples of important chants, hymns, and sacred songs from each religion. As "sacred songs," the examples conform very well to the description of this genre by Stephen Marini in his recent work, *Sacred Song in America: Religion, Music, and Public Culture* (2003): "Sacred Song is music that expresses religious meanings through the interaction of mythic content and ritual performance."[21] The lyrics of these examples each reflect the mythic content of the respective religious tradition, while the performative context of these songs is tied to a specific ritual or liturgy, whether personal or public. Almost all examples are considered obligatory—sometimes statutory—for the believers to chant, sing, or hear, and are generally mandated by authorities within each religious tradition. Sacred songs—such as the Shema, the Psalms, and the Haggadah (Judaism); the Kyrie, Sanctus, "Salve Regina," and "A Mighty

Fortress" (Christianity); the Call to Prayer and *al-Fātiḥa* (Islam); the "Gāy-atrī Mantra," *Bhagavad Gītā*, and *nām-kīrtan* (Hinduism); *Japjī*, "Kaisī Āratī," and "So Dar" (Sikhism); *Mangalacharanam, Trisaranam,* the "Maṇi Mantra," and the *Heart Sūtra* (Buddhism)—are all considered typical or normative for the traditions. Thus, in their original contexts, these songs are not viewed in the sense of "art-for-art's sake," or as high technical achievements. On the contrary, they represent and express the close and delicate bonds between the divine word and ritual action that serves to keep hope and faith alive, and to animate and sustain the religious consciousness of millions of devout followers. Each sacred song example first is transliterized into Roman characters, then given in an English translation. While the repertoires of religious music within each tradition are exceedingly vast and always changing, the items selected also represent what one might still encounter in a congregation or a religious meeting, rather than those that are extinct or otherwise obscure. Beyond this, students and readers are urged to explore the abundance of recorded music suggested in the discography.

The first chapter, on Judaism and music by Joseph A. Levine, begins with references to music in the Hebrew Bible, establishes the role of song in synagogue services, and then takes us all the way to the present day, with splendid examples and insights into the musical worship of the Lord Most High. The author's historical approach combines biblical references with actual practices at various periods in Jewish history. Key Jewish prayers and songs are highlighted, along with the mystical tradition of Hasidism and a discussion of post-Holocaust music and beyond.

In chapter 2, Gerald Hobbs describes the historical role of music in Christian traditions of worship. From early Gregorian chant through Protestant hymns and church practices, he emphasizes the saving dimension of Christian singing with the added feature of folk hymnody and African-American gospel traditions. Beginning with the background of Hebrew psalmody and the early theology of the Triune God, he discusses the various influences that provide form and function to the ever-evolving religious art forms of classical and liturgical Christian music.

In chapter 3, Regula Qureshi discusses music in the religion of Islam, providing an accurate picture of the nature of the debate regarding the use of "religious" music. Despite orthodox hesitation and even prohibitions regarding music, monotheistic religious chant and music devoted to the One God have flourished throughout the Islamic world. In this chapter, the nature of Qur'ānic chant, as well as the use of music of other genres, is presented within a historical framework. After introducing primary and secondary sources, the author discusses the Call to Prayer in public liturgy, and proceeds to analyze a variety of Islamic songs, including hymns to celebrate the Prophet, hymns of mourning, and songs of the widely popular Sufi tradition of *qawwālī*.

Chapter 4, by Guy L. Beck, focuses on the religious and mythological roots of sacred sound and music in India as a central part of Vedic and Hindu traditions. This rich and timeless legacy has been very influential within the various branches of Hinduism and beyond, such that Indian musical styles and instruments have been adopted by all of the other major religions in South Asia, including Jain, Buddhist, Sikh, Islamic, and even Christian communities. Ranging from ancient times through the medieval period and up to current sectarian practices, this chapter provides insights into the development of Hindu music as a fundamental religious expression in the form of both Sanskrit prayers and vernacular devotional music. The author first describes Vedic chant and the relationship between music and the Hindu gods and goddesses in the context of sacred myth. He then discusses devotional singing in North India, including *dhrupad*, Hindi *bhajan*, Bengali *kīrtan*, and chanting of the names of God. The chapter closes with references to film music and the recent commercialization of religious songs in India and the Hindu Diaspora.

Chapter 5, on Sikhism and music by Pashaura Singh, outlines the role of music in the Sikh faith and tradition, with appropriate examples of the *Japjī*, *shabads* and their use in Sikh worship, and the veneration of Akāl Purakh and Sat Nām, or the One True Name. Sikhism is unique in being the only major world religion in which the founder himself, Guru Nānak, was a musician who spread his message through music and song. As this emphasis has remained unchanged for over half a millennium, the prevailing importance of music for this religion cannot be overestimated.

In chapter 6, Sean Williams provides a historical overview, as well as in-depth studies, of two major traditions of Buddhist music. Despite the Buddha's initial reservation about music as "amusement," and the existence of monastic vows of abstention, the role of chant in the early formation of the Buddhist sangha and its development within the various communities that spread throughout Asia was formidable, including both Theravāda and Mahāyāna traditions. Framed within the spiritual quest for ultimate nirvana, this chapter discusses the chanting of the Pali Canon, the Theravāda *paritta* services, Tibetan Buddhist multiphonic chanting known as *dbyangs*, and Japanese Buddhist chant or *shōmyō*. The six chapters are followed by an annotated discography.

Finally, I close this introduction with some interesting reflections on music and the sacred from the last two centuries. The first is from the musicologist Edmund Gurney, who stated, toward the end of the nineteenth century, that "The link between sound and the supernatural is profound and widespread.... Possibly sound—like the gods a powerful unseen presence—is an unacknowledged model for our concept of the other-worldly.... If we are believers, then we can believe that the spirit is moving us in our ritual music. Ritual sound makes the transcendent immanent. It is at the same time ours, our own sounds pressing in around us and running through us like a vital current of belief, molding us into a living interior that is proof against the unbelieving emptiness that lies around."[22]

More recently, at the end of the twentieth century, the intellectual historian George Steiner affirmed his belief in the important role of music in the higher mystical dimensions of the human condition: "I believe the matter of music to be central to that of the meanings of man, of man's access to or abstention from metaphysical experience. Our capacities to compose and to respond to musical form and sense directly implicate the mystery of the human condition. To ask 'what is music?' may well be one way of asking 'what is man?'"[23]

Notes

1 A Dictionary of Comparative Religion, ed. S.G.F. Brandon (1970), s.v. "Music."
2 Rudolf Otto (1923), 49. Otto examines the link between music and the numinous in three places: see music compared to the numinous, 48–49; Appendix II, "The Numinous in Poetry, Hymn, and Liturgy," 189–90; and Appendix III, "Original Numinous Sounds," 190–93.
3 Gerardus Van der Leeuw (1938), 453.
4 Gerardus Van der Leeuw (1963), 225, 227.
5 Oxford Dictionary of World Religions, ed. John Bowker (1997), s.v. "Music."
6 Theodore Ludwig (2001), 19.
7 Gary E. Kessler (2003), 144.
8 Vivian Lee-Nyitray (2001), 4.
9 Stephen A. Marini (2001), 3; see also Carol Babiracki (2001), 5.
10 Bruno Nettl (2001), 9.
11 Joshua R. Jacobson (2001), 7.
12 The importance of the oral form of scripture is explained in Harold Coward (2000), introduction.
13 Jon Michael Spencer (1994), 45.
14 Ibid., 46.
15 Robin Sylvan (2002), 6.
16 Vatican Council II: The Conciliar and Post Conciliar Documents (1975), 81, 84.
17 Robin A. Leaver and Joyce Ann Zimmerman, eds. (1998), 8.
18 Edward Foley (1990), 868–69.
19 William E. Paden (1988), 93.
20 Louis Bouyer (1963), 53.
21 Stephen A. Marini (2003), 8.
22 Edmund Gurney (1880), 25–26.
23 George Steiner (1991), 6.

Bibliography

Babiracki, Carol. "Religion, Musically Speaking." In "Spotlight on Teaching/Religion and Music," ed. Tazim R. Kassam, special issue, *Religious Studies News* 16 (Spring 2001): 5.

Beck, Guy L. *Sonic Theology: Hinduism and Sacred Sound.* Columbia: University of South Carolina Press, 1993.

Bell, Catherine. *Theory, Ritual Practice.* New York: Oxford University Press, 1992.

———. *Ritual: Perspectives and Dimensions.* New York: Oxford University Press, 1997.

Bouyer, Louis. *Rite and Man: Natural Sacredness and Christian Liturgy.* Notre Dame, IN: Notre Dame University Press, 1963.

Bowker, John, ed. *Oxford Dictionary of World Religions.* Oxford: Oxford University Press, 1997.

Brandon, S.G.F. *A Dictionary of Comparative Religion.* New York: Charles Scribners, 1970.

Braun, Willi, and Russell T. McCutcheon. *Guide to the Study of Religion.* London and New York: Cassell, 2000.

Burrows, David. *Sound, Speech and Music.* Amherst: University of Massachusetts Press, 1990.

Coward, Harold. *Experiencing Scripture in World Religions.* Maryknoll, NY: Orbis, 2000.

Crim, Keith, ed. *The Perennial Dictionary of World Religions.* San Francisco: Harper and Row, 1989. First published 1981 by Abingdon Press.

Doniger, Wendy, ed. *Merriam-Webster's Encyclopedia of World Religions.* Springfield, MA: Merriam-Webster, 1999.

Eliade, Mircea. *Patterns in Comparative Religion.* New York: Sheed and Ward, 1958.

———. *The Sacred and the Profane: The Nature of Religion.* New York: Harcourt Brace, 1959.

———. *A History of Religious Ideas.* 3 vols. Chicago: University of Chicago Press, 1978–1985.

———, ed. *The Encyclopedia of Religion.* 16 vols. New York: Macmillan, 1986.

Ellwood, Robert S., and Barbara A. McGraw. *Many Peoples, Many Faiths: Women and Men in the World Religions,* 8th ed. Upper Saddle River, NJ: Prentice-Hall, 2005.

Fenton, John Y., et al. *Religions of Asia.* 3rd ed. New York: St. Martin's Press, 2001.

Fisher, Mary Pat. *Living Religions,* 5th ed. Upper Saddle River, NJ: Prentice-Hall, 2002.

Foley, Edward. "Music, Liturgical." In *The New Dictionary of Sacramental Worship,* ed. Peter E. Fink, S.J., 854–70. Collegeville, MN: Liturgical Press, 1990.

Gaster, Theodore H. *Thespis: Ritual, Myth and Drama in the Ancient Near East.* New York: Harper Torchbooks, 1961.

Greeley, Andrew. *God in Popular Culture.* Chicago: Thomas More Press, 1989.

Grimes, Ronald L. *Ritual Criticism: Case Studies in Its Practice and Essays on Its Theory.* Columbia: University of South Carolina Press, 1990.

Gurney, Edmund. *The Power of Sound*. London: Smith, Elder, 1880.

Harned, David Baily. *Theology and the Arts*. London: Westminster Press, 1966.

Hopfe, Lewis M., and Mark R. Woodward. *Religions of the World*, 8th ed. Upper Saddle River, NJ: Prentice-Hall, 2001.

Irwin, Joyce, ed. *Sacred Sound: Music in Religious Thought and Practice*. Chico, CA: Scholars Press, 1983.

Jacobson, Joshua R. "Experiencing Jewish Music." In "Spotlight on Teaching/Religion and Music," ed. Tazim R. Kassam, special issue, *Religious Studies News* 16 (Spring 2001): 7.

Jones, Lindsay, ed. *Encyclopedia of Religion*. 2nd ed., 15 vols. Detroit: Macmillan Reference USA, 2005.

Kessler, Gary. *Studying Religion: An Introduction through Cases*. Boston: McGraw-Hill, 2003.

Kitagawa, Joseph M. *Religion in Japanese History*. New York: Columbia University Press, 1966.

———, ed. *The History of Religions: Essays on the Problem of Understanding*. Chicago: University of Chicago Press, 1967.

———. *The History of Religions: Understanding Human Experience*. Atlanta, GA: Scholars Press, 1987.

Leaver, Robin A., and Joyce Ann Zimmerman, eds. *Liturgy and Music: Lifetime Learning*. Collegeville, MN: Liturgical Press, 1998.

Leeuw, Gerardus van der. *Sacred and Profane Beauty: The Holy in Art*. New York: Holt, Rinehart and Winston, 1963. (See in particular part 6, "Music and Religion," 211–62.)

———. *Religion in Essence and Manifestation*. 2 vols. Gloucester: Peter Smith, 1967. First published 1938 by Allen and Unwin.

Livingston, James C. *Anatomy of the Sacred*. 5th ed. Upper Saddle River, NJ: Prentice-Hall, 2005.

Ludwig, Theodore. *The Sacred Paths of the East*. Upper Saddle River, NJ: Prentice-Hall, 2001.

Marini, Stephen A. "Sacred Music in the Religious Studies Classroom." In "Spotlight on Teaching/Religion and Music," ed. Tazim R. Kassam, special issue, *Religious Studies News* 16 (Spring 2001): 3.

———. *Sacred Song in America: Religion, Music, and Public Culture*. Urbana and Chicago: University of Illinois Press, 2003.

Merriam, Alan P. *The Anthropology of Music*. Evanston, IL: Northwestern University Press, 1964.

Monti, Anthony. *A Natural Theology of the Arts: Imprint of the Spirit*. Burlington, VT: Ashgate, 2003.

Muck, Terry. "Psalm, Bhajan, and Kirtan: Songs of the Soul in Comparative Perspective." In *Psalms and Practice: Worship, Virtue, and Authority*, ed. Stephen Breck Reid, 7–27. Collegeville, MN: Liturgical Press, 2001.

Nettl, Bruno. *Excursions in World Music*. 3rd ed. Upper Saddle River, NJ: Prentice-Hall, 2001.

Nielson Jr., Niels C., et al. *Religions of the World*. 3rd ed. New York: St. Martin's Press, 1993.

Noss, David S. *A History of the World's Religions*. 11th ed. Upper Saddle River, NJ: Prentice-Hall, 2003.

Nyitray, Vivian-Lee. "In Pursuit of Active Listening." In "Spotlight on Teaching/ Religion and Music," ed. Tazim R. Kassam, special issue, *Religious Studies News* 16 (Spring 2001): 4.

Olson, Carl, ed. *Theory and Method in Religious Studies: A Selection of Critical Readings*. Belmont, CA: Thomson Wadsworth, 2003.

Ong, Walter. *The Presence of the Word*. New Haven, CT: Yale University Press, 1967.

Otto, Rudolf. *The Idea of the Holy: An Inquiry into the Non-rational Factor in the Idea of the Divine and Its Relation to the Rational*, 2nd ed. New York: Oxford University Press, 1958 (1923).

Paden, William E. *Religious Worlds: The Comparative Study of Religion*. Boston: Beacon Press, 1988.

Pals, Daniel L. *Seven Theories of Religion*. New York: Oxford University Press, 1996.

Parrinder, Geoffrey, ed. *World Religions: From Ancient History to the Present*. New York: Facts-on-File, 1971.

Pettazzoni, Raffaele. *Essays on the History of Religions*. Leiden: E.J. Brill, 1967.

Ralls-MacLeod, Karen, and Graham Harvey, eds. *Indigenous Religious Music*. London: University of London, School of Oriental and African Studies Musicology Series, 2000. With accompanying CD.

Randel, Don Michael, ed. *The New Harvard Dictionary of Music*. Cambridge: Harvard University Press, 1986.

Renard, John. *The Handy Religion Answer Book*. New York: Barnes and Noble, 2002.

Rouget, Gilbert. *Music and Trance*. Chicago: University of Chicago Press, 1986.

Ryba, Thomas. *The Essence of Phenomenology and Its Meaning for the Scientific Study of Religion*. New York: Peter Lang, 1991.

Segal, Robert A. *Explaining and Interpreting Religion: Essays on the Issue*. New York: Peter Lang, 1992.

Shelemay, Kay Kaufman. *Soundscapes: Exploring Music in a Changing World*. New York: W.W. Norton, 2001. (chapter 5, 153–80, "Music of Worship and Belief," covers Tibetan chant, Santeria, and Ethiopian Christian liturgical chant.)

Smart, Ninian. *The Phenomenon of Religion*. New York: Herder and Herder, 1973.

Smith, Huston. *The Religions of Man*. New York: Harper and Row, 1964 (1958). Revised and reprinted as *The World's Religions: Our Great Wisdom Traditions*. New York and San Francisco: HarperSanFrancisco, 1991.

Smith, Jonathan Z., ed., with the American Academy of Religion. *The HarperCollins Dictionary of Religion*. San Francisco: HarperSanFrancisco, 1995.

Spencer, Jon Michael. *Theological Music: An Introduction to Theomusicology*. Westport, CN: Greenwood Press, 1991.

———. "Musicology as a Theologically Informed Discipline." In *Theomusicology*, ed. Jon Michael Spencer, 36–63. Durham, NC: Duke University Press, 1994.

Stebben, Gregg. *Everything You Need to Know About Religion*. New York: Pocket Books, 1999.

Steiner, George. *Real Presences*. Chicago: University of Chicago Press, 1991.

Sullivan, Lawrence E. *Enchanting Powers: Music in the World's Religions*. Cambridge, MA: Harvard University Press, 1997.

Sylvan, Robin. *Traces of the Spirit: The Religious Dimensions of Popular Music*. New York: New York University Press, 2002.

Taylor, Mark C., ed. *Critical Terms for Religious Studies*. Chicago: University of Chicago Press, 1998.

Tillich, Paul. *Theology of Culture*. New York: Oxford University Press: 1959.

Titon, Jeff Todd. *Worlds of Music: Introduction to the Music of the World's Peoples*. New York: Schirmers, 1984. (chapter 4, 106–17, "Music of Worship," deals with Black American gospel hymns and sermons.)

Turner, Victor. *The Ritual Process: Structure and Anti-Structure*. Chicago: Aldine, 1969.

Vatican Council II: The Conciliar and Post Conciliar Documents. Ed. Austin Flannery, O.P. Northport, NY: Costello, 1975.

Viladesau, Richard. *Theology and the Arts: Encountering God through Music, Art, and Rhetoric*. New York: Paulist Press, 2000.

Waardenburg, Jacques, ed. *Classical Approaches to the Study of Religion: Aims, Methods, and Theories of Research*. New York and Berlin: Walter de Gruyter, 1999 (1971). (There is no mention of "Music" in the vast Index of Scholarly Concepts, 686–736.)

Wach, Joachim. *The Comparative Study of Religions*. New York: Columbia University Press, 1958.

Young, William A. *The World's Religions*. 2nd ed. Upper Saddle River, NJ: Prentice-Hall, 2005.

Zaehner, R.C. *The Concise Encyclopedia of Living Faiths*, 1st ed. New York: Hawthorne, 1959.

Zuckerkandl, Victor. *Man the Musician*. Princeton, NJ: Princeton University Press, 1973.

———. *Sound and Symbol: Music and the External World*. Princeton, NJ: Princeton University Press, 1956.

1
JUDAISM AND MUSIC

Joseph A. Levine

The study of Judaism and music has often been relegated to the periph-ery of Western music history, which tends to favour theory and conse-quently has given credit to the Greeks as its primary predecessors. Ancient Greek music is no longer extant, however, and current studies have shown that the Hebrew Bible has been transmitted and received for centuries primarily through the medium of chant and musical intonation, showcasing a living religious musical tradition that originated in the Mid-dle East and is still thriving throughout the world over two millennia later. The study of Jewish music provides modern scholars with a link to the ancient world: many types of musical instruments currently in use, for example, were used in Judaism's ancient temple worship and even before, in biblical times. Jews have contributed, without a doubt, to West-ern classical music, but not at the expense of creating their own rich her-itage of liturgical music for synagogue services and festivals, and of paraliturgical music for life-cycle rituals and domestic observances.

The fact that musical instruments were banned by the rabbis after the destruction of the Second Temple by the Romans and the subsequent loss of Jewish national sovereignty in 70 CE, and that regional dispersion neces-sitated the adaptation of foreign folk musical traditions to religious texts, has provided Jewish music with a somewhat disjointed historical continu-ity. Indeed, while the form and context of music in worship, especially with regard to instruments and the use of foreign melodies, has been vig-orously debated by rabbinical authorities over the years, unaccompanied chanting of Scripture has been accepted within all Jewish communities since the beginning. Whereas regional musical practices in synagogue worship have been deeply influenced by the sounds of specific host cultures, they still reflect a creative combination of perceived ancient customs in the Judean homeland. Any successive approach to the study of Judaism and music, therefore, must attempt to blend the historical with the ideological in order to understand the complex role of music in the Jewish experience.

Origins

The Hebrew Bible is the primary and most fertile source for our knowledge of music in ancient Israel. Besides containing descriptions of some sixteen musical instruments, numerous references are found in it with regard to the role of music in various dimensions of life, including ritualistic, prophetic, therapeutic, magical, ecstatic, military, official, and folk aspects. In addition, post-biblical sources like the Talmud, the Mishnah, the Dead Sea Scrolls, the writings of Josephus, and archaeological fragments enable scholars to reconstruct musical life in biblical times.

The book of Genesis (4:20–21) credits a man named Jubal with fashioning the first musical instruments: "Jubal was the father of all those who master the *kinnor* (lyre) and *ugav* (pipe)." This reference is traditionally understood to mean that Jubal invented music: that is, that music was a human invention. The Hebrew Bible considered music important enough to be mentioned alongside a staple of Bronze Age economy, cattle raising: Jubal's older brother, Jabal (Yaval in Hebrew), is described as "the father of those who dwell in tents and have cattle." This implies widespread use of the ram's horn (*shofar*), mentioned sixty-nine times in scripture and upon which ancient performers must have blown expertly. The *shofar* was steamed, bent, and flattened, with its smaller tip cut off and pierced to allow the production of perfect fourth and fifth intervals.

A ram's horn first appears in Exodus 19, when the Israelites, awaiting God's revelation at the foot of Mount Sinai, perceived thunderings and lightnings "and the continuous sound of the *shofar* that grew ever louder." Only a multitude of expert blowers could have produced and sustained such extraordinary volume. Aside from the *shofar's* permanently fixed pitches, its martial quality made it the ideal public instrument; it was employed by magistrates, tribal chieftains, and army captains. It announced the removal of the Holy Ark, reinforced general rejoicing, called warriors to battle, and proclaimed divine judgment upon erring nations. According to Jewish tradition, "God will sound a *shofar*" signaling Israel's redemption at the End of Days (Zechariah 9:14). The *shofar* remains the only quasi-

"King David Playing His Harp" (from medieval manuscripts). Watercolour by Kajal Beck. Courtesy of the artist.

musical instrument—used for signalling purposes only—sounded during worship in all Jewish communities.

Worship

Scripture first mentions worship when Cain and Abel bring grain and animal offerings (Genesis 4:4). Vocal offerings appear six generations later: "That was when humankind began to call upon the Lord" (Genesis 4:26).

Two generations after that, Noah was the first to acknowledge God in worship: "Blessed be Adonai, God of Shem" (Genesis 9:26). Blessings that connected God with individuals or groups followed: "Blessed be Adonai, God of Abraham" (Genesis 24:27); "Blessed be Adonai, God of Israel" (Psalms 72:18). The traditional phrase for chanting such blessings—even today, with the wording "Blessed be Adonai, Sovereign of the Universe"—is a rising fifth inflecting up to the octave, the characteristic heralding signal of the biblical *shofar*. It is chanted almost exclusively in the context of a public prayer service, a preference expressed in the book of Proverbs (14:28), "A Sovereign is glorified in the midst of the people."

Musicologist Curt Sachs believed that Jewish music progressed from an initial era of pure vocalism to a time when singing was accompanied by a wind instrument like the *shofar*, whose sounds the voice then imitated.[1] In addition, a rising fifth—followed by its descending mirror image—conforms with normal speech inflection. This sequence of intervals still occurs in two of Jewish worship's oldest ritual moments. The ascending *shofar* blasts on Rosh Hashanah (the Jewish New Year), are mirrored in the descending questions that the youngest child asks during a seder meal on Passover Eve. The first question addresses the biblical command to eat *matsah* (unleavened bread) exclusively on that night.

⊩ EXAMPLE 1 (Track 1)

The Youngest Child's First Question on Passover Eve[2]

> sheb'chol haleilot anu ochelin
> chameits umatsah,
> halailah hazeh kulo matsah.
>
> ∿
>
> Why on all other nights may we eat
> either leavened or unleavened bread,
> but on this night only unleavened bread?

Israel's first communal religious expression came as an involuntary reaction to its liberation from Egyptian bondage: "God ... split the Red Sea for us; He led us through it dry-shod, and engulfed our foes in it."[3] When the immensity of this deliverance sank in, Moses led the Israelites in a general laudation (Exodus 15:1–20): "I sing to the Lord for He has triumphed ..." As indicated by its opening words ("I sing"), the hymn was performed in unison. It was echoed by another unison song at the end of Moses' life, "Give ear, O Heavens, Listen, O Earth," which he taught the people (literally "put it in their mouths and ears") (Deuteronomy 31:19, 30; 32:43). The final instance of massed song in the Hebrew Bible occurred at the

First Jerusalem Temple's inaugural service, almost five centuries later. Hundreds of brass players, percussionists, and singers "were as one to make a single sound in praising the Lord" (2 Chronicles 5:13).

Prayer that is sung in unison singing alternates with prayer that is sung responsively in Scripture. The first instance of a call and response is Miriam's reworking of the sea song "And Miriam answered the people" (Exodus 15:21), apparently after they had sung her new refrain "You sing to the Lord." Her version of Moses' song must have alternated between a leader and a congregation. When Israel was ruled by judges (Judges 5), Deborah the prophetess, and Barak, who had led the fighting men of the Naphtali tribe, echoed Miriam's antiphonal scheme in praising God for bringing them victory over Canaanite forces at Kishon Brook. Barak calls, "Awake, Deborah, utter your song"; Deborah responds, "Arise, Barak, take your captives!" Several centuries later, King Solomon reinstituted unison worship at the First Temple's inauguration. As stated above, he had hundreds of instrumentalists and singers all performing together while thousands joined in unbridled rejoicing as an equal number of sacrifices was simultaneously offered (2 Chronicles 5).

Oscillation between spontaneous unison singing and calculated call-and-response stems from the fact that public prayer is a form of art, subject to the same process by which all works of art are created. Psychologist Anton Ehrenzweig likens an artist's perception of the world to the wide-eyed stare of a very young child: all-encompassing. He found that only as children mature does their view of things narrow, becoming more analytical and conscious of detail. Adults, on the other hand, have learned to move back and forth between these two types of awareness, alternating the open stare of early childhood with the focused attention that comes from life experience. By doing so, adults can grasp at once everything the artist has included: figure and background, melody and harmony.[4]

The creative process includes two phases, which are spelled out in Exodus 35. When instructing the artisan Bezalel on how to design a wilderness sanctuary, God says, "Free your imagination" (35:32), and then, "Teach the fruits of your imaginings to others" (35:34). First comes discovery, an instinctive and solitary event. Systematic modification comes later, as a byproduct of sharing the discovery.[5] There is a constant alternation in scripture between the two phases. Moses' song exemplifies the conceptual phase. Miriam's reworking of it epitomizes the refinement phase, as does the antiphonal laudation of Deborah and Barak. The First Temple's explosive inauguration signals a recycling of the conceptual phase.

The role of music in public liturgy and private devotion

References to the public worship of God through offerings of animals, grains, or libations appear throughout the Hebrew Bible. The book of Leviticus gives instructions on how the Aaronite priests should administer sacrificial rites on behalf of the people. Chapter 16, for example, describes an elaborate Day of Atonement (Yom Kippur) ritual in which the High Priest sought absolution for inadvertent transgressions committed by himself, by his tribe, and by the entire house of Israel. In delineating both communal and individual worship through various types of sacrifice, the first ten chapters of Leviticus also detail every step of the initiation ceremony for priests, laying a foundation for the ritual in both Jerusalem Temples later on.

At the daily morning, afternoon, and holy day offerings, a Levitical choir and orchestra performed psalms, many of them responsively.[6] Levites in the First Temple (900 BCE–586 BCE) evidently sang at top volume in order to be heard above the din of 128 cymbals and 120 trumpets (2 Chronicles 5:12). Proceedings in the Second Temple (516 BCE–70 CE) were significantly quieter, as an eyewitness reported that sacrifices were offered in "the most complete silence."[7] Moreover, the singing was now accompanied only by stringed instruments, the harp and lyre (Mishnah, *Arakhin* 2.3), which yielded a softer sound.[8]

By late in the Second Temple era, in the first century BCE, the synagogue (from the Greek *synagein*, "to bring together") had been institutionalized.[9] Before this, existing gathering spots such as open areas fronting upon city gates were used as venues where prayers were offered. This occurred at the exact times and in the exact manner as in the Jerusalem Temple,[10] for the Temple itself contained a synagogue.[11] According to the Mishnah (*Tamid* 5.1), the daily prayer service held in that hall was led by an appointed precentor who alternated with the choir-supported congregation in chanting the liturgy, without sacrificial offerings and without instruments. The Temple synagogue's repertoire of prayers and biblical excerpts provided a framework for the liturgy that is still universally sung today. Its twin pillars were the Shema (Israel's Credo, from Deuteronomy 6 and 11 and Numbers 15), and the *Amidah* ("Standing Devotion," the number of whose benedictions varies with the liturgical occasion). Other statutory elements are: *Emet V'yatsiv* ("True and Certain," one of the earliest rabbinically composed statutory prayers), the Priestly Blessing (in the liturgy, consisting of a petitionary verse introducing Numbers 6: 24–26), and the Ten Commandments (Exodus 20: 2–14).

Following the Roman destruction of the Temple, the intonation of prayer by a precentor—in alternation with a responding group—persisted through the long exile, the offerings of Israel's lips having replaced bullocks, grain, or libations (as predicted in Hosea 14:3). An appointed *chazzan* (cantor) inherited the role of precentor, while worshippers assumed the role of Levitical choristers. Rabbis, up until the emergence of Reform Judaism in modern times, played no part in the conduct of public worship unless they happened to serve as *chazzan* at a given service. From the seventh century on, a metrical form of religious hymn—or *piyyut* (from the Greek *poietes*, "poet")—entered the liturgy. It was patterned after hymns created a bit earlier by Byzantine Christian poets, the most prominent being Romanus, a Syrian-born Jew who had converted in the fifth century.[12] By means of alphabetically sequenced lines and recurring refrains, it enabled worshippers to remember the words and to participate at a time when prayer books had not yet been invented.[13] Gradually, special prayers for sabbaths, festivals, holy days, and fast days were added to an order of prayer that has remained remarkably uniform to the present day.

The wordings of private benedictions for every daily act, from rising in the morning to retiring at night, also date from this period and remain standardized in Jewish usage everywhere. What varies is the skill with which they are sung, privately or—when called upon—in leading a quorum of ten adults (a minyan) in prayer so that anyone remembering a deceased relative can officially recite Kaddish (a "Sanctification" of God, despite adversity), to which all respond "Amen; may God's great name be blessed forever and ever." Educator Steven Lorch points out that the music which Judaism uses in the performance of ritual is not hierarchic, in the sense of being reserved for a separate class of ministers. "At all times, each Jewish music consumer is a past and potential future producer. He can, at any time, be called upon to act as *chazzan* or Scripture reader, and his experience in these non-hierarchic roles provide a base in common with the current producer, so that the improvisational alternatives available to one in practice are simultaneously available to the other in theory."[14] The "improvisational alternatives" that are available to an individual, whether praying privately, leading others in prayer, or Scripture reading, are a choice of modes ("ways" of chanting), motifs within each mode, metres, tempos, volumes, voice qualities, sudden variations, and every other element that makes music "the universal language of human emotion, the expression of the unexpressable."[15]

Jewish music's medieval decline and modern renewal

Chroniclers of Jewish worship confirm a periodic shifting between uninhibited unison song and dignified responsive chant throughout the Middle Ages. In 883, a Jew from Southeast Africa, Eldad the Danite, reported how his own warlike tribe—descendants of Samson—kept shouting a single phrase, *Shema Yisrael Adonai Eloheinu Adonai Echad* ("Hear O Israel, the Lord our God is One," Deuteronomy 6:4), at the top of their lungs in preparation for battle. He contrasted this with the tribe of Reuben, which chanted in methodical antiphony from a Torah scroll—the text in Hebrew, its translation in the vernacular—one thousand miles northward on the Red Sea coast.[16] In 930, a Babylonian Jew, Nathan, described how his co-religionists all joined in lustily singing out whole sections of the service.[17] Two centuries later, the oldest *piyyut* to be written down with primitive musical notation ("Who Stood on Horeb's Mountain?") was composed in sedate Gregorian style by Obadiah the Proselyte, a Norman monk who converted to Judaism in 1102.[18]

Over the next five hundred years, synagogue worship would grow increasingly more uninhibited. When King Charles II openly readmitted Israelites to the British Isles in 1660 after their banishment since 1290, enterprising exiles from the Iberian peninsula (*Sepharad* in Hebrew) were the first to return. Initially allowed to worship only in the cramped confines of private homes, Jews of Spanish/Portuguese descent shocked the famous diarist of Restoration London, Samuel Pepys, with the offhandedness of their worship: "But Lord, to see the disorder, laughing, sporting, and no attention but confusion in all their service, more like brutes than people knowing the true God. I never...could have imagined there had been any religion in the world so absurdly performed as this."[19]

Nor was synagogue practice in *Ashkenaz* (the Hebrew word for Germany) immune to criticism, mainly by Jews themselves. Two centuries after Samuel Pepys's disparagement of Sephardic ritual, Ashkenazic leader Meyer Israel Bresselau criticized the Hamburg community's prevalent style of service in an ominously titled pamphlet, "Avenging Sword of the Covenant": "Three stand; one raises a lion's voice that can cause cows to bear calf...the second roars, the third chirps...will God listen to your yelling?"[20] This generic trio must have brought German synagogue music to its low point, for communities referred to the ensemble facetiously as *klei chomos,* or "instruments of violence."

Yet, at the very moments when both main branches of synagogue practice had succumbed to relative anarchy, they would undergo rebirths that stand as systematic paradigms even today. In seventeenth century Mantua, in northern Italy, synagogues heard four-part choral music with orchestral accompaniment during worship for the first time, written in Western notation by the Sephardic court composer Salomone Rossi (1565–1628).[21] Services at which these compositions were performed, including the Sabbath service and on other holy days, avoided the rabbinic injunction against musical instruments being played on the Sabbath through extremely dexterous scheduling: they either concluded just before the Day of Rest began or commenced an hour after it ended.

The following century saw elaborate processions wind their way through Amsterdam's Jewish quarter on the eve of holy days in celebration of community landmark events, and featuring original cantatas with string, woodwind, and brass accompaniment. If surviving manuscripts are any indication,[22] these public observances by Sephardic synagogues in eighteenth-century Amsterdam managed to achieve an exquisite blend of ritual observance and artistic expression. That self-assurance pervades a Sephardic hymn, sung on Rosh Hashanah, that recounts Isaac's "binding" upon a sacrificial altar (based on Genesis 22).

‖ EXAMPLE 2

Sephardic Hymn based on Genesis 22, opening verse[23]

> Eit sha'arei ratzon
> lehipatei'ach.
> yom eheyeh chapai
> le'eil shotei'ach,
> ana zechor na li
> beyom hochei'ach,
> okeid vehane'ekad
> vehamizbei'ach.
>
> ⁓
>
> Now let the Gates of Mercy
> Be opened on high.
> At this hour
> We ask You, God, to
> Remember the beloved son
> Who, at Your command,
> Was bound by his father
> Upon the altar.

Abraham prepares the wood and binds Isaac, his tears turning the day into night. The boy begs his father to "tell Mother Sarah to turn her face away from the son born to her in old age; who gave himself up to the knife and the flame. Take my ashes and tell her, 'This is what remains of Isaac, who was bound upon the altar.'" As that passage was recited, a collective shudder swept through the women's gallery. On high, the angels plead before God's Mercy Throne, "Let not the world be without its light!"

⊩ EXAMPLE 3
Sephardic Hymn, closing verse

> Amar le'avraham
> adon shamayyim
> al tishlechayad
> el shlish utayim;
> shuva leshalom,
> mala'chei shamayim.
> yom zeh zechut
> livnei yerushalayim;
> bo cheit benei ya'akov
> ani Solei'ach.
> okeid vehane'ekad,
> vehamizbei'ach.
>
> ⁓
>
> Then to Abraham
> God relented, saying:
> Do not lay your hand
> Upon the lad; return
> To your place in peace.
> For every year on this day
> I shall show mercy
> To your descendants.
> The sins of My people
> Will be forgiven
> In remembrance of the son
> Who was bound upon the altar.

Isaac is released from his bindings the same way that he was bound: at God's command. Abraham's unquestioning willingness to relinquish his most precious possession earns his offspring an equally unconditional promise. The covenant that God had made with them earlier (Genesis 17:7) would now last "throughout the ages."

During the nineteenth century, another cycle of creativity occurred in Hapsburg Vienna, and afforded Ashkenazic Jewry the opportunity to secure its own moment in the sun. After an exile of 111 years, the re-established community fashioned a compromise ritual that satisfied the demands of both impulse and predictability. The brilliant baritone cantor Salomon Sulzer (1804–90) reclaimed an age-old stock of prayer melodies that dated back hundreds of years.[24] He balanced them as antecedent and consequent phrases for cantor and congregation that matched the parallelistic strophes of biblical Hebrew, and the Psalms above all, from which ninety per cent of the liturgy derives. Psalm 145:1 typifies biblical parallelism, a single thought expressed in two different ways: "I exalt You, my God and Sovereign; I bless Your name forever and ever."

Salomon Sulzer and his psalmodic approach to prayer chant—essentially musical questions and answers—served as a model for disseminating the Ashkenazic tradition throughout Europe and North America. It is found in his arrangement of a forgiveness prayer from Neilah, the closing high holiday service on Yom Kippur, the Day of Atonement. In this setting, the bracketed opening of each verse was sung by worshippers led by a choir of men and boys, and the cantor responded with the second half of each verse.

⁞ EXAMPLE 4 (Track 2)
Responsive High Holiday Forgiveness Prayer[25]

    [Adonai, Adonai]
    Eil rachum vechanun
    [erech apayim]
    verav chesed ve'emet
    [notseir chesed la'alafim]
    nosei avon vafesha vechata'ah venakeh
    [vesalachta la'avoneinu]
    ulechatateinu unechaltanu
    ~

    [The Lord, the Lord,]
    merciful and compassionate,
    [patient One,]
    abounding in love and faithfulness,
    [assuring love for thousands of generations,]
    forgiving iniquity, transgression and sin,
    [pardon our iniquity]
    and our sin; claim us for Your own.

Psalmodic recitation lends solemnity above all to Judaism's declaration of faith—the Shema (Deuteronomy 6:4)—which is sung first by the cantor and then repeated by the congregation. During morning and evening services on weekdays, when worshippers must rush off to work or get home for supper, a simple chant works best. At Sabbath morning services, when the Torah Scroll is removed from the Holy Ark to be publicly read, there is time for more ornate psalmody.

⊦ Example 5 (Track 3)
Judaism's Declaration of Faith, the Shema:
Weekday and Sabbath (*twice each*)[26]

> Shema Yisrael,
> Adonai Eloheinu,
> Adonai Echad
>
> ∿
>
> Hear, O Israel
> The Lord is our God
> The Lord is One!

The role and structure of chant in Judaism

Three techniques are traditionally employed in transmitting the Hebrew liturgy orally: cantillation, psalmody, and modal chant. The word "chant" derives from the verb "enchant" in both English and Hebrew: "enchantment" (Hebrew: *manganah*) is achieved through "chant" (Hebrew: *n'ginah*).[27] Synagogue song has traditionally drawn its motifs from the musical declamation of Hebrew scripture, a practice at least twenty-five hundred years old.[28] In order for biblical texts to sanctify both the moment and the worshippers who hear them, those who cantillated Scripture intoned the words melodically from before the Christian Era.[29]

Cantillation—the first technique which comprises chant in Jewish practice—depends for its effect as much on rhetoric as on music; each word is sung to a tiny melody of its own, often consisting of no more than two or three notes. Special signs—called neumes (from the Greek *pneuma*, meaning "breath")—were later used to indicate the melodies, called neume motifs. "Neume" in Hebrew is *ta'am*, whose root has several meanings: "taste," "accent," and "sense." Neumes impart taste to scripture through the tiny melo/rhythmic figurations whose contours they signify. They denote accent through their placement above or below certain syllables, and they convey sense by creating pauses or running words together. This system of neumes dates from a tenth-century school centred in Tiberias, on the Sea of Galilee.[30] Eleven hundred years later, congregations still cantillate the passage presented below (Leviticus 16:1–2) to the same neumes. Yet, depending on the community's geographical location, motifs to which those neumes are sung might sound entirely different. Turkish Jewry, living in a Middle Eastern cultural sphere, prefer a free and ornate cantillation that maintains listeners' interest through an ever-changing succession of rapidly delivered and closely spaced tones. German Jews, living in a culture steeped in the rich sonorities of Bach chorales, would relate better to a regular and unadorned chant marked by long-held notes spaced a third apart (as in D-F, F-A, A-F), implying underlying harmonies.

∥ EXAMPLE 6 (Track 4)
Biblical Cantillation of Torah in Two Traditions:
Turkish and German.[31]

> Vaidabeir adonai el mosheh,
> acharei mot
> shenei benei aharon
> vayomer adonai
> ∿
>
> And God spoke to Moses,
> after the death
> of Aaron's two sons...
> and God said

The second technique, psalmody, follows no prescribed cantillation motifs, yet quotes them freely in order to stimulate the worshippers' imagination. The passing musical references serve to remind people of other moments in their religious lives and in the lives of those who preceded them. The texts to which Jewish prayer chant is applied consist of balanced half-verses either quoted directly from the book of Psalms or patterned after it, and are performed as a steady intonation of many syllables on one note, a "reciting" tone whose rhythm and poetic metre are determined by its word-accents. This ends in a flourish of many notes on a single syllable, called a melisma, which traditionally punctuates every verse or semi-verse of prayer chanted in the synagogue. Melismas traditionally borrow their musical contour from neume motifs associated with biblical cantillation.

The first two techniques, cantillation's short vertical outcroppings and psalmody's long horizontal lines, combine to form the third technique: modal chant, or chanting according to fixed musical modes. There are three principal modes. The laudatory mode—*Adonai Malach* ("Adonai Reigns")—is a bright-sounding major mode, with its seventh and tenth degrees lowered a half-step. It perfectly suits a passage from the Passover Eve Haggadah ("retelling") of God's role in redeeming ancient Israel from Egyptian bondage, illustrated in example 7.

‖ EXAMPLE 7 (Track 5)
Passage from the Passover Eve Haggadah[32]

Avadim hayinu,
lefar'oh bemitsrayim,
vayotsi'einu adonai eloheinu
misham beyad chazakah
uvizro'a netuyah.
Ve'ilu lo hotsi
hakadosh baruch hu
et avoteinu mimitsrayim,
harei anu uvaneinu
uvenei vaneinu
meshubadim hayinu
lefar'oh bemitsrayim.
Va'afilu kulanu chachamim,
kulanu zekeinim,
kulanu yodeim et hatorah,
mitsvah aleinu
lesapeir bitsi'at mitsrayim.
Vechol hamarbeh
lesapeir bitsi'at mitsrayim
harei zeh meshubach.

～

Once we were slaves
to Pharaoh in Egypt,
and Adonai our God brought us forth
from there with mighty hand
and outstretched arm.
Had our ancestors
not been delivered
by God from Egypt,
we and our children
and our children's children
would still be slaves
to Pharaoh in Egypt.
And no matter how learned
any of us may be
in the Law,
it is our duty
to retell the Exodus story.

And any who dwell
upon the story at length
are to be commended.

The didactic mode—*Magein Avot* ("Protector of Our Ancestors")—is a pastoral-like minor mode that works effectively in a night prayer that anchors the *Ma'ariv* (Evening) service (example 8).

⫽ EXAMPLE 8 (Track 6)
A Night Prayer[33]

Hashkiveinu, adonai eloheinu,
Leshalom;
veha'amideinu, malkeinu,
lechayim…
vehagein ba'adeinu,
vehaseir mei'aleinu; oyeiv…
uvetseil kenafecha tastireinu…
uferos aleinu
sukat shelomecha…

≈

Cause us, our God,
to lie down in peace,
and raise us, our Sovereign,
to life…
protect us,
rid us of our enemies…
shelter us beneath Your wings…
spread over us
Your tabernacle of peace…

The supplicatory mode—*Ahavah Rabah* ("With Great Love")—is a major mode with its second and sixth degrees lowered a half-step. This adds fervour to the Priestly Blessing's introductory liturgical verse, seen below in example 9.

⫽ EXAMPLE 9 (Track 7)
The Priestly Blessing's Introductory Liturgical Verse[34]

Eloheinu veilohei avoteinu,
borcheinu vabrachah hamshuleshet,
batorah haktuvah
al yedei mosheh avdecha,
ha'amurah mipi

aharon uvanav, kohanim
am kedoshecha, ka'amur.

～

Our God and God of our forebears,
bless us with the three-fold blessing
written in the Torah
by Your servant, Moses,
and pronounced aloud by
Aaron and his priestly descendants,
Your holy people, as it is written.

Cantors used to improvise new settings for given texts by combining motifs from three secondary prayer modes—for study, forgiveness, and yearning—with motifs from the three principal modes and with each other. They also quoted neume motifs from the six sets of biblical cantillations for different occasions, of which there are at least eight regional variants. This created innumerable opportunities for renewing a fixed liturgy by constantly varying the way it was performed: in other words, by inventively rearranging seemingly unrelated phrases into unexpected sequences, tempos, rhythms, and voice qualities to evoke a specific ethos or atmosphere. In short, the prayer modes carry moods, in line with the ancient Greek doctrine set forth by Aristotle (*Metaphysics* 8.5). The ethos of *Adonai Malach* supposedly led to righteousness, that of *Magein Avot* to learning, and that of *Ahavah Rabah* to contrition.

Licence for creating new prayer melodies as well as variations on old ones derives from the Talmud: "Do not make your prayer predictable" (Mishnah, *Avot* 2:18). Since the amount of actual chanting during contemporary services has been severely curtailed in favour of metrical tunes deemed conducive to congregational participation, synagogue composers have tried to meet the need for accessible new music, with varying degrees of success. Many have attempted to fit prayer book wordings to pop song formats, adding original Hebrew lyrics that are often grammatically suspect. The following have been among the rhythmic subheadings chosen: mariachi, reggae, soft shoe, calypso, funky, and bouncy. Hardly any American synagogue composers have adapted motifs from biblical cantillation or prayer modes and—using the standard liturgy—woven them into balanced psalmodic recitative that can be sung by both professional cantors and lay worshippers. A few exceptions are Edward Stark ("Let Us Adore"),[35] Arthur Yolkoff ("Tov Lehodot"),[36] and Craig Taubman ("Yigdal").[37]

The role of instruments in Judaism

While there are elaborate descriptions of the varieties of musical instruments that were employed in the Jerusalem Temple, the final collapse of Jewish sovereignty in 70 CE created the diasporic situation in which the rabbis who compiled and canonized both Talmuds (Palestinian ca. 400 CE, Babylonian ca. 500 CE) forbade the use of musical instruments in worship. Both out of a sense of grief for this monumental loss and as a safeguard against tendencies toward sensuality, Jews in exile restricted their religious expression to vocalization. While most religious traditions that originated in the Middle Eastern cultural sphere gave priority to vocal music, with instruments playing a secondary role, the synagogue banned musical instruments outright. This was also in deference to the Second Temple's discontinued rite, in which singing took precedence over instrumental playing at the sacrificial service (Babylonian Talmud, *Arakhin* 11a) as well as at the daily prayer service (Babylonian Talmud, *Sukkah* 51a).

During the long national exile, rabbinic authorities like Maimonides (1135–1204 CE) forbade Jews even to listen to instrumental music while the Temple lay in ruins.[38] The issue did not arise again until early in the nineteenth century when, following political emancipation in Western Europe, several communities introduced the organ along with other worship reforms. Innovators like Rabbi Aaron Chorin of Arad in Hungary,[39] pointed to a seventeenth-century precedent for synagogue prayer accompanied by an organ in Prague.[40] The counter-reformers, championed by Rabbi Moses Sofer of Pressburg (also in Hungary), prohibited organ playing during worship as "conforming to the statutes of other nations" (Leviticus 18:3).[41] Despite the ban, organ music has steadily entered European and North American synagogues over the past two centuries. The main reason for this was given by Louis Lewandowsky, chief choirmaster of the Berlin synagogues from 1876 until his death in 1894: "There is not a greater evil than ... the inability of the choir to control the congregation's mainly jumbled singing.... The time has come to add a strong support to the choral aspect of the service."[42]

Synagogue ritual reform began in Westphalia, Germany, in 1810, when Israel Jacobson exchanged the traditional rabbinic role of legal authority for that of minister. Jacobson eliminated the *chazzan* and "conducted" services in the manner of a Christian clergyman. He drastically cut the liturgy, removing every *piyyut* and all references to a national restoration in Zion. But when he also discontinued the responsive chanting of prayer, Jacobson stripped Jewish worship of its primary motive force. In a feeble attempt to replace it, he borrowed one or two hymns from Protestant usage, most notably "O Head, All Bruised and Wounded," the principal chorale of Johann Sebastian Bach's *St. Matthew Passion*.[43]

That sort of complete overhaul proved an exception.[44] The service in most German Liberal synagogues, while slightly abbreviated when compared to its Orthodox counterpart, was still sung entirely in Hebrew. A *chazzan*—assisted by organ and mixed or boys' choir—led prayer. It was an unusual blend of progressive thought and traditional practice, and it remained as a model in Central European liberal synagogues right up to the Second World War.[45]

The first American synagogue to install an organ was Beth Elohim of Charleston, South Carolina, in 1841. When New York's Temple Emanuel adopted the organ in 1847, the die was cast for American Reform congregations and, eventually, for about 10 per cent of those that affiliated with the Conservative (middle-of-the-road) movement. Orthodoxy, which accounts for 9 per cent of contemporary Jewry, shuns the use of instruments during worship. Reconstructionism, a 1930s offshoot of Conservatism that established itself as an international movement in 1996, avoids the organ but invites voluntary congregational accompaniment on folk instruments like the guitar. The World Center for Progressive Judaism in Jerusalem sets the pattern for Israeli Reform practice. It adheres to as much tradition as is compatible with liberal ideology; the liturgy is in Hebrew (since that is the Jewish state's official language), sung sometimes with and sometimes without instrumental accompaniment.

The role of music in American Judaism: Foreign borrowings and use of hymnals

Viewed from the perspective of an endlessly rotating creative cycle, Jewish worship in the New World has faithfully mirrored the changing preferences of its distant past, ranging from the impromptu excitement of Moses' song at the Red Sea through the Second Temple's highly organized psalmody. Continuing changes in North American synagogue procedure are traceable largely to the freedom that North American citizens enjoy to observe the religion of their choice in a manner with which they are comfortable. The changes are also due to the specificity of Jewish immigration there during different periods. The first to arrive, in 1654, were Sephardic Jews of Portuguese descent, whose meticulously performed ritual (see example 2) prevailed for almost two hundred years among the ten thousand Jews scattered in a vast and untamed land.

Around 1840, Sephardic practice was eclipsed by a wave of Ashkenazic immigration to the United States from the German-speaking lands of Central Europe—two hundred and sixty thousand by the end of the Civil War. That meant another turn of the worship cycle because, in the absence of qualified leadership, the newcomers' prayer practice was totally disorganized. It was the crudest sort of synagogue service that held sway in the United States in the mid-nineteenth century, when many newly arrived German Jews had no choice but to rough it along a frontier that was moving rapidly westward. In the absence of trained cantors, those who took it upon themselves to lead prayer were generally unversed in Jewish law or custom, and were relying instead on raw emotion and their own quick wits. Not surprisingly, they drew criticism from one of the first ordained rabbis to arrive, Isaac Mayer Wise.

In his memoirs, Rabbi Wise recounts the debut of a choir he formed at his first synagogue in Albany, New York. "Yes, the choir sang; but I pray you, do not ask how. It made no difference to our chazzan whether he began or ended a few notes lower or higher; he passed with surpassing ease from one key to another, and the choir was expected to keep up with him. The shipwrecked notes were mixed up fearfully and wonderfully, until finally everyone sang ad lib, and stopped only when the text was finished."[46]

Wise's organizational skills, however, led the Reform movement to adopt a non-participatory, church-inspired service. Liturgy was established along the lines of a readily accessible Protestantism, with services stressing reading and preaching. Congregants sank comfortably into cushioned pews while surrounded by a wall-to-wall carpet of organ music. They were content to maintain a silence of glacial proportions except when joining in hymns, typically sung to church or secular tunes, like "I Know That My Redeemer Liveth," "Hark! The Herald Angels Sing," and "Deutschland über Alles."[47] The distinguished twentieth-century composer Hugo D. Weisgall (1912–96), who as a young music student had been organist and choirmaster in Baltimore's Temple Ohab Shalom, observed how the Reform service also borrowed tunes from Italian opera and German oratorio. "Thinly disguised, completely platitudinous versions of the *Miserere* from *Il Trovatore* or the *Sollene in Quest'Ora* from *La Forza del Destino*[48] were sung to the text of Shiviti [Psalm 16:8–9; 'I have set the Lord ever before me'] in the Memorial service for Yom Kippur."[49]

Until the nineteenth century Jewish hymnals did not exist; all texts were sung from prayer books as they occurred in the liturgy. When the Reform temple in Hamburg, Germany radically abridged its prayer book in 1818, it also published a hymnal that contained modified Lutheran chorales with organ accompaniment. In 1848, the first American Reform hymnal appeared in Charleston, South Carolina. It set the pattern for others in New York City (1868), Chicago (1876), Evansville, Indiana (1878), Rochester, New York (1880), and Cincinnati, Ohio (1895). In 1897, the Central Conference of American Rabbis (Reform) issued its own *Union Hymnal*, the first in a series intended for all congregations affiliated with the

Reform movement. The Orthodox, Conservative, and Reconstructionist national organizations have never formalized their musical repertoires beyond the periodic compilation of song booklets used in summer camps and by families around the Sabbath table.

Just as the creative pendulum of North American Jewish worship swung back to non-participation at the nineteenth century's close, more than two million Jewish immigrants arrived, fleeing from religious and economic persecution in Eastern Europe. Once established in their new surroundings, the so-called "greenhorns" initiated a groundswell of sentiment for the homespun culture they had left behind. The earthy language and small-town conventions of that civilization were obligingly brought to life by Yiddish theaters that flourished in immigrant neighborhoods like New York's Lower East Side. The authentic sounds of Eastern European-style Jewish prayer were faithfully reproduced by a host of accomplished cantors, who emigrated in numbers sufficient to prompt claims for a Golden Age of synagogue song. Too often, though, brilliant solo cantorial efforts were undone by ragtag male choirs, whose shrieking adult falsettos and yowling boy altos fell far short of musical refinement. It was a failed attempt to transplant a highly ornamented religious chant that had travelled from the Middle East to Europe one thousand years before, and from there to the inhospitable soil of America's machine-age culture.

Constant change in the way synagogue prayers were offered continued through the first two decades of the twentieth century, with each group of newcomers advocating a regional preference from the old home. Those who had preceded them by a few years and had already become Americanized tried to tone down elements that they already considered outdated. In the 1930s, a near-total clampdown on Eastern European immigration to the United States and Canada disrupted this sequence just as the liturgical swing from one extreme to the other paused at its halfway mark. In the face of rampant anti-Semitism at home and abroad, a beleaguered North American Jewish community sought solace in more understated devotions. In 1934, the Swiss/Jewish composer Ernest Bloch produced his *Sacred Service* for cantor, choir, and orchestra in response to a commission from Temple Emanuel of San Francisco.[50] Its spacious treatment of the liturgy and transparent musical texture made it appear as if a workable middle ground between hit-or-miss excitement and boring consistency had again been attained. Very few congregations of the Depression era could afford the luxury of a full symphonic chorus and orchestra to accompany prayer, however. Bloch's landmark achievement was relegated to occasional concert performances, while synagogue services of every persuasion were kept under tight control as the international situation worsened.

Mysticism in Judaism: Hasidism and music

Historically, whenever Jewish worship over-organized itself, a clamor for deregulation arose in protest. From the eighth to the fifth centuries BCE, the rallying cry of every Hebrew prophet was that God prefers rambunctious righteousness to unblemished sacrifice (Hosea 6:6). Between the first and seventh century of this era, Talmudic authorities declared that the All-Merciful One looks to the heart rather than to the mind (Babylonian Talmud, *Sanhedrin* 106b). Jewish mystical thinking has always maintained that "in the Hereafter, rules and prohibitions will no longer hold sway" (Babylonian Talmud, *Niddah* 61b).[51]

That teaching resurfaced in eighteenth-century Poland, where bloody pogroms and grinding poverty had removed all hope from the impoverished Jewish masses. Amid this pervasive misery arose a group of saintly religious teachers, known as Tzaddikim, who lifted the yoke of ritual requirements so that their devout adherents—the Hasidim—might have easier access to God. Rather worry over failure to fulfill every minute provision of rabbinic law, the founder of Hasidism, Israel Ba'al Shem Tov ("Master of the Good Name," 1700–60), stressed joy and ecstasy as being closer to God's presence,[52] and music as the medium by which joy and ecstasy was to be aroused. One of Hasidism's more innovative dispensations was to permit singing melodies without words, known as *niggunim*, as an acceptable form of prayer when worshippers could not read the liturgy. Filler syllables (e.g., ai-di-di-di dai) were sung and danced to steadily accelerating tempos—and to rising volumes and pitches—until a crescendo was reached. Then the music dropped an octave, and the whole process started again.

The explosive Hasidic approach to ritual still survives in mainstream synagogues as emotional prayer (*tefillat haregesh*). Its opposite—elegant but detached worship—is called orderly prayer (*tefillat haseder*). So, in addition to an ongoing worship cycle of rabbinically imposed conformity that discouraged individual expression, recent centuries have witnessed a see-sawing between the pietistic fervour of Hasidism and the staunch propriety of its mainstream Orthodox opponents. This opposition has softened considerably since a very small number of Hasidic survivors arrived in the United States and Canada after the Second World War. At first, they served mainly as a reminder of what had been lost—the life piously lived without expectation of earthly reward. In time, their example provided the impetus for a general effort to recapture elements of that lifestyle in North America, and lately in the decimated but slowly reviving Jewish centres of Europe.

Current trends and the future of music in Judaism

In the mid-twentieth century, when North American Jewry realized that its European counterpart of six million souls had been obliterated, a feeling of remorse over the failure to prevent the slaughter paved the way for openly emotional worship. European-born cantors—even those who had emigrated to America decades before and had thus escaped the Holocaust—seized upon any text that could express the despair they felt over those who perished. A Sabbath Eve text that welcomes the Day of Rest as Israel's Bride—*Lo Teivoshi*—was treated as a memorial dirge even though it promises redemption (example 10).

‖ EXAMPLE 10
    A Text of Sabbath Welcome—*Lo Teivoshi* (treated as a dirge)[53]

> Lo teivoshi velo tikal'mi,
> mah tishtochachi umah tehemi;
> bach yechesu aniyei ami,
> venivnetah ir al tilah.
>
> ᙏ
>
> Zion, be not ashamed [says God];
> My afflicted people
> Will re-enter your gates
> And rebuild the ancient ruins.

The relentlessness of that litany—in a poignant mode begging forgiveness—made the Sabbath feel like Yom Kippur! Yet the approach proved effective until 1968, when nightly television news started showing the bloody results of American napalm bombing in Vietnam. At the moment when police at the Democratic Party's National Convention in Chicago clubbed demonstrators who protested those air strikes, many young people of draft age lost all respect for authority. Even their songs rejected the four-square congregational anthems their parents sang. They began "pushing the beat," anticipating the accent a fraction ahead of time, and holding that note through the actual beat.[54] This was especially true of 1960s "peacenik" songs like "Where Have All the Flowers Gone?" by Pete Seeger.[55]

   In the 1970s, young North American-born cantors began imitating not only the "pushed" beat but also the melodic motif just cited, which every pop and rock singer seemed to be featuring. Paul Simon's "Bridge over Troubled Water" comes to mind, particularly the line "all your dreams are on their way."[56] That motif had permeated American life for 150 years, in folk songs like "Singing Polly Wolly Doodle All the Day"[57] and "Hal-

leluyah, I'm a Bum."[58] It happened to mesh seamlessly with the lauda-
tory mode's optimistic mood (*Adonai Malach*: see example 7, earlier). By the
1980s, cantorial students at the Reform Hebrew Union College's School of
Sacred Music, the Conservative Jewish Theological Seminary's H.L. Miller
Cantorial School, and the Orthodox Yeshiva University's Belz School of
Jewish Music had plugged the motif—together with its characteristic
American syncopation—into prayers. The new offbeat rhythm gave clas-
sical Hebrew prayers the stress pattern of colloquial speech.

At the twentieth century's conclusion, that kind of musical inventive-
ness had run its course. Synagogue practice had become timid, afraid of
showing too much emotion in an age when being "cool" was considered
"in." The worship cycle now tilted toward the intellectual. Those who led
prayer began enlisting structuralism, a methodology developed by the
French anthropologist Claude Levi-Strauss,[59] to uncover the hidden message beneath the surface narrative of the mythic tales of various cultures.
This new understanding of ancient metaphor and its place in religious
belief was taken as licence to dissect the Hebrew liturgy. Prayer was converted into instruction through deconstruction, a rigorous form of analysis that sets out to reveal the underlying ideological assumption of a given
text.[60]

Congregations proved willing audiences because, unlike other ethnic
groups, North America's Jews had forsaken their hereditary language
in order to fit in better with society at large.[61] Minute analysis not only
of prayer wordings but of everything that took place during worship
suited their needs perfectly. Regular synagogue goers, however, faced
with endless information about a liturgy they had prayed hundreds of
times in their lives, learned to play dumb. Along with the neophytes, they
responded only on command, and then only grudgingly.

On the bright side, American Reform and Conservative Judaism began
ordaining women as cantors during the 1980s, after seven hundred years
of men exclusively leading synagogue prayer. Liturgist Lawrence A. Hoffman documents the fact that women had played active roles in the synagogue as early as the ninth century and as late as the thirteenth century, but
were not permitted to do so thereafter.[62] This despite the fact that a woman
prophetess, Miriam (Exodus 15:20-1), and a woman judge, Deborah
(Judges 5), had led mixed gender communal prayer in biblical times, and
that the hundreds of levitical singers whom King Cyrus of Persia repatri-
ated to Judea from Babylonian exile in the fifth century BCE had included
both men and women (Ezra 2:65).

In American Jewish religious practice, change emerges from below in
a popular groundswell, and is then canonized by rabbinic decree from on
high.[63] So it has been with the ever-growing number of women cantors

who now serve in Judaism's liberal movements worldwide. Without prior role models among their own gender, they have been forced to imitate the prayer-leading style and mannerisms of male cantors. Furthermore, although these women officiate in Reform, Conservative, and Reconstructionist congregations, the style most widely admired and disseminated through recordings is the Orthodox style from the early through mid-twentieth century, with its superstar tenors like Josef Rosenblatt (1882–1933) and Moshe Koussevitzky (1877–1966). The high-flying vocal pyrotechnics (such as sailing on the high c's) at which those virtuosos excelled do not suit many female voices, and young women seminary graduates often find difficulty in reproducing them.

Currently, American pop song influences have diluted the ethnic flavour of synagogue prayer, almost eliminating the exotic modal intervals of sacred chant. It has also levelled the playing field for some women new to cantorial practice. Since male cantors lately sound remarkably similar to the musical entertainers on radio and television, women cantors can now follow suit with impunity. Singing in more comfortable lower registers to a supportive metred rhythm, they bring innovative dimensions along with nurturing reassurance to the congregants. And, whether they tend toward a tranquil or passionate style, the leadership of public worship by women is now increasingly welcomed by forward-thinking congregations, and will eventually be accepted even by Orthodoxy (although that may not happen in the near future).

Surprisingly, a revival of frenzied Hasidic-style worship is currently underway in the former Soviet Union among Jews who have chosen to remain rather than join the million who have already emigrated to Israel. In September 2000, on the three hundredth anniversary of the Ba'al Shem Tov's birth, Russian President Vladimir Putin came out of the Kremlin to help open the first Hasidic synagogue in Moscow since 1917. An estimated ten thousand people watched on a video screen set up in the street as Putin stood at attention and a shofar was sounded. Natan Scharansky, a former refusenik who epitomized Russian Jewry's struggle for freedom from Soviet repression and who now heads a political party in Israel, spoke, saying "These are the streets where they tried to destroy our identity; we once thought we were the last Jews, without a future or a past."[64]

The Moscow synagogue's Friday night devotions no longer have to express lamentation: they are the most cheerful services imaginable. Beginning with *Lo Teivoshi* ("Zion, Be Not Ashamed," the Sabbath-welcoming verse presented in elegaic style as example 10), hundreds of young Russian Jews dance in the aisles to a merry Hasidic tune (example 11) that is far removed from cantorial chant. It uses a recognizable tempo—allegro—instead of depending on the words of a recitative for its rhythm. Its melodic fingerprint suggests both Russian folk dances and French military marches. It features a sprightly realization of *Magein Avot*, rather than the poignant forgiveness mode. Its melismatic figurations—articulated a third of the time through filler syllables—derive from harmonic sequences instead of biblical neume motifs. Example 11 also adds the three verses that follow *Lo Teivoshi* in the Friday Night *piyyut* known by its refrain, "Lecha Dodi."

‖ EXAMPLE 11

Verses 6–9 of "Lecha Dodi," including its refrain[65]

Lo teivoshi velo tikal'mi,
mah tishtochachi umah tehemi
bach yechesu aniyei ami,
venivnetah ir al tilah.
Lecha Dodi, likrat kalah,
penei shabbat nekab'lah!
Vehayu limshisah shosayich
verachaku kol meval'ayich;
yasis alayich Elohayich
kimsos chatan al kalah.

Lecha Dodi …

Yamin us'mol tifrotsi,
ve'et Adonai ta'aritsi;
al yad ish ben partsi,
venism'cha venagilah.

Lecha Dodi …

Bo'i veshalom ateret ba'alah,
gam besimcha uv'tsoholah
toch emunei am segulah;
bo'i chalah, bo'i chalah.

Lecha Dodi …

Zion, be not ashamed [says God];
My afflicted people
Will re-enter your gates
And rebuild the ancient ruins.
Come, My Beloved, to
Greet the Sabbath Bride!
Those who oppressed you
Will themselves be oppressed;

God will rejoice over you
As a newly wed bridegroom.

Break out of your shackles
And render glory to God;
Messiah will come at last,
Bringing cheer and happiness.

Let the Bride now enter,
Greeted with gladness
By God's faithful, who plead:
Come, beloved Sabbath Queen!

Hasidic fervour is increasingly evident in the synagogue services of other movements within Judaism that have adopted the practice of singing and dancing to filler syllables as their prime medium of religious expression. This is so widespread now that, along with Hebrew prayers and English readings, visitors to synagogues of almost any persuasion—no matter where in the world—will hear an equal number of newly composed Hasidic-style melodies. This cross-over trend is not simply an attempt to make the liturgy accessible to those unfamiliar with Hebrew; transliteration would accomplish the same end. It is another recycling of the Jewish people's initial reaction to its unexpected salvation at the Red Sea: the unbridled passion of unison hymnody. Judaism's current re-embrace of passion in its sacred music is symptomatic of that recycling—a shift from pulpit micromanagement to congregational self-expression in the synagogue.

Notes

1 "The exchange between text, words, and instrumental sounds can ... assume two phases: vocal, instrumental–vocal." Curt Sachs (1962), 37.
2 Joseph A. Levine (2000), 117. Ex. 6.6a, CD 2:11.
3 *The Passover Haggadah* (1953), 45.
4 Anton Ehrenzweig (1967), 5–6, 31–35.
5 R.G. Collingwood, in *The Principles of Art* (1938), 306, characterizes the first phase of artistic creativity as "imaginative experience." The second phase involves an audience, whose function is "not merely a receptive one, but collaborative."
6 More than half of the 150 Psalms either mention a *m'natsei'ach* ("leader"), or else shift personal pronoun from "I" to "We" before the end.
7 "The Letter of Aristeas," in *The Apocrypha and Pseudepigrapha of the Old Testament in English* (1966), verse 95.
8 The Second Temple's orchestra included two harps and nine lyres for accompanying the Levites' song. A single cymbal cued the music as well as the people's prostrations in the outer courtyard. Two flutes were added on twelve holy days during the year, plus four harps and a limitless number of lyres.

9 Hebrew University professor Ehud Netzer unearthed a synagogue—complete with benches and Torah scroll niche—adjoining the Hasmonean Winter Palace in Jericho. See Bizhrano (1998).

10 Solomon Zeitlin (1931): 78.

11 "Chamber of Hewn Stone" in Mishnah, *Sanhedrin* 11.2, Babylonian Talmud, *Yoma* 25a; "Solomon's Portico" in the Christian Bible, Acts 3:11; it doubled as headquarters of the Great Sanhedrin (High Court of Justice).

12 Romanus is remembered today chiefly for his "Hymn for the Second Coming of Christ," which prefigures theological motifs in the eighth-century Jewish doomsday threnody for Rosh Hashanah and Yom Kippur, *Un'taneh Tokef* ("Let us recount the awesome holiness of the day"). Wordings from that *piyyut* reappear in Tomas of Celano's Dies Irae (1200), a staple of the Roman Catholic requiem mass. In Eric Werner (1959), 252–55.

13 *High Holiday Prayer Book* (1951), 261.

14 Steven Lorch (1977), p. 147.

15 Theodore Reik (1953), 8.

16 "The Travels of Eldad the Danite," in *Masterpieces of Hebrew Literature*, edited by Curt Leviant (New York: Ktav Publishing, 1969), 151.

17 Eric Werner (1959), 136, citing Adolf Neubauer, *Medieval Jewish Chronicles*, vol. 2, 83–88.

18 Israel Adler (1969), 5–16.

19 Diary entry for October 14, 1663.

20 Cherev Nokemet Nekam Brit (1819). See Michael A. Meyer (1991).

21 "Hashirim Asher Lishlomo" (Venice, 1623), transcribed and edited in *Cantiques de Salomon Rossi*, vol. II (1876).

22 Israel Adler (1966).

23 Isaac Levy (1974), 270, 276–78. Single-selection audio cassette, "Eit Sha'arei Ratson," excerpted from Inter-Choir Festival, Southgate Centre, 1995. London, Male Choir of the Bevis Marks Congregation, directed by Maurice Martin.

24 Max Grunwald (1936), 219–20. Among the by-laws of the United Viennese Jewry was a stipulation that all melodies sung in the Temple had to approved by the municipal authorities and deposited in the archives of the Tolerated Jews of Vienna.

25 Salomon Sulzer, *Schir Zion*, No. 457 (Vienna, 1865). Joseph A. Levine (2000), 110. Ex. 6.2d, CD 2:7.

26 Joseph A. Levine (2000), 28. Ex. 2.12a, b, CD 1:20.

27 David Wulston (1971), 7.

28 Hanoch Avenary (1963), 8.

29 Sifra on Leviticus 23:44: "And Moses declared the set feasts of the Lord unto the children of Israel." On Acts 15:21: "From early generations Moses had in every city those who preach him, for he is read every Sabbath in the synagogue." For fuller documentation, see Hyman I. Sky (1977), 23–24. See also Babylonian Talmud: *Megillah* 32a, *Sanhedrin* 14a.

30 Max L. Margolis, "Accents in Hebrew," in *The Jewish Encyclopedia*, vol. I (1901), 156.

31 Joseph A. Levine (2000), 47. Ex. 3.10, CD 1:27.

32 Joseph A. Levine (2000), 159. Ex. 7.6c, CD 3:6.

33 Joseph A. Levine (2000), 181. Ex. 8.4, CD 3:13.

34 Joseph A. Levine (2000), 102. Ex. 5.12C, CD 2:5.

35 *Anim Zemiroth* (1911).

36 *Shirat Atideinu* (1966).

37 *Friday Night Live!* (1993).

38 In a responsum. In Henry George Farmer (1941), 15.

39 Nogah Hazedek (Dessau, 1818), in Jakob J. Petuchowski (1968), 93–95.

40 Alfred Sendrey (1970), 349–50. The synagogue's organ had been built by Rabbi Maier Mahler.

41 Akiva Zimmermann (1992), 131–45.

42 See Morton Gold (2000), citing Lewandowsky's January 1, 1862 stand in the controversy over permitting an organ in the new Berlin synagogue then being built on Oranienburgerstrasse.

43 Eric Werner (1976), 195.

44 Jakob J. Petuchowski, "Reform Judaism." In *Encyclopedia Judaica*, vol. 14 (1972), 24–26.

45 Steven M. Leowenstein (1989), 33.

46 Rabbi Isaac Meyer Wise (1901), 53.

47 *Union Hymnal* (1897), 5, 102, 158–59.

48 Giuseppe Verdi: 1853, libretto by Salvatore Cammarano, after a Spanish drama by Antonio Garcia Gutierrez; 1862, libretto by Francesco Piave, after a Spanish drama by the Duke of Rivas.

49 "Jewish Music in America," in Theodore Friedman and Robert Gordis (1955), 249.

50 *Avodath Hakodesh* (1934).

51 Horodetzky (1947), s.v.v. "The Aggadah," "The Kabbalah."

52 Max L. Margolis and Alexander Marks (1978), 582–83.

53 Sixth of the nine verses in Solomon Alkabetz's hymn, "Lecha Dodi" (Safed, sixteenth century). Audio cassette: *The Art of Cantor Yehoshua Wieder* (1973), A, 1.

54 Jeffrey Gutcheon, *Improvising Rock Piano* (1983), 14.

55 Pete Seeger (1961).

56 Paul Simon and Art Garfunkel (1970).

57 *New American Song Book* (1941).

58 Margaret Bradford Boni (1947).

59 Gordon Graham (2000), 191–92.

60 Laurence Lerner (1983), 3.

61 Leon Weiseltier (1999) in "The Ties That Bind," a speech while accepting the National Jewish Book Award for Non-Fiction, said "The Jews of the United States are the first great Jewry in the history of the Diaspora that believes it can receive, develop and transmit the Jewish tradition not in a Jewish language. For this, our historians will judge us severely."

62 Lawrence A. Hoffman (1996), 193–98.

63 See Leon A. Jick (1976), 186–91.

64 Jonathan Mark (2000).

65 *Songs of the Gerer Hasidim* (1962), Track 1.

Bibliography

Adler, Israel. *La practique musicale savante dans quelques communautees juives en Europe aux XVII et XVIII siecles.* Vol. 1. Paris: Mouton, 1966.

———. *Three Synagogue Chants of the Twelfth Century.* Tel Aviv: Israeli Music Publications, 1969.

Alkabetz, Solomon. "Lecha Dodi," *The Art of Cantor Yehoshua Wieder.* Brooklyn, NY: Greater Recording Company (audio cassette).

Anim Zemiroth. New York: Bloch, 1911.

Aristeas. "The Letter of Aristeas." In *The Apocrypha and Pseudographia of the Old Testament in English*, ed. R.H. Charles, 2: verse 95. Oxford: Clarendon Press, 1966.

Avenary, Hanoch. *Studies in the Hebrew, Syrian and Greek Liturgical Recitative*. Tel Aviv: Israel Music Institute, 1963.

Avodath Hakodesh. Boston: C.C. Birchard, 1934.

Bizhrano, Osnat. "Oldest Synagogue…Discovered in Jericho," *Israel Shelanu* March 27, 1998.

Boni, Margaret Bradford. *Fireside Book of Folk Songs*. New York: Simon and Schuster, 1947.

Braun, Joachim. *Music in Ancient Israel/Palestine: Archaeological, Written, and Comparative Sources*. Grand Rapids, MI: William B. Eerdmans, 2002.

Cantiques de Solomon Rossi. Vol. ii. Transcribed and edited by Samuel Naumbourg. Reissued in *Out of Print Classics of Synagogue Music*, no. 16. New York: Bloch, 1954.

Collingwood, R.G. *The Principles of Art*. Oxford: Clarendon Press, 1938.

Ehrenzweig, Anton. *The Hidden Order of Art*. Berkeley and Los Angeles: University of California Press, 1967.

"Eit Sha'arei Ratson." Single-selection audio cassette excerpted from *Inter-Choir Festival*, Southgate Centre, 1995. London, Male Choir of the Bevis Marks Congregation, directed by Maurice Martin.

Encyclopedia Judaica, 18 vols. Jerusalem: Keter, 1972.

Farmer, Henry George. *Maimonides on Listening to Music*. Bearsden, Scotland, n.p., 1941.

Friday Night Live! Sherman Oaks, CA: Sweet Louise Publications, 1993.

Friedman, Theodore, and Robert Gordis, eds. *Jewish Life in America*. New York: Horizon Press, 1955.

Gold, Morton. "Praise for Lewandowsky." *Jewish Post and Opinion*, November 1, 2000.

Gradenwitz, Peter. *The Music of Israel: From the Biblical Era to Modern Times*. Portland, OR: Amadeus Press, 1996.

Graham, Gordon. *Philosophy of the Arts*. 2nd ed. London: Routledge, 2000.

Grunwald, Max. *Vienna*. Trans. Solomon Grayzel. Philadelphia: Jewish Publication Society, 1936.

Gutcheon, Jeffrey. *Improvising Rock Piano*. New York: Amsco, 1983.

Heskes, Irene. *Passport to Jewish Music: Its History, Traditions, and Culture*. New York: Tara, 1994.

High Holiday Prayer Book, ed. Philip Birnbaum. New York: Hebrew Publishing, 1951.

Hoffman, Lawrence A. *The Art of Public Prayer: Not for Clergy Only*. Washington, DC: Pastoral Press, 1988.

———. *Covenant of Blood: Circumcision and Gender in Rabbinic Judaism*. Chicago: University of Chicago Press, 1996.

Horodetzky, Samuel Abba. *Yahadut Haseichel Veyahadut Hagaresh*. Vol. 1. Tel Aviv: N. Tverski, 1947.

Idelsohn, Abraham Z. *Jewish Music in Its Historical Development*. New York: Tudor, 1948.

Jacobson, Joshua R. *Chanting the Hebrew Bible: The Art of Cantillation*. New York: Jewish Publication Society, 2002.

The Jewish Encyclopedia. Vol. 1. New York: Funk and Wagnalls, 1901.

Jick, Leon A. *The Americanization of the Synagogue, 1820–1870*. Hanover, NH: University Press of New England, 1976.

Lerner, Lawrence. *Reconstructing Literature*. Oxford: Basil Blackwell, 1983.

Leowenstein, Steven M. *Frankfurt on the Hudson: The German-Jewish Community of Washington Heights, 1933–1983, Its Structure and Culture*. Detroit: Wayne State University Press, 1989.

Levine, Joseph A. *Synagogue Song in America*. Northvale, NJ: Jason Aronson, 2000. Available from pbs@pathwaybook.com. A set of three one-hour compact discs recorded as a study aid for the book bearing the same title is also available from pbs@pathwaybook.com.

——. *Rise and Be Seated: The Ups and Downs of Jewish Worship*. Northvale, NJ: Jason Aronson, 2001.

Levy, Isaac. *Antologica de Liturgia Judeo-Espanol*. Vol. 6. Jerusalem: Ministry of Education and Culture, 1974.

Lorch, Steven. "The Convergence of Jewish and Western Culture as Exemplified through Music: Some Educational Consequences." PhD dissertation, Columbia University, 1977.

Margolis, Max L., and Alexander Marks. *A History of the Jewish People*. Philadelphia, PA: Jewish Publication Society, 1978.

Mark, Jonathan. "Chabad's Russian Revolution." *The Jewish Week*, December 1, 2000.

Meyer, Michael A. "The Early 19th Century and Viennese Jewry." In *The Legacy of Solomon Sulzer*. Proceedings of a conference at Hebrew Union College, New York, December 8–10, 1991.

Munk, Elie. *The World of Prayer*. 2 vols. Trans. Gertrude Hirschler. New York: Philipp Feldheim, 1963.

Nulman, Macy. *The Encyclopedia of Jewish Prayer*. Northvale, NJ: Jason Aronson, 1996.

Oberndorfer, Anne and Max, eds. *New American Song Book*. Chicago: Hall and McCreary, 1941.

The Passover Haggadah, ed. and trans. Philip Birnbaum. New York: Hebrew Publishing, 1953.

Pasternak, Velvel. *Holidays in Song*. New York: Tara, 1985.

Petuchowski, Jakob J. *Prayer Reforms in Europe*. New York: World Union for Progressive Judaism, 1968.

Reik, Theodore. *The Haunting Melody: Psychoanalytical Experiences in Life and Music*. New York: Farrar, Straus, and Young, 1953.

Rosh Hashanah. A compact disc of excerpts from the New Year liturgy as sung in Holy Blossom Temple, Toronto (available from benyzm@rogers.com).

Sachs, Curt. *The Wellsprings of Music*. The Hague: M. Nijhoff, 1962.

Seeger, Pete. "Where Have All the Flowers Gone?" Fall River Music, 1961.

Sendrey, Alfred. *The Music of the Jews in the Diaspora*. New York: Thomas Yosselof, 1970.

Seroussi, Edwin, et al. "Jewish Music." In *The New Grove Dictionary of Music and Musicians*. 2nd ed. Ed. Stanley Sadie, 13: 24–112. New York: Macmillan, 2001.

Shiloah, Amnon. *Jewish Musical Traditions*. Detroit: Wayne State University Press, 1992.

Shirat Atideinu. New York: Transcontinental, 1966.

Simon, Paul, and Art Garfunkel. "Bridge over Troubled Water," *Bridge over Troubled Water*. Charing Cross Music, 1970.

Sky, Hyman I. "The Development of the Office of Hazzan through the Talmudic Period." PhD dissertation, Dropsie University, 1977.

Songs of the Gerer Hasidim. A compact disc produced by Aderet Music (New York, 1962). Available from mostlymusic.com.

"The Travels of Eldad the Danite." In *Masterpieces of Hebrew Literature*, ed. Curt Leviant. New York: Ktav, 1969.

Union Hymnal. Cincinnati, OH: Central Conference of American Rabbis, 1897.

Werner, Eric. *Sacred Bridge: The Interdependence of Liturgy and Music in Synagogue and Church during the First Millennium*. New York: Columbia University Press, 1959.

———. *A Voice Still Heard: The Sacred Songs of the Ashkenazic Jews*. University Park: Pennsylvania State University Press, 1976.

Wise, Rabbi Isaac Mayer. *Reminiscences*. Trans. David Philipson. Cincinnati, OH: Leo Wise, 1901.

Wulston, David. "The Origin of the Modes." In *Studies in Eastern Chant*, vol. 2, ed. Milos Velimirovic, 5–20. London: Oxford University Press, 1971.

Zeitlin, Solomon. "The Origins of the Synagogue." *Proceedings of the American Academy for Jewish Research* (1931): 69–82.

Zimmerman, Akiva. *Sha'arei Ron: The Cantorate in Rabbinic Responsa*. Tel Aviv: B'Ron Yahad, 1992.

2

CHRISTIANITY AND MUSIC

Gerald Hobbs

With gratitude in your hearts
sing psalms, hymns and spiritual songs to God.[1]

From the origins of the Christian religion, music has been integral to the common life of its believers. Any description of Christian musical practice, however, must take into account the wide range of the Christian experience, which ranges across twenty centuries and among dramatically diverse cultures throughout the world. It must seek to do justice to the formal beliefs and practices of a faith and to the place of music in its rites of public worship. It must also acknowledge that there is a certain common tradition, but also that liturgical celebrations vary widely among the different families into which the Christian church is divided. At the same time, significant attention must be paid to a parallel tradition, the vast corpus of songs or hymns written in some instances as paraliturgical texts, but in others as personal meditation, or as unofficial and lay expressions of the faith.[2] For the past two centuries, most, though not all, Christian denominations have sponsored an official selection of these in hymnals used in public worship, books that are periodically re-edited to reflect changing cultural norms as well as shifting religious emphases. These officially sanctioned collections are, moreover, outnumbered by unofficial publications, whose use ranges from less formal church gatherings to meetings in private homes. Recordings of "pop" hymns are also given regular airplay on commercial radio, particularly in the United States. It would therefore be a serious deformation of the subject not to represent both these official and unofficial dimensions.

Basic teachings and primary sources

The Christian religion was, for many centuries, the formally established faith of Europe. Its myths and liturgy have, at least until the modern era, profoundly shaped the core of the Western musical tradition as a whole. Many of the greatest composers practiced their art primarily as church musicians, writing as well as performing for public worship. Yet, from the first centuries, the Christian faith also had significant communities of adherents in regions of Asia and Africa, while, since the sixteenth century, moving steadily from its European and North American strongholds into all corners of the globe. It is probably inevitable that a Western historian writing for a Western audience will place principal emphasis upon the historical mainstream, but to ignore the practice of millions of adherents in every corner of the globe, or to speak of only one cultural tradition—even that of the (until recently) predominant Western European civilization— would be to repeat the self-centredness of nineteenth-century North Atlantic imperialism. North Americans are only now beginning to discover these traditions, but still must endeavour, at least, to name them as an increasingly significant dimension of the Christian story.

Christianity is a religion whose beginnings lay in the lands of the eastern Mediterranean littoral. Historians and biblical scholars continue to debate the factual reliability of the traditions associated with Jesus of Nazareth, for whom the faith was named. What is indisputable, however, is that he was a Jew living in a border province of the Roman Empire early in the first century of the Common Era. This simple statement expresses Christianity's dual origins, and those of its music. While almost nothing is said within these traditions on the subject of Jesus and music, we are told that he and his disciples "sang the hymn" at the end of their celebration of Passover, at what became known as the Last Supper.[3] As this example suggests, Christian music can best be understood as a direct heir of the Psalms of ancient Israel. By the time of Jesus, the Psalms figured in several dynamic centres of Jewish life and faith. They were sung in the liturgy of the Jerusalem Temple (until it was destroyed by the Romans in 70 CE), in the local synagogues where Jews both in Palestine and throughout the diaspora met for weekly study and prayer, in rituals of the home like the annual *Pesah*, or Passover, celebration, and they were studied by scholars for whom their purported author, the king David, was one of Israel's greatest prophets. Detailed consideration of the Psalms is beyond the scope of this chapter, but a few observations will help to show their contribution to

Christians singing hymns in church. Photo courtesy of Guy L. Beck.

the development of Christian music. The earliest Christians were Jews, although in time the Jewish presence would be reduced to that of a tiny minority. Their conviction that David and many of the Psalms pointed to Jesus as the promised Messiah ("the Christ" in Greek) meant that it was natural to carry forward into Christian assemblies both the reading and the singing of the Psalms. Christians' beliefs were, in their own firm conviction, the fulfillment of all Israel's history and hopes.

Moreover, as the faith of Jesus spread to non-Jews, or Gentiles, it did so initially among those who had already been attracted to Jewish monotheism, so that these worshippers too found it natural to join in singing the Psalms with their allusions, particularly obvious in the Greek translations used in Christian assemblies, to the Christ. Thus, almost seamlessly, Christianity inherited a substantial corpus of hymns and traditions for their use. How natural this faith expression would have seemed is attested in early Christian literature like the Gospel of Luke, which adds new "psalms"—the Magnificat, the Benedictus and the "Nunc Dimittis"[4]— texts that were utterly Jewish in character, and set on the lips of the key figures in the birth narratives of Jesus. These songs, usually termed canticles, became and remain a central part of the customary repertoire of public worship in the church.

Two further remarks should be made. First, far from being straightforward songs of praise, the Psalms are of a remarkably diverse character. From the liturgical life of ancient Israel they present individual as well as communal perspectives: they are bold in their pleas for divine aid as well as in thanksgiving for help received; they confess fault; they state and celebrate the demands of the covenant; and they recite the founding epics and myths of the Hebrew people. In addition, the Temple practice of the Psalter involved priestly choirs, and was evidently rich in musical accompaniment of the human voice: "Praise God with trumpet, lute and harp, with tambourine and dance, with strings and pipe, with clanging cymbals."[5] Such was hardly possible in the local synagogue, let alone in the home, where a simpler form of chant had become the rule. This musically complex Temple tradition bequeathed, in effect, a dual heritage to Christianity alongside the more modest practice of the synagogue, one that must be remembered for an understanding of the ambivalences felt by practitioners around performance and musical accompaniment in the history of Christian music.

Oral transmission: Chant and music in early Christianity

Song was a defining characteristic of worship among the first Christian generations. One of the earliest independent (i.e., non-Christian) reports of their behaviour comes from the correspondence of a Roman governor in what is now central Turkey with his friend, the emperor Trajan, around 112 CE. The governor, Pliny the Younger, reports that he has learned that, in the illicit early morning gatherings of these "Christians," they sing a hymn "to Christ as it were to a God."[6] This engagement in some form of song accords with the testimonies of the first Christian texts. In the New Testament, the already largely non-Jewish followers of Paul in Corinth are advised that their religious enthusiasm finds best expression not in an alcohol-induced trance, but in a chanting of "psalms, hymns and spiritual songs" that is guided by God's Spirit.[7] The precise distinction between these three forms of music is not clear today, but the apostle's directions on worship to the community in Corinth give us a glimpse into practices that certainly differed from those of the synagogue. Individual members could draw upon immediate personal inspiration to contribute a song of praise "in tongues" to the assembly, a song that might well be unintelligible to the others present.[8] Occurring alongside structured psalmody, this element of spontaneity is new, and probably attributable to the influence of ecstatic Greek religious practices familiar to the Corinthian converts. What precisely was meant by this speaking and praising "in tongues" and "with the Spirit" has been vigorously debated, particularly since the emergence and world-wide spread of the Pentecostal movement in the early twentieth century. Whether it was similar to the remarkable instances of spontaneous singing that can be experienced in today's Pentecostal gatherings, or among the numerous independent charismatic Christian churches of southern Africa, is unknown. But the faithful in these churches are at least right in claiming a first-century precedent for a free worship style that has never been an altogether comfortable fit for those who prefer Paul's dictum that "all should be done decently and in order" (1 Corinthians 14:40)! Discomfort with charismatic spontaneity may help to explain the disappearance of these ecstatic expressions of faith from most Christian assemblies by the second century, despite the short-lived efforts of the Montanist movement to revive it.

What is well-attested to, however, is the continuity of the psalmody tradition, together with a practice of intoning prayers and even the scripture lessons themselves. Edward Foley has underlined the essentially musical character of *all* early Christian worship,[9] which points to an emerging, more formalized liturgical tradition. It should be noted that there is solid evidence that singing was done by the full assembly, that is, by both men and women. Furthermore, despite the musical traditions of Temple worship, Christians agreed widely on the exclusion of all musical instruments from their worship during the first centuries as did post-Diaspora Jews at this time. While there may have been some local exceptions, there is a broad consensus among early writers that divine worship should privilege the glory of the unaccompanied human voice. This seems to have taken the form of unison singing, judging by the frequent references among authors to the symbolic strength of song *una voce*, "with one voice"; of course, given the reality of male and female voices united, there also would have been the harmony of the octave.

Behind these choices—the preference for set texts, the rejection of instrumental accompaniment—was a Christianity manifestly seeking to distinguish itself sharply, by the sobriety, chastity and clarity of its worship, from the general cultural, as well as religious, practices of its Mediterranean environment. This was a world that Christianity considered idolatrous, and that it associated with an orgiastic cult devoted to demonic spirits. In the process of this self-identification, however, it seems fair to suggest that its Hebraic heritage was significantly influenced and modified by the Hellenistic Greek philosophical environment, and in particular by the body-soul dualism inherent in Platonic thought. Disparagement of the body in favour of the spirit has implications for the practice of music in public worship, in attitudes relating to rhythm and to dance as well as to instruments, and even in some cases to song itself. The misogyny of the later patristic period needs also to be seen in this light. A genuine, if neurotic, mistrust of human sexuality found an easy target in the participation of women with men in the assembly, and women were excluded more and more from choral singing.

Ritual context: Music in public liturgy

Public worship or "the liturgy," with rare exceptions, has maintained a large place for music,[10] although there have been considerable variations within the details. To begin with, there is a significant polarity between the liturgy as performed by professionals—whether the clergy or associated musicians—and the unrehearsed participation of the congregation. One is struck by the similar Temple-synagogue divide in the Hebraic tradition, although, given the destruction of the Temple in 70 CE and the termination henceforth of all its rituals, this is not an adequate explanation for the clericalization of Christian music. A better explanation is provided by sociocultural factors, such as the desire by larger congregations for a more sophisticated and polished performance of the sacred rites.

It is probable that, from earliest times, a cantor was used to direct the congregational singing. This role took on a new form in sixteenth-century Reformed churches, which attached great importance to congregational singing of the Psalter as personal engagement with the word of God. Confronted, however, with the difficulties of a low literacy rate and unfamiliar texts, a precentor "lined out" the Psalms for congregational repetition, thereby not only indicating the melody, but leading with the words.[11] The song leader of modern evangelical American Protestantism is an heir to this tradition, although, as literacy has become widespread, cheap pew books have become customary, and the songleader's function is more one of stirring-up congregational enthusiasm. Closer to the older models was the American frontier preacher—typically Baptist or Methodist—who would carry a worship book in his saddlebags to remote settlements and line out the words of an English hymn, to which the faithful would respond with a refrain. These refrains were, as a rule, not from the author of the verses; tending towards repetition of a single phrase, they enabled a simple dialogue between leader and congregation. The pattern of call-and-response in African and some African American worship song is similar to this.

Over the centuries, however, a variety of factors has constantly encouraged the professionalization of the music in clergy and choir. Wherever the language of the liturgy was not the vernacular—as when Latin was used in medieval Western Europe, or Old Church Slavonic in Russia—participation by the assembly in the music occurred only to a limited degree.

The cycle of frequent services in the Catholic tradition, and an increasingly sophisticated liturgy and musical accompaniment in large churches like cathedrals, had a similar result. Moreover, urban congregations in Lutheran Germany also developed correspondingly high expectations of performance in their Sunday worship. More recently, Protestant churches in America, theoretically committed to a populist and participatory liturgy, have given significant place alongside congregational singing to the performance of anthems by prominently positioned choirs and soloists since the mid-nineteenth century. Radio and television have significantly accentuated this trend, presenting and thereby encouraging worship experiences where little or no participation in the music is expected of the audience, save for appreciative applause at its conclusion.

Since the establishment of Gregorian chant as an official aspect of the Catholic liturgy—first in the monasteries with the Divine Office of daily prayers and then among the parish congregations—by about the eighth century CE, there have been strong, and in many periods overwhelming, forces in favour of a liturgy sung only by the clergy and their paraprofessional associates. Gregorian chant refers to the traditional monophonic chant named after Pope St. Gregory the Great (540–604 CE), who, rather than composing the chants under divine inspiration according to Christian legend, was in reality more of a codifier or systematizer of the existing chant repertoire. This repertoire remained relatively fixed until modern times. While the chant in its original Latin has been removed from the official rite since Vatican II (1963–65), Gregorian chant has risen in popularity in recent years, and the splendour of it must be acknowledged. In medieval Europe, the daily Catholic Mass consisted of the Proper, prayers and readings specific to a holiday or event in the liturgical calendar, and the Ordinary, a series of five sections that remained relatively unchanged throughout the year: Kyrie, Gloria, Credo, Sanctus, and Agnus Dei. These five parts were interlaced with the Proper in the Mass, but later became an independent structure that many composers used for settings of polyphonic masses from the Renaissance to modern times. Below, in Example 1, are three sections of the Ordinary in Gregorian style.

⏴ EXAMPLE 1 (Track 8)
Roman Catholic Mass Ordinary: *Kyrie, Sanctus, Agnus Dei.*
Latin text and translation from Richard L. Crocker (2000), 202–208.

Kyrie
(Source: ancient Greek hymn to the sun, adapted by early Christianity)

Kyrie eleison	(3×)	Lord, have mercy
Christe eleison	(3×)	Christ, have mercy
Kyrie eleison	(3×)	Lord, have mercy

Sanctus
(Source: Isaiah 6:3)

Sanctus, sanctus, sanctus, Dominus Deus Sabaoth
Pleni sunt coeli et terra Gloria tua. Hosanna in excelsis

~

Holy, holy, holy, Lord God of hosts.
Heaven and earth are full of thy glory. Hosanna in the highest.

Agnus Dei
(Source: John 1:29)

Agnus Dei, qui tollis peccata mundi: miserere nobis (2×)
Agnus Dei, qui tollis peccata mundi: dona nobis pacem

~

O Lamb of God, that takest away the sins of the world, have mercy upon us.
O Lamb of God, that takest away the sins of the world, grant us thy peace.

While these portions were generally unvarying, the additional elements of the Proper varied in textual content in relation to the season and lessons of the day. A large part of these texts continued to consist of portions of the Psalms, taken from the Latin translation of the Bible, known as the Vulgate, by St Jerome. The Western European musical tradition developed initially within this setting, and mass texts became increasingly intricate as the requirement of unison singing was abandoned in favour of polyphony, the weaving of two or more voices. While plainchant or Gregorian chant, sung in unmetred unison style, never disappeared from the sung liturgy, there were periods when a glorious intricacy and musical elaboration upon the base melody (*cantus firmus*) threatened to overwhelm the liturgical acts themselves. From this repertoire came many of the foundational master-works of Western European music, such as the Catholic masses of Palestrina, Haydn, and Mozart, the innumerable liturgical contributions of Vivaldi, and the *Mass in B Minor* of the Lutheran J.S. Bach. Lutheran and Anglican reformers in the sixteenth century strove to restore a greater simplicity to the music by translating the liturgy from Latin into the vernacular, and encouraging participation by the whole assembly, yet their success was limited by the ongoing evolving complexity of European music in general. For the same reason, Roman Catholic liturgical reform in the early twentieth century, known as the Liturgical Movement, encouraged the revival of plainchant, and focused attention primarily upon the words of the text that accompanied the actions of the liturgy.

Christian hymns

The hymn traditions of the Christian church are central to the theme of Christianity and music. Their form and content will be discussed later on in this chapter, but here they will be considered as being at the opposite pole to a professionally sung liturgy; that is, worship song offered by the assembly as a whole. Although often associated with Protestant reform of the liturgy, the practice of assembly singing began in the Eastern churches during the first few centuries CE. In a celebrated incident, Ambrose, a fourth-century bishop of Milan, was able to sustain the courage of his flock, while all were barricaded inside a cathedral surrounded by hostile troops, by encouraging the singing of hymns in the Eastern fashion.[12] This lay participation largely disappeared from the public liturgy during the Middle Ages, but re-emerged on the margins of formal practice—in pilgrimages, festival processions, and drama—as a folk tradition of song and dance using religious themes, using a text more joyous than reverent, and with snatches of melody from the formal liturgy, often again with a call-and-response pattern. The carol stems from this marginal practice, and has remained a folksong only partially assimilated into formal liturgy.[13]

It was against this background, in 1523, that Martin Luther issued his call to poets and composers to join him in writing German song for the people to sing within the liturgy.[14] He had no intention of replacing the church's liturgy, which continued to be sung to traditional settings, with some parts in Latin and other parts translated into German. Rather, for Luther, new hymns would accompany the liturgy and strengthen the people's participation. This activity, so central to Lutheran identity from that day to this, may be understood as complementary hymnody: that is, a sacred music intended to form an integral part of the liturgy, though not constituting the whole. A very important Lutheran hymn is "Ein' Feste Burg," or "A Mighty Fortress Is Our God." Otherwise known as the "Battle Hymn of the Reformation," this famous tune, written by Martin Luther himself, is set to words in paraphrase of Psalm 46 and in the Minnesinger metrical form of 8/7/8/7 syllables per line. The meaning revolves around the cosmic theme of the triumph of God, through Jesus Christ, over Satan.

| EXAMPLE 2 (Track 9)
"A Mighty Fortress Is Our God." Martin Luther, 1529, adapted from *The Worship Book: Services and Hymns* (1972), 274–75. English version adapted from original German.

1 A mighty fortress is our God, a bulwark never failing;
   Our helper He amid the flood of mortal ills prevailing:
   For still our ancient foe doth seek to work us woe; His craft
   and power are great, And, armed with cruel hate, on earth is not His equal.

2 Did we in our own strength confide, our striving would be losing;
   Were not the right man on our side, the man of God's own choosing:
   Dost ask who that may be? Christ Jesus, it is He; the Son of Hosts His Name,
   from age to age the same, and He must win the battle.

3 That word above all earthly powers, no thanks to them abideth;
   The spirit and the gifts are ours through Him who with us sideth:
   Let goods and kindred go, this mortal life also; The body they may kill:
   God's truth abideth still, His kingdom is forever. Amen.

On the other hand, in Strasbourg and Geneva, John Calvin actively encouraged the development of a complete psalter in French, sung unaccompanied in metrical verse. In his case there were a few additional liturgical pieces—the Ten Commandments, and the New Testament canticles—but for the Reformed tradition that grew from his ministry, the congregational singing of the Psalms would constitute the heart of popular participation in public worship, in effect replacing the older liturgical elements with a renewed psalmody. To this day a few churches in the Reformed tradition maintain this exclusive emphasis on sung psalms.

Such hymnody has been, on occasion, subversive. There are numerous accounts of groups creating and using song against persecuting authorities: the Hussite hymns of fifteenth-century Bohemia, for example, or the Anabaptist (precursor to the Hutterite and Mennonite movements) songs of the sixteenth century. People witnessing the courage of such singing before public executions were sometimes converted to the faith of the victim. The black spiritual tradition of America certainly belongs in this category of subversive song. When African-American slaves, kept illiterate in a bondage that would end only with death, sang to one another "When Israel was in Egypt's land, let my people go! Oppressed so hard they could not stand, let my people go!" they claimed the heritage of the ancient Exodus liberation as their spiritual refusal of the tyranny of slavery. Similarly, nineteenth-century Mormons stiffened their resolve to follow the prophets Joseph Smith and Brigham Young through years of wandering, mockery, and even violent opposition, by the singing of an alternative hymnody: "Come, come, ye saints!"

Between these positions stands a third category of this essentially lay music: supplementary hymnody. In an England whose formal Anglicanism only rarely had pew space, let alone pastoral care, for the shifting, poverty-stricken population displaced as a result of the emerging forces of the early Industrial Revolution, the several thousand songs written by Charles Wesley inspired a new sense of worth, dignity, and hope in the poor who joined Methodist societies. Such evangelical hymnody can hardly be termed subversive, insofar as Wesley and his brother John encouraged their converts to participate regularly in Church of England services. Yet, practically speaking, their societies became a second, even primary, faith home for thousands, and their hymns were a vital supplement to an Anglican psalmody whose practice as the people's music had fallen upon evil days.[15]

Into this broad category can also be placed the songs of the Salvation Army, directed at the lowest of the urban poor in the late nineteenth century. Considered an outrageously vulgar musical expression by much of the Christian world, their fresh, plain lyrics and noisy, enthusiastic melodies provided the spiritual tonic needed by many on the streets of the great cities. One could say the same of the hymns of various sectarian groups, such as the Pentecostals of the early twentieth century. Initially understanding their songs to be supplementing the spiritual fare being served in so-called mainstream Protestant churches, in the long run, these groups formed a new religious tradition, their songs ceased to be marginal, and their song became their public liturgy.

Ritual context: Music in private devotion

Christianity has made extensive use of music as a vehicle for personal prayer. It is in this light that the older, Western Protestant practice of prefacing public worship with a quarter-hour of purely instrumental music, most commonly from an organ, should be understood. Culturally conditioned by the easy-listening sounds piped into shopping malls, the contemporary worshipper may assume this to be a form of "sacred muzak." Its significance derives, however, from the piety of an earlier age, when worshippers expected to be spiritually uplifted by the reminiscences sparked by familiar hymns. This benefit depends upon the common phenomenon of association, whereby a snatch of melody overheard, even subconsciously, draws into the conscious mind the words with which the listener has associated that melody.

A major musical genre linked to this devotional practice is the chorale prelude. For example, composer Johann Christoph Bach suggestively weaves themes from an early Lutheran hymn, "Wenn wir in höchsten nöten sein" ("When in the hour of deepest need"), into a musical tapestry that brings particular elements of the words to mind, and thereby awakens liturgical, personal, and spiritual associations.[16] For most Christians, the ultimate practitioner of this art was his nephew, Johann Sebastian Bach (1685–1750). Among the scores of his chorale preludes and variations on hymn themes, his *Orgelbüchlein* (Little Organ Book), a collection of forty-five (or so) short preludes on well-known Lutheran chorales, or hymns, is one of the greatest monuments to Christian spirituality in music.[17] Here, it is precisely the association of text and melody that carries the spiritual force; it is not even necessary for the composer to employ the entire melody. Preludes that do this have a rather more explicit pedagogical function: they prepare a community for the singing of a less familiar hymn tune. But, evocation of the opening line, as spiritual artists like Bach understood, can suffice to draw the hearers into the art of meditation, what the ancient Hebrews called *higgayon*.

What is true of the chorale preludes applies as well to Bach's much longer masterworks, the *Passions* of St. Matthew and St. John. Here, Bach created a musical narration of the respective Gospel versions of the Passion and death of Jesus Christ. The timbres of different voices portray the biblical narrative as recitative but also invite the hearer into reflective arias, where an immediate identification is created between listener and bystander at the crucial event of the Christian story. Finally, the whole is punctuated at intervals by well-known chorales, or hymns, in which the congregation is expected to join. Here, as in his more than two hundred cantatas, however, Bach conducts Lutherans alone into the inner sanctum of the Temple; non-Lutheran Christians, unfamiliar with most of the hymns that he uses, may be deeply moved by the spiritual energy of the composition, but the evocative element escapes them. They remain, as it were, in the Temple court of the Gentiles.

Probably the closest analogy for English-speaking Protestants to this meditative force of text-melody association comes from the oratorio the *Messiah*, composed by Bach's great contemporary, George Frederick Handel (1685–1759). There are many for whom the approach of the sacred seasons of Christmas and Easter is spiritually incomplete without a listening to that work. A moving instance of this devotion can be found in the remote Nass valley of northern British Columbia. Among the elders of the Nisga'a people, there is still a deep affection for the choruses of the *Messiah* and Haydn's *Creation*, which earlier generations had learned "by heart" thanks to the teaching of a musically talented woman missionary. In turn, this music can bring for believers an intimate association of the victory of Christ with their personal triumphs. African Americans meeting in the ruins of a bombed church in Montgomery, Alabama, signalled their trust in life beyond racist oppression by breaking spontaneously into the "Hallelujah" Chorus.[18]

Until recently, within Roman Catholicism, the hymn has played a much less prominent part in the life of the congregation. In the nineteenth century, Catholics like the great French composers Charles Gounod, César Franck, and many others, built their preludes as spiritual meditations around the familiar elements of the Mass. In developing this musical tradition, they stand within a vital tradition of Catholic and Orthodox devotion, where those witnessing the Eucharistic celebration use their eyes and ears within the drama of the Mass itself, in such a way that, though they might seem passive to the casual observer, participants may actually enter meditatively into the heart of the mystery. Historically, the Roman Catholic Church long sought to strengthen this meditative participation through the provision of printed companions such as books of hours in the late medieval period. Protestants had their personal copies of the hymnal, one of the purposes of which was a similar meditative reading, where, of course, the words would bring the familiar melody to mind.

The Catholic dimension of personal devotion reaches its zenith in the veneration of the Virgin Mary, Mother of Jesus Christ. Marian "antiphons" originally formed part of monastic daily prayers, known as the Divine Office, during the thirteenth century. Chanted after evening Vespers on special days, they gradually became popular among the laity. The most famous antiphon is of course the "Ave Maria," or "Hail Mary," based partly on a combination of the angel Gabriel's salutation to Mary in Luke 1:28, and Elizabeth's greeting of Mary in Luke 1:42. Recited primarily as part of private rosary prayers since the fifteenth century, it has also been set to music in both Latin and vernacular by great composers like Schubert and Gounod. The English, familiar to many believers, is as follows:

> Hail Mary, Full of grace, The Lord is with thee.
> Blessed art thou among women,
> and blessed is the fruit of thy womb, Jesus.
> Holy Mary, Mother of God, Pray for us sinners,
> Now and at the hour of our death. Amen.

Another famous Marian antiphon that has retained one of the best-known melodies from the Middle Ages is the "Salve Regina," composed by monks in the twelfth century. According to Gregorian chant scholar Richard L. Crocker, "Salve Regina, an antiphon addressed to the Virgin Mary, is the most famous of many such chants in European monasteries in the twelfth and thirteenth centuries."[19] The Marian antiphons were generally more ornate or melismatic than the Ordinary chants, containing many notes per syllable. Example 3 below of "Salve Regina" is normally sung in its standard tune, which is in a minor mode known as Dorian.

EXAMPLE 3 (Track 10)
  "Salve Regina." Latin text and translation from Richard L. Crocker (2000), 219.

> Salve, Regina, mater misericordia: Vita, dulcedo, et spes nostra, salve. Ad te clamamus, exsules, filii Hevae. Ad te suspiramus, gementes et flentes

in hac lacrimarum valle. Eia ergo, Advocata nostra, illos tuos miseri-
cordes oculos ad nos converte. Et Iesum, benedictum fructum ventris tui,
nobis post hoc exsilium ostende. O Clemens: O pia: O dulcis Virgo Maria.

～

Hail, queen, mother of mercy: our life, sweetness and hope, hail. To thee
we cry, as exiles, children of Eve. To thee we sigh, groaning and weeping in this vale of tears. Come, then our counselor, turn those merciful
eyes upon us. And show Jesus, the blessed fruit of thy womb, to us after
this exile. O gentle: O pious: O sweet virgin Mary.

The intercessory prayers in both of the antiphons, "Pray for us sinners," and
"To thee we sigh, groaning and weeping in this vale of tears," are indica-
tive of the rise of the notion of Purgatory, a "third" place for Christians to
"burn off' their sins before reaching Heaven. By the thirteenth century, a
connection had developed between Marian devotion and the relief of suffering for all deceased Christians who were destined to reside there. The
idea was that the Virgin Mary controlled a vast storehouse of Divine Grace,
and, if she were properly approached, would intercede with her Son on
behalf of the penitent in order to lessen the pain and anguish. As such, a
large corpus of music developed around Mary, including hymns of praise
and petition like "Stabat Mater," "Salve Regina," "Ave Maris Stella," "Alma
Redemptoris Mater," and "Regina Coeli." In addition, the Requiem Mass,
or Mass for the Dead, which was originally recited in monasteries by
monks, became the means by which the suffering of the deceased already
in Purgatory could be mitigated. It gradually became widespread as a
polyphonic musical setting by the fifteenth and sixteenth centuries, beginning with Ockeghem and Palestrina. Fascination with the Requiem Mass,
and with its sequence known as "Dies Irae," ("Day of Wrath"), continued
unabated among great composers through the nineteenth (Berlioz,
Gounod, Verdi, Dvorak) and twentieth centuries (Duruffle, Howells, Rutter, Lloyd Webber) in both Latin and vernacular versions. Even so-called
"pagan requiems," without allusions to Jesus or Mary, were composed
by such figures as Brahms, Delius, and Hindemith.

The Hymnal and the songbook

Gutenberg's invention of movable type in the fifteenth century made possible the wide dissemination of relatively inexpensive literature. The Protestant churches of the Reformation era took advantage of this to create a
new spiritual genre, the small volume of hymns and psalms destined for
the lay public. These were followed within a few years by official collections, wherein the reader found text and sometimes melodies for the songs

approved by church authorities for use in public worship. That these were genuinely "people's books" and central to lay piety is attested by the numerous copies, today usually found in library Rare Book rooms, of small editions of the Bible and the hymnal which the owner had bound together in one volume, frequently with the prayer book or official liturgy as a third component. Inscriptions on the fly-leaves attest that these books were often passed from generation to generation as family treasures.

The enlargement of hymnals by the inclusion of recommended tunes has meant that, since the eighteenth century, the hymnal has emerged as a fully independent volume in many churches. As in earlier times, authors as well as publishers would issue particular collections, which then are sometimes adopted for congregational use. Most typical is the denominational hymnal, a collection edited by a formally appointed committee to meet the liturgical needs of congregations with texts that correspond to the church's particular understanding of the Christian message. In North America, it has become a working rule to prepare a new collection every twenty years or so; elsewhere, the interval probably is longer. While this was once primarily a Protestant concern, the Roman Catholic Church has followed a similar pattern since the Second Vatican Council (1962–65). Typically, a hymnal will contain between four and six hundred songs and psalms; some hymnals are structured liturgically, others thematically, and most are a combination of these two. In contrast with the practice of earlier generations, the trend of recent decades has been away from private ownership of the hymnal. Instead, parishes customarily purchase sufficient copies to supply all worshippers during the service, and these are intended to remain in the church.

Earlier, in the chapter, hymnody was shown to have functioned as a lay counterweight to the clericalized liturgy, and as a vehicle of reform or even of revolutionary change across the broad Christian tradition. Two points were made that contribute to an understanding of the role played by this incredibly diverse and vast corpus of material: first, that much of the basic character of Christian hymnody continues to flow out of its model, the Hebrew Psalms. Secondly, the hymn, as an instrument of congregational participation in the liturgy, must be in the language of the community. This last point will certainly be contested by some, who will point to Latin or Greek hymns in the tradition that are sung with fervour; they might also note the very recent practice of encouraging the use of versions in other languages contained in the latest generation of hymnaries. Yet, both of these practices are deliberate exceptions, and do not invalidate the general rule: hymns are in the people's language. It is this intimate bond with communal and personal identity that leads to a third point: the act of singing a hymn in public worship is itself a faith statement. The blending of male, female, adult, and infant voices—the uniting of practised and off-key singers—actualizes the theological claim that lies at the heart of the Christian faith community, namely that, as it assembles in one location, the body of Christ, its Head, is reincarnated. Moreover, because this not only takes place in a local unity of immediate time and place, but also employs the music of earlier generations, the whole people of God is present, from the ends of the earth, from ages past and yet to come. While singing in parts also demonstrates this unity, albeit in a different manner, one can understand why the earliest Christians laid such emphasis upon "with one voice."

Some examples will illustrate, although certainly not exhaust, the rich diversity of Christian hymnody. The central motif of the Psalms of Israel is certainly the praise of the Creator, and Christian hymnodists have followed their lead, often borrowing wholesale from their antecedent. While pure praise adores the One in a gesture of absolute simplicity—a giving back of the breath/spirit of life[20]—Hebrew and Christian praise have often incorporated into their song the qualities of deity that make praise "comely, or becoming for the upright" (Psalms 33:1).

In 1737 the Anglican John Wesley edited a metrical version of Psalm 146 by Isaac Watts, an English Congregationalist, "Praise We Our Maker While We've Breath." The melody of "Old 113" comes from the first Strasbourg psalters (1525), and is the work of the cathedral organist, Matthaus Greiter. While not the only tune to which these words have been sung, its majestic simplicity fits the strain of praise well. Greiter's original is more elaborately repetitive, and some would argue more musically stimulating, but experience has shown that North American congregations prefer the simpler version. The first strophe testifies to the singer's sense of a vocation of praise; the second and third elaborate the reasons why the community praises its Maker, namely because God is also the deliverer of all in distress; and the last strophe makes personal the opening affirmation. It is said that, in his final hours before death, Wesley repeatedly voiced the opening line.

｜ EXAMPLE 4 (Track 11)
"Praise We Our Maker While We've Breath." Adapted from
The Worship Book: Services and Hymns (1972), 558.

> I'll praise my Maker while I've breath;
> And when my voice is lost in death,
> praise shall employ my nobler powers.
> My days of praise shall ne'er be past,
> while life, and thought, and being last,
> or immortality endures.

Happy are those whose hopes rely
on Israel's God who made the sky;
the earth and seas with all their train.
His truth forever stands secure;
God saves th' oppressed, God feeds the poor,
and none shall find his promise vain.

The comments on the melody of this hymn suggest a further word on the literary structure of hymns. Luther, as mentioned earlier, appealed to the poets and musicians of his day to contribute their gifts to the creation of a popular German hymnody. In contrast with the prosaic, non-metrical, and free-flowing character of plainchant, European and subsequent North American hymnody has tended to follow the models familiar in Indo-European epic poetry and folk song: that is, to use various patterns of metre and rhyme. The example above uses six four-foot lines in iambic metre, which features two syllables in an unstressed-stressed pattern, and a rhyme scheme of "aabccb." This is more sophisticated than the patterns used in the English and Scottish psalters, which used almost exclusively four-line patterns in one of three metrical forms in the name of simplicity, and most commonly possessed an "abab" rhyme scheme.[21] These "short," "common," and "long" metre patterns had the advantage of simplicity of access: a community need only know a handful of tunes to sing the whole Psalter. That same simplicity, however, could also induce monotony and bring psalm-singing into disrepute. In contrast, continental Protestants employed a much wider range of poetic patterns, and the music is correspondingly more interesting.

A poignant example of how an Old Testament paradigm has provided substance to both Roman Catholic chant as well as Protestant hymnody is found in the nineteenth-century hymn, "Holy, Holy, Holy! Lord God Almighty!" This, of course, is the English rendition of the Latin Sanctus, used in the Ordinary of the Catholic Mass. The original Hebrew is "Kadosh, Kadosh, Kadosh," and expresses the song rendered by the angels of God around the Holy Throne in Isaiah's dramatic vision (Isaiah 6:3). The English Christian hymn, centred around praise of the Holy Trinity, has become a basic staple in most Protestant congregations.

| EXAMPLE 5 (Track 12)
"Holy, Holy, Holy! Lord God Almighty!" By Reginald Heber (1826) and John B. Dykes (1861). From *The Worship Book: Services and Hymns* (1972), 421.

1 Holy, holy, holy! Lord God Almighty!
Early in the morning our song shall rise to thee;

Holy, holy, holy! Merciful and Mighty!
God in three Persons, blessed Trinity!

2 Holy, holy,holy! all the saints adore thee,
Casting down their golden crowns, around the glassy sea;
Cherubim and seraphim, falling down before thee,
Who wert, and art, and evermore shalt be.

3 Holy, holy, holy! though the darkness hide thee,
Though the eye of sinful man thy glory may not see,
Only thou art holy; there is none beside thee
Perfect in power, in love, and purity.

4 Holy, holy, holy! Lord God Almighty!
All thy works shall praise thy name, in earth and sky and sea;
Holy, holy, holy! Merciful and mighty!
God in three Persons, blessed Trinity!

The American biblical scholar Walter Brueggemann comments on how praise which celebrates the goodness of life may serve as a buttress of the status quo, promoting (if unconsciously) the interests of those who benefit from order and stability.[22] Christian hymns are not exempt from this criticism. What seems a simple children's hymn rejoicing in the God-given beauty of nature, "All Things Bright and Beautiful," published in 1846 by Cecil Frances Alexander, is a particularly striking example of this. This hymn (with an admittedly rather idyllic view of nature) is found in almost all new English-language hymnals, and generally is set to the tune "Royal Oak," English composer Martin Shaw's adaptation of a seventeenth-century folk tune. The form, using a recurrent refrain that makes it ideal for children, employs the versicle-and-response pattern of those earlier Christian hymns that developed along folk lines.

❘: EXAMPLE 6 (Track 13)
"All Things Bright and Beautiful." Adapted from *The Hymnal of the Protestant Episcopal Church* (1943), 311–12.

Refrain: All things bright and beautiful, all creatures great and small,
all things wise and wonderful, the Lord God made them all.

1 Each little flower that opens, each little bird that sings;
God made their glowing colors, God made their tiny wings.

2 The purple-headed mountain, the river running by,
the sunset, and the morning that brightens up the sky.

3 The cold wind in the winter, the pleasant summer sun,
the ripe fruits in the garden, He made them every one.

4 He gave us eyes to see them, and lips that we might tell
  how great is God Almighty, Who has made all things well.

In a pluralistic world where the songs "everybody knows" are increasingly rare, much new hymnody at the end of the twentieth century employed this style. In its original form, however, the hymn included the following verse:

> The rich man in his castle,
> The poor man at his gate,
> God made them, high and lowly,
> And gave each his estate.

Because it was a favourite hymn for use in schools, British and Canadian children imbibed this propaganda for a divinely mandated social inequality, written by the wife of a Church of Ireland dignitary, well into the twentieth century!

Hymns fulfill various functions for the Christian community, and this means that celebration and praise of God is not their only form. Some are catechetical, placing basic affirmations of the religious creed on the singers' lips and thereby, it is hoped, in their hearts. Others recite the key elements of the Christian faith, showing the saving presence of God in human history. Most of the hymns inherited from the early and medieval church are of this character; translated into English by High Church Anglicans like John Mason Neale, scores of these have passed into the repertoire of modern English-speaking Christians, Catholic and Protestant. Like their model, the Psalms, hymns speak for both the community and the individual. Much of the hymnody of eighteenth- to early twentieth-century Protestantism sought deliberately to voice the spiritual experience of the singer, endeavoring by the phenomenon of identification to move the singer from conviction of sin and despair to an act of trust in God's salvation, and a joyous commitment to follow the path of obedience and discipleship. These hymns have often been criticized for their subjectivity. Yet, when they are seen as instruments of spiritual transformation, their role in the formation of the faithful becomes understandable. Recent hymnal collections have sought to discriminate in retaining the best of this tradition.

In the twentieth century, hymnody took on a stronger prophetic role, calling upon the community to engage in the building of a world that corresponded to the biblical vision of the justice of God. The verse of the Dutch-English contemporary poet Frederick H. Kaan is distinguished by the artful passion with which it critiques the ways of our society. The first verse of the following hymn, in widespread use in the most recent hymnals, sets biblical imagery on the lips of worshippers, who call upon their God to help them participate in the bringing of a just and peaceful world:

> All that kills abundant living,
> Let it from the earth be banned,
> Pride of status, rank or schooling,
> Dogmas that obscure your plan.
> In our common quest for justice
> May we hallow life's brief span.[23]

A more striking contrast with the affirmation of the status quo in the earlier selection could hardly be found.

As shown earlier, in the midst of an oppressive present, folk hymnody can enable its singers to glimpse and construct for themselves an alternative vision of reality. What gives folk hymnody its power is that it sings out of authentic human experience. It allows the basic faith convictions of a people to take flesh and find expression in a way individuals recognize as their own, in the melodies and rhythms of their daily lives. Here is a convergence of sacred and secular that may even be unsettling for those on the outside.

The African-American experience is one of the most powerful and influential instances of this convergence. Slaves used the musical idiom of their African homelands to voice their identification with past sufferers, and also their hope in a Lord who has been known to break chains and set prisoners free. The authenticity of this music meant that it genuinely remained a people's song, evolving with the black experience in America beyond slavery, both within churches and outside in the blues bands on urban street corners. The repertoire of African-American spirituals that was transmitted orally during the nineteenth century comprised work and religious songs sung in unison, sometimes with polyphonic and rhythmic accompaniment. They were generally rendered as short refrains in call-and-response pattern, and expressed deep melancholy. The shared and living history of suffering and oppression ensured that the old songs still had galvanizing power in the struggles of the mid-twentieth century against civil segregation based on race.

Influenced by spirituals and blues, the twentieth century saw the rapid development of Black Gospel music, wherein simple Protestant hymns were embellished with florid and spontaneous vocal elements, including the use of falsetto, shouts, moans, groans, whispers, screams, and cries. These were often punctuated with the phrases "Lord Have Mercy," amen, and hallelujah. The Golden Age of Gospel (1930–69) was dominated by the Baptists, and gained visibility under Thomas A. Dorsey, a converted blues-singer, and Rev. James Cleveland, among others. The steady theme of sin and despair was gradually uplifted into hope and transformation of the world during the Modern Gospel Era (1969–present), whereby Pentecostal artists of the Church of God in Christ, especially Edwin and Walter Hawkins, Sandra and Andrae Crouch, and the Clark Sisters, brought fervent optimism into the public sphere through their songs of God's praise and human redemption. The splendid career of Mahalia Jackson spanned both eras of this vital and uniquely American music.

In a remarkable cultural transference, African-American song also contributed significantly to the emergence of an authentic white American folk hymnody. One particular example, "Life's Railway to Heaven," takes the singer into the world of American folk gospel.[24] The metaphor and tune are folksy, evoking the era when rail first entered the remote valleys of southern Appalachia and lessened their isolation. Today, many Christians find the poetry crude and dismiss the theology as simplistic. This example should, however, be a reminder of the existence of an immense world outside the church structures of urban, middle-class, North American culture groups whose members belong to another social order, and who likewise identify themselves as followers of Jesus.

Written in 1779 by a white man from England, John Newton, the hymn "Amazing Grace" has a achieved a status in the gospel repertoire, both white and black, that is unparalleled. Yet the tune is drawn from American folk sources, and so represents the anguished experiences of pioneer life at its fullest. John Newton lived the life of the proverbial sinner, even engaging in slave trade atrocities. Then, with a change of heart and deep remorse, he composed this simple yet moving lyric.

⊦ EXAMPLE 7 (Track 14)
"Amazing Grace." From *The Worship Book: Services and Hymns* (1972), 296.

1 Amazing grace! How sweet the sound that saved a wretch like me!
   I once was lost, but now am found, was blind, but now I see.

2 'Twas grace that taught my heart to fear, and grace my fears relieved;
   How precious did that grace appear the hour I first believed!

3 When we've been there ten thousand years, bright shining as the sun;
   We've no less days to sing God's praise, than when we first begun.

Christianity has not had a good track record of recognizing the way in which its majority traditions are both shaped and limited by their social and cultural contexts. The nineteenth-century mission movement carried the Christian faith from a North Atlantic base to the furthest corners of the planet, helping to make it a genuinely global religion. But while some missionaries sought to be sensitive to the cultural differences they encountered, on the whole the Christian worship traditions they brought with them, including sacred music, were overtly imperialistic. They assumed that the most appropriate manner, texts, and instruments with which to worship God were those from Europe and America. They disparaged local music traditions they did not understand, undoubtedly because they felt them hopelessly culture-bound and therefore corrupted by the non-Christian world they were seeking to overcome for Christ. They exported organs, or at least harmoniums, to the four corners of the earth. And, it must be said, that they did their work thoroughly. Among the First Nations of Canada, for example, it has been a hard task to encourage exploration of traditional dance and song to the accompaniment of the drum within the setting of Christian liturgy; to the community's elders, in particular, the drum often seems unchristian and inappropriate in the church! Wherever one goes on this planet, one is likely to encounter in local translation most of the Christian songs discussed in this chapter.

This is beginning to change, however. Worship at the Sixth Assembly of the World Council of Churches, meeting in Vancouver in the summer of 1983, was led by musician-theologians like I-to Loh of Taiwan and Pablo Sosa of Argentina, who sought to make the liturgies genuinely global in character. The astonishingly positive response at that assembly has meant that new music is appearing in hymnals everywhere. For example, in a new Kyrie from Central America,[25] one can hear the folk music rhythms and the yearning of the native peoples of Nicaragua for their God to bring liberation from oppression and a world without fear of violence.

The forms of text and music

As the previous examples have shown, Christianity, unlike some religious traditions, has had no one sacred literary style. Certainly, the words of scripture do have a privileged place in Christian imagery and story, and the language of the formal liturgy reflects this. Hymns draw freely upon many sources, however, and this diversity is, in fact, considered an appropriate reflection of the belief that all human experience is made sacred by the incarnation of the Son of God. Similarly, while free verse characterizes the poetic form of the liturgy, the hymn tradition has been able to employ the full range of poetic metre. The preference for only a few metres in the older British traditions may have been determined by the simplicity of popular ballad styles; other European traditions felt no such restraint, and that limitation has long since been abandoned.

The origins of Christian chant are ancient, perhaps owing something again to synagogue practice. Recent interest in the revival of plainchant has encouraged contemporary musicians to develop new patterns for this form, especially for the intoning of psalms. Now plainchant ignores that powerful component of music which is rhythm, or, to be more precise, the rhythm of the chant is completely dictated by the sense-cadence of the words rather than by an innate rhythmic pattern within the music itself. This is a music that to many Christians feels "sacred." On the other hand, the tunes to which hymns are set often have their origin in folk music, although this is not always the case. Luther's appeal to composers has echoed across the centuries; many of the great names of Western music, from Bach and Handel to Ralph Vaughan Williams and Aaron Copland, have contributed by writing or arranging tunes for hymns. The form of these tunes has usually been dictated by existing hymn texts, although some of the many poet/hymn-writers have done the reverse, and have written their hymns with a particular tune in mind. Unlike plainchant, hymns are most typically written in patterns of metrical rhymed verse, and so are sung to tunes that are at least, in theory, rhythmic. Practically, however, the old Christian fear of the attraction of the sensual—attributed earlier to the influence of Platonic thought—has discouraged the overt recognition of rhythm in church music, particularly in the mainstream bourgeois denominations. That there is a serious disjuncture between this reality and the incarnational theology of Christianity is regrettable, but this has, at least until very recently, been an accepted norm. European missionaries condemned absolutely the use of the drum, so common among the peoples to whom they brought the faith. The African-American tradition, on the other hand, perhaps because it emerged as a countercultural form, is richly rhythmic, and the American white gospel tradition that was derived from it has been so as well. The new hymnody from Latin America and Africa is unabashedly sensual.[26]

The same ascetic impulse that caused early Christians to condemn the use of the rhythmic drove them to ban instrumental music within the liturgy. This condemnation was renewed by some Protestant reformers, who echoed Plato's strictures against the polyphonic organ music of their day. Catholics, Anglicans, and Lutherans, on the other hand, encouraged the use of the organ; and, as the older strictures were abandoned, this instrument enjoyed an unofficial but real reign as the sacred instrument par excellence. The force of this tradition is best illustrated by the universal popularity in America of the electronic organ, or keyboard, where a pipe organ was found to be impractical. In a distant second place, at least until recently, have been all other instruments, including the piano, although the last decades of the twentieth century saw a major change in this respect.

The music of the communities that style themselves post-denominational, as well as that of the "contemporary" services of many traditional denominations, uses shorter texts with considerable repetition, and is accompanied by guitars, drums, and keyboards.

Music as a spiritual discipline

To write about Christian sacred sound and not to at least identify the distinctive character of it in monastic life would be a serious omission. Within the Christian tradition, there have been monastic communities, more or less cloistered according to the communal rule, since at least the fifth century. While its patterns may vary considerably, a central element of the ascetic life has been the celebration of the offices. Ideally, a monastic community will meet seven times daily, from long before dawn until mid-evening, for the singing of psalms and prayer. The cycle is termed the Opus Dei, "the work of God," an offering before God of the entire world in sung prayer. Here, the Psalter alone provides the text of sacred song, the form is chant and not metred hymn, and the entire Psalter is sung through over the course of each week.

Since the 1940s, an ecumenical community founded by Swiss Protestants has lived a version of the monastic life in Taizé, a tiny village in the hills of eastern Burgundy. The French composer Jacques Berthier created a particular style of psalmody for this community that has come to be practiced not only at Taizé but in similar prayer services around the world. The style is simple, and most typically consists of a short phrase of scripture, often from the Psalms, which is repeated in *ostinato* fashion for several minutes. The language sung often is not the vernacular, but Latin. This recognizes the polyglot character of the Taizé community, but, more importantly, the diminished role given to verbal signifiers means that, in repeated singing, the mind relaxes more quickly and moves into a body-spirit rhythm that makes the song itself a deep inner prayer.

Current trends and the future of Christian music

At the beginning of the twenty-first century, several issues are being raised by change both within and without the Christian churches regarding the future of music in the Christian tradition.

Christian music has been reshaped profoundly in the past three decades by the liturgical changes in Roman Catholicism following the Second Vatican Council, as well as by the strength of the ecumenical movement. Major steps have been taken to break down the clergy-lay polarization in liturgy in favour of popular participation. In all churches, the hymns sung no longer reflect a particular denominational origin. It is too soon to state the long-term effects of these changes, and there are strong voices calling for some retrenchment, but it is inconceivable that the churches will return to the status quo *ante*.

A second religio-cultural shift has been the disappearance of the established translation of scripture. There is a plethora of new, easily available translations to meet every taste. While this may suit the spirit of postmodern individualism, it raises major questions for the Christian tradition, not least in liturgy and music. How will the intimate association of music and text function in a world where there is no longer a universally agreed version of the word of God?

Third, the centre of gravity in Christianity has shifted from the North Atlantic world of Europe and North America to the southern hemisphere, even with the revival of Orthodoxy in Russia. Will the long hegemony of North Atlantic civilization, not least in the churches, affect those churches' ability to welcome, as equals, voices that speak and sing in very different modes and tongues?

Finally, there are fundamental shifts concerning the place of music in popular culture. Musical training, for centuries a characteristic of a good education, increasingly has only a limited place in many schools. Will this mean a resurgence of professionalization at the expense of an enfeebled people's song? Furthermore, North Americans have experienced a general devaluation of the musical idiom, a consequence of the ubiquitous and pervasive genre called "elevator music," sound piped into malls, telephone call-waiting queues, and public places. Many have learned to resent, if not screen out, "easy listening." In some quarters there is a preference for silence over all music. Will there be a place in the religious world of the twenty-first century for the music of prayer, in any manner that would be considered a continuation of its heritage?

The gap between the growing edge of classical music and the forms being employed by and finding acceptance within the churches has never been so great. It is easy to dismiss the trivialization and the shoddiness of some religious music, including that being promoted for the music of the church, and to contrast it disparagingly with the greatness of the past. It is more difficult to discern the appropriate path as the Christian churches move into the secular and pluralistic society of the twenty-first century.

Notes

1 Colossians 3:16. All biblical references are to the New Revised Standard Version.
2 Charles Wesley (1709–88), a Church of England clergyman, wrote by best count at least six thousand such texts. They were intended not for public worship in his denomination—which at the time did not permit the singing of other than biblical

texts—but for less formal gatherings of converts to the Methodist revival movement, as well as for private devotion.

3 Matthew 26:30; Mark 14:26. These would certainly have been one or more of the *Hallel* psalms sung at Passover.

4 These are found in Luke 1:46–55, 68–79; 2:29–32.

5 From Psalm 150. 1 Chronicles 25 gives a fifth-century BCE picture of priestly choirs and musicians.

6 The expression used seems to mean antiphonal singing. See Pliny the Younger, *Epistulae x*, 96, in J. Stevenson (1965), 13–15.

7 In canonical New Testament texts, whether from Paul or from one of his disciples. See Ephesians 5:19; cf. Colossians 3:16, quoted at the beginning of this chapter.

8 1 Corinthians 14, especially verses 13–18, 26–40.

9 Quoted in Paul Westermeyer (1998), 60.

10 One striking exception occurred in Reformation Zurich, where the reformer Zwingli banned music altogether from public worship, using Platonist arguments that prayer is essentially a matter of the Spirit and therefore to be done in silence. Early Quaker worship was also conducted without community song.

11 During the first generations of Protestantism, the rate of literacy in the urban general population would not have exceeded 20 per cent, and in rural areas would have been much lower.

12 This incident occurred in 386 CE. See Augustine, *Confessions* (1955), book IX, chap. VII–VII, 187.

13 For a superb collection, see *The New Oxford Book of Carols*, ed. Hugh Keyte and Andrew Parrott (1992).

14 Luther to George Spalatin, in *Luther's Works: Letters* (1972), 2:68–70.

15 In 1780, John Wesley edited a selection of his brother's writings under the title, *A Collection of Hymns for the Use of the People Called Methodist*; see *The Works of John Wesley*, vol. 7, (1983).

16 Johann Christoph (1642–1703) was one of the numerous musicians in the talented Bach family of north-central Germany from the seventeenth to the nineteenth century. The prelude, based on a sixteenth-century tune by Louis Bourgeois, is found in *Eighty Chorale Preludes* (1937), no. 76.

17 As with that of other church musicians, Bach's work lay about parishes like St Thomas, Leipzig, where he served, and has survived in an imperfect state. Musicologists differ on the precise number of the preludes belonging to this collection.

18 Ralph David Abernathy (1990), 187.

19 Richard L. Crocker. Personal Communication to Guy L. Beck, February 1, 2005.

20 Note that, in Hebrew, *ruach* means "breath," "wind," and "spirit." Psalm 150 is a good instance of such praise.

21 The three metres were: Short (6-6-8-6), Common (8-6-8-6) and Long (8-8-8-8). Numbers refer to syllables per line.

22 In Walter Brueggemann (1988), chapters 4–5.

23 "For the Healing of the Nations," written in 1965. Frederick H. Kaan (1968).

24 M.E. Abbey and C.D. Tillman copyrighted this version of an older poem in 1890; see http://www.cyberhymnal.org.

25 From an English translation used in Christ Church Cathedral, Vancouver, of *La Mesa Capeskin Nicaraguans* (c. 1970). An arrangement can be found in *The Book of Praise* of the Presbyterian Church of Canada, 1997, no. 713.

26 I appreciate the thoughtful reflections on this topic sent to me after my public lecture on this theme by Professor Robert Manger, visiting research fellow from the Université du Québec at the Centre for Studies in Religion and Society, Victoria.

Bibliography

Abernathy, Ralph David. *And the Walls Came Tumbling Down: An Autobiography.* New York: Harper Perennial, 1990.

Adey, Lionel. *Hymns and the Christian Myth.* Vancouver: University of British Columbia Press, 1986.

Augustine. *Confessions.* Trans. Albert Outler. Library of Christian Classics 7. London: SCM, 1955.

Bach, Johann Christoph. "Prelude." In *Eighty Chorale Preludes,* ed. Hermann Keller. Leipzig: Peters, 1937.

Brueggemann, Walter. *Israel's Praise: Doxology against Idolatry and Ideology.* Philadelphia: Fortress Press, 1988.

Cone, James H. *The Spirituals and the Blues.* New York: Seabury Press, 1972.

Crocker, Richard L. *An Introduction to Gregorian Chant.* New Haven, CT: Yale University Press, 2000.

Dickinson, Edward. *Music in the History of the Western Church.* New York: Charles Scribner's Sons, 1902.

Hoffman, Lawrence A., and Janet R. Walton, eds. *Sacred Sound and Social Change: Liturgical Music in Jewish and Christian Experience.* Notre Dame and London: University of Notre Dame Press, 1992.

The Hymnal of the Protestant Episcopal Church. New York: The Church Pension Fund, 1943.

Kaan, Frederick H. "For the Healing of the Nations." Carol Stream, IL: Hope Publishing, 1968.

Leaver, Robin A., and Zimmerman, Joyce Ann, eds. *Liturgy and Music: Lifetime Learning.* Collegeville, MN: Liturgical Press, 1998.

Luther, Martin. *Luther's Works.* Vol. 2, ed. Gotfried G. Krodel. Philadelphia, PA: Fortress Press, 1972.

McKinnon, James W. "Christian Church, Music of the Early." In *The New Grove Dictionary of Music and Musicians,* 2nd ed., ed. Stanley Sadie, 5:795–807. New York: Macmillan, 2001.

New Oxford Book of Carols, ed. Hugh Keyte and Andrew Parrott. Oxford and New York: Oxford University Press, 1992.

Pelikan, Jaroslav. *Bach among the Theologians.* Philadelphia: Fortress Press, 1986.

Pliny the Younger. *Epistulae* x. In *A New Eusebius: Documents Illustrative of the History of the Church to A.D. 337,* ed. J. Stevenson. London: SPCK, 1965.

Quasten, Johannes. *Music and Worship in Pagan and Christian Antiquity.* Washington DC: National Association of Pastoral Musicians, 1983 (German edition, 1973).

Routley, Erik. *A Panorama of Christian Hymnody.* Collegeville, MN: Liturgical Press, 1979.

———. *The Music of Christian Hymns.* Chicago: GIA Publications, 1981.

Spencer, Jon Michael. *Protest and Praise: Sacred Music of Black Religion.* Minneapolis, MN: Fortress Press, 1990.

Wesley, John. *The Works of John Wesley.* Vol. 7, ed. Franz Hildebrandt and O. Beckerlegge. Oxford: Clarendon Press, 1983.

Westermeyer, Paul. *Te Deum: The Church and Music*. Minneapolis, MN: Fortress Press, 1998.

Wilson-Dickson, Andrew. *The Story of Christian Music: From Gregorian Chant to Black Gospel. An Authoritative Illustrated Guide to All the Major Traditions of Music for Worship*. Minneapolis, MN: Fortress Press, 1996. First published 1992 by Lion Publishing.

The Worship Book: Services and Hymns. Philadelphia: Westminster, 1972.

3
ISLAM AND MUSIC
Regula Qureshi

uslims, like Jews and Christians, are a "people of the book" (*ahl-al-kitāb*). Their scripture, the Qur'ān (Koran), contains the word of God. His divine message was revealed to the Prophet Muḥammad, who is also called the Messenger of God. The Muslim creed encapsulates this powerfully simple foundation of Islam: *Lā ilāha illa'Allāh, Muḥammad al Rasūl Allāh* ("There is no God but Allāh, and Muḥammad is His Messenger"). This utterly monotheistic creed is the last of the three "revealed" religions originating in the Middle East, and completes the three "Abrahamic" faiths: Judaism, Christianity, Islam. Islam is also universally accessible to anyone ready to submit to its teachings. *Islam* means "submission," and a Muslim is one who submits to its creed and follows its five "pillars": (1) *shahāda*, or creed, (2) *ṣalāt*, the ritual prayer practised five times a day (3) *zakāt*, or a tithe for charity (4) fasting during the month of Ramadān; and (5) *hajj*, or pilgrimage to the Ka'ba, Abraham's sanctuary in Mecca.

The Prophet Muḥammad is also called the last prophet, for the Qur'ān recognizes the Jewish prophets as well as Jesus. Muḥammad, however, is but a man; the gulf between God and human beings is absolute. The Qur'ān was revealed to Muḥammad, starting when he was forty years old (610 CE), through the archangel Jibrā'īl (Gabriel). Jibrā'īl voiced the message to make it audible to a human ear, for God cannot be seen or heard. Alone, Prophet Muḥammad heard a voice command: "Recite." The message from God was made accessible to human perception and comprehension not through cognition, inspiration, or a vision, but through sound: the sound of the spoken word in Muḥammad's language, Arabic.

Islamic mosque in Calcutta. Courtesy of Guy L. Beck.

The Prophet Muḥammad received the words of the Qur'ān in retainable portions over a considerable span of time. He kept them in his memory and transmitted their message to his followers through oral recitation. By the time he died (632 CE), many others had memorized the entire message. It was not until later that the present text of the Qur'ān was committed to writing during the reign of the Calīph Uthmān (644–56), third of the four companions of the Prophet who were chosen to succeed him as leader of the community. However, the written words of the Qur'ān remain inseparably linked to their utterance in recitation. Muḥammad had spread the message by sending out reciters, not texts, and Calīph Uthmān sent with each copy of the standard text a reciter who could teach its recitation.[1]

Even today, the pages of the Qur'ān are as much an aid for the memory as a direct access to the message of Islam. Learning how to read the Qur'ān means learning the sound as well as the meaning of the words, so that they can be remembered and recited. That the written words continue to live both phonetically and in writing can be seen clearly from the standard practice of teaching Muslim children to read and recite the Qur'ān in its original Arabic form. The ultimate achievement is to retain the entire message by memory with the aid of its sounded form; such reciters are honoured with the title of *Ḥāfiz al-Qur'ān*.

As a text, the Qur'ān is a testimony to the power and glory of God, a clear statement of His will, and a guide to believers that also includes instructive narratives of past prophets shared by the Judeo-Christian tradition. It is also a text of unequalled poetic beauty, which is itself considered a proof of its divine origin. For 1,400 years the language of the Qur'ān has served as the exalted standard for classical literary Arabic. As a poetic text, the Qur'ān abounds in a wealth of rhyme, assonance, rhythmic patterns, and recurring phrases, all of which enhance the meaning, and provide structure to the text as well as sonic impact. It has been observed that the way the text is structured is highly commensurate with recitation.

References to recitation are found in the Qur'ān itself, stating that the Qur'ān was transmitted to Muḥammad in the mode of recitation (*tartilan*) (25/31), and that Muḥammad was directed to recite it in the same manner (*wa rattili l-qur'āna tartilan*, 73/4). Does that make the Prophet a musician? For Muslims, this very question is anathema, if not defamatory, and it reveals two premises that are entirely inappropriate to Islam. The first premise is that all sonic cultural expression fits the common (Greek-derived) category of music. The second premise is that musicians are highly valued individuals, and they can transmit even divine messages through music—after all, some Christians call Bach "the fifth evangelist."

In Islam, to maintain the "abiding intrinsic orality" of the Qur'ān, an exclusive and exquisite melodic-rhythmic system has been developed to sound the divine word and articulate its uniqueness, different from any other words or music. This sonic form stands in conceptual opposition to all non-religious musical sounds, both vocal and, especially, instrumental. In fact, Islamic tradition considers secular music spiritually suspect; hence, Qur'ānic recitation, even if it sounds musical, is not conceived of as music. It falls into a permitted category of chant or cantillation where musical features are subordinated to religious text and function.

The Qur'ān, the revealed word of God, is uncontested as the only primary source of Islam. Next in importance, but not always uncontested, are the practices or Sunna of the Prophet Muḥammad recorded in the Ḥadīth. Extant in collections that were recorded over two centuries after the Prophet's death, the Ḥadīth take the form of the Prophet's sayings or actions that serve as interpretation of and guidance on matters of practice, but there is not always full agreement on the authenticity of all the ḥadīth (the two major collections are by Bukhari and Muslim). Third in importance is the body of Islamic jurisprudence, or *fiqh*, established during the eighth and ninth centuries, with a continuing discourse of theological interpretation which today is concentrated at the ancient Al Azhar University in Cairo, the most highly regarded institution of Islamic theology, as well as at Islamic institutions in Mecca and Medina. Regarding the admissibility of music in Muslim life, both the Hadīth and *fiqh* have been used to argue divergent positions, but no definitive interpretation can be established.

The important point to make about the structure of Islam is its egalitarian conception of the religious community. There is no central authority or religious hierarchy in Islam, and even the Calīphs represented the Prophet only as leaders of the Umma or Islamic community, not as its religious head. There is no ordained priesthood in Islam; every Muslim can be equally close to God and requires no intermediary. This does not change even where Muslims have joined special communities or sects that observe spiritual hierarchies. What unites all Muslims are the Qur'ān in its Arabic form and the five pillars of the faith, especially the call to prayer and the recitation of the ritual prayer, both of which are based on words from the Qur'ān. Every Muslim, regardless of social status, can learn to become a reciter of the Qur'ān or lead the congregational prayer.

Like Christians, Muslims have also formed distinct religious communities or sects. Apart from the great majority of believers, called Sunnī or "orthodox" Muslims, the most prominent community is that of the Shī'a or Shī'ites; this group also includes the Ismaīlis. The Shī'a believe in the Prophet's descendants as his spiritual successors or imāms. In contrast to the Sunnī exclusive focus on the Prophet, Shī'a practices particularly stress the martyrdom of the Prophet's grandson, Imām Husain. Sufis, or mystics of Islam, are largely Sunnī, but are also found in other communities; they even include non-Muslims. Their focus is on a search for God through lineages of spiritual guidance and religious ecstasy.

Sectarian, as well as regionally based practices, find expression in religious texts that are devotional rather than liturgical. Collectively called hymns, or *inshād*, they express above all devotion to the Prophet and to other religious figures. They also express aspects of personal faith, including supplicatory prayer or *du'ā*. Above all, these hymns are performed in recitation in a rich variety of sonic devotions. While *inshād* is not part of the essential core of Islamic religious practice, it is a form of worship as broadly defined. The emotional impact of *inshād* draws upon both the affective influence of music and the spiritual power of Islam. Because of their non-liturgical character, hymns tend to draw more eclectically from local and secular music and share features of the musical vernacular of particular regions. At the same time, hymns, like Qur'ān recitation, are conceptually considered religious recitation, not music.

Historically and collectively, "Islam has adopted a restricted view toward the use of music as a means of religious expression; the terms used both reveal and protect the conceptual boundaries constructed to surround various kinds of vocalization, all of which would naively be labelled 'singing' or 'music' by the English-speaking non-culture bearer."[2] This conceptual barrier has also kept most music scholars unaware of the spiritual, aesthetic, and affective richness of sonic Islamic practices. To move beyond generalizations, specific traditions of Sunnī, Shī'a, and Sufi recitation in different languages will be explored here. Throughout the Muslim world, Qur'ān and hymn recitation constitutes a domain of sonic religious experience that needs to be discovered through performance and participation, as well as through study and understanding.

Oral transmission: The role of chant in the early community

Kristina Nelson, in her study of the art of reciting the Qur'ān, posits that the prominence of the recitation or chant and its characteristic sound may be explained by three widely recognized concepts of the Qur'ān: (1) The Qur'ān is meant to be heard—therefore, the most common means of transmission is oral; (2) It is of divine and inimitable beauty—therefore, listeners approach it with expectations of heightened experience; (3) It is held to be the last of God's revelations—therefore, it must be preserved, and high value is placed on its accurate transmission. The importance of recitation can be seen from the development of *tajwīd*, an elaborate rule system to govern recitation. *Tajwīd* is believed to be the codification of the sound of the revelation as it was revealed to the Prophet Muḥammad and as he subsequently rehearsed it with the Angel Jibrā'īl (Gabriel). In the words of an authoritative manual widely used in Cairo: "Knowledge of Tajwīd is a collective duty and the practice of it is a duty prescribed for all who wish to recite something from the Holy Qur'ān."[3]

Another striking role of recitation is directly linked to its emotional effect on the listener, and to the ability of a reciter to "make people weep," for weeping is a response to the truth. The Qur'ān states: "When the signs of the All-Merciful were recited to them [the Prophets], they fell down prostrate, weeping" (19/58) "And when they hear what has been sent down to the Messenger, thou seest their eyes overflow with tears, because of the truth they recognize (5/86)." There are a number of reports that testify to the Prophet and his companions weeping on hearing the Qur'ān recited.

The same emotional effect is explicitly associated with Sufi poetry that is performed musically. There is a vast literature several centuries old which explores the truth of ecstasy caused by a spiritually focused listening or *samā'* that will transport the Sufi to a higher plane of unity with (or nearness to) God. And, in a famous Indian music treatise, the author challenges the artistry of music to match the emotional impact of Shī'a hymns of mourning.[4]

Yet another role of recitation is congregational and social: it creates a shared religious experience out of listening to a religious message whether the recitation is performed jointly or solo, though each is aesthetically distinct. Exploring that experience involves moving from a consideration of the text to its enactment in specific recitational genres and their contexts of performance.

Ritual context: Chant in public liturgy

Public ritual contexts for Qur'ānic recitation are connected to its location in the mosque. The beginning is the Call to Prayer (*Adhān*), recited by the muezzin, a respected designated male reciter in the tradition following the first muezzin named Bilāl, an Ethiopian man appointed by Muḥammad. *Adhān* (also pronounced *azān*) is sounded from the minaret of the mosque for people to join in prayer; then it is sounded again at the start of the prayer ritual in the mosque. The text is a simple set of repeated phrases containing the Islamic creed (*kalima*) and praise to God. These same words are heard from mosques throughout the world, reminding Muslims to remember God in prayer at five designated times each day: dawn (*fajr*), after midday (*zuhr*), late afternoon (*aṣr*), sunset (*maghrib*), and night (*ishā*) (see example 1). The sound of *adhān* ranges from simple intonation to elaborated melody, depending on the vocal ability and training of the reciter; it creates an Islamic soundscape somewhat analogous to Christian church bells, but here the message is verbal and explicit.

⊦ EXAMPLE 1 (Track 15)
Adhān (Call to Prayer). Text (Arabic); translation by author.

> Allāhu Akbar (4×)
> Ashadu an lā ilāha illa 'llāh (2×)
> Ashadu anna Muḥammadan Rasūl Allāh (2×)
> Hayya 'ala 'ṣ-ṣalāti (2×)
> Hayya 'ala 'l falāh (2×)
> Allāhu Akbar (2×)
> Lā ilāha illa 'llāh
>
> ⁓
>
> Allāh is the Greatest,
> I bear witness that there is no God except Allāh
> I bear witness that Muḥammad is the Messenger of Allāh
> Come to prayer
> Come to prosperity / salvation
> Allāh is the Greatest
> There is no God except Allāh.

Today, muezzins are increasingly being replaced by recorded broadcastings over loudspeakers mounted on the minarets, but *adhān* remains a powerful sonic symbol of Islamic presence; certainly, Western media reports from the Islamic world regularly use it as a sonic signature.

Qur'ānic recitation (*qir'āt*) is the Islamic vocal idiom par excellence; it frames religious rituals, and is performed formally in the mosque and informally at home by professional reciters (*qāri*), religious functionaries, and Muslim laymen and laywomen. The first message that reaches the ear of a newborn infant is the recitation of the Islamic creed. In homes, older family members recite from the Qur'ān at night or after *fajr*, the early morning prayer, but the real season of Qur'ān recitation is Ramadān, the month when Muḥammad's revelation was completed. Mosques resound with *qirā'a* every night when the faithful assemble there to say the day's last prayer (*ishā*), and then take part in this daily recitation (*tarāwīh*) in order to complete the entire Qur'ān within the holy month of Ramadān.

A ubiquitous form of individual *qirā'a* is the reading of chosen passages from the Qur'ān following prayer or at any other suitable time. Normally silent, such recitation may also be chanted, depending on the reciter's inclination and vocal skill. What is essential is that uttering God's word in the Qur'ān and, by extension, in other religious texts, is an oral-aural activity, with its full implication of internal and external participation. Words are not a transparent conduit of meaning; their sound is deeply implicated in the experience of their meaning. Hence, the sounds of the words are also set apart in recitation by making them sonically appealing (*khush ilhān*, literally "well-sounding"). Recitation means making the words one's own and making them live by actually saying them, whether aloud or silently to oneself.

Qur'ān recitation is a highly developed art governed by both religious and formal standards, which are taught in special institutions. The style of trained reciters or *qāris* is melodious and deliberately "affecting in its beauty." In Muslim countries, it is heard on radio and television in early morning or late evening broadcasts. It is also presented in public recitals, especially in Egypt. Termed *mujawwad*, this melodically elaborate style stands in contrast with the unadorned "simple" or *murattal* style of recitation that is used by lay people and also by trained reciters when reciting extended portions of the Qur'ān in the mosque during Ramadān. Both simple and elaborated *qirā'a* styles are based on the same rules of phonetic representation of the Qur'ānic text (*tajwīd*). The most commonly recited portion of the Qur'ān is Chapter One, verses 1–7. This short sūra, called *al-Fātiḥa*, marks the beginning of the Qur'ān and is recited during daily prayers, and also frequently at public gatherings. Like every sūra of the Qur'ān, it begins with the traditional injunction *Bismillāhi 'rahmān ir rahīm*, "In the Name of God, the Compassionate, the Merciful."

ǀ Example 2 (Track 16)

Qur'ān recitation (sūra 1.1–7), *al-Fātiḥa*. Text (Arabic); translation from *The Koran*, trans. N.J. Dawood (London: Penguin, 1956).

> Bi-'smi 'llāhi 'r-rahmāni 'r-raḥīm
> Al ḥamdu li-'llāhi Rabbi 'l-'ālamīn
> Ar-raḥmani 'r-rahīm Māliki yawmi 'd-dīn
> Iyāka na'budu wa-iyāka nasta 'īn
> Ihdinā 'ṣ-ṣirāta 'l-mustaqīm
> Ṣirāta 'lladhina an 'amta 'alaihim
> Ghairi 'l-maghdūbi 'alaihim walā 'ḍ-ḍāllīn
>
> ∿
>
> In the Name of Allāh the Compassionate, the Merciful
> Praise be to Allāh, Lord of the Creation,
> The Compassionate, the Merciful,
> King of Judgment Day!
> You alone we worship, and to You alone we pray for help.
> Guide us to the straight path,
> The path of those whom You have favoured,
> Not of those who have incurred Your wrath,
> Nor of those who have gone astray.

Vernacular, non-canonical recitation (*Inshād Dīni*)

Based on the word of the Qur'ān, and made explicit in Sufi writings since the thirteenth century, the Muslim ideology of the sounded word also extends to vernacular religious hymns. These hymns can be recited by anyone anywhere, but their primary context of performance is devotional assemblies centred on spiritual content as well as on principal religious figures of Islam. Believers directly identify them with these assemblies as the ritual context of performance.

The devotional hymns and their contexts presented in this chapter belong to Sunnī, Shī'a, and Sufi practices prevalent in Pakistan and India, and also among South Asian diasporic communities. Their principal language is Urdu, and they are musically South Asian, meaning that there is the use of Indian *rāga* scales and *tāla* rhythms with accompaniment by Indian musical instruments such as the harmonium and barrel-drum (*dholak*), especially during *qawwālī*. The devotional assemblies are held mostly in homes, and also in larger and more public venues, but not in mosques. A lead reciter, often with a supporting group, presents a series of hymns to an audience of devotees, who respond in specific ways to the religious listening experience. While the three hymn genres differ from each other

and from the language and recitation of the Qur'ān, they are invariably permeated with scriptural references and phrases in Arabic, so that the connection with the primary message of Islam remains audible.

Milad assembly and hymns in praise of the Prophet: *Na't*

Na't is a poem in praise of the Prophet Muḥammad, chanted in the *milad*,
or *mawlid*, the devotional assembly celebrating the birth of the Prophet
Muḥammad. The primary season for this is the month of *Rabī-ul-Awwal*,
and most auspiciously on the twelfth day, the Prophet's actual birthday. But
many Muslims, especially among the Sunnī majority, also hold a *milad* in
celebrating auspicious events in a family or an individual's life. Families
host *milads* at home; they are, particularly, a women's event. Among Sunnīs
especially, everyone is familiar with many well-known *na't*, or hymns in
praise of the Prophet. For most Muslim girls and women, such recitation
is the only approved way of expressing musicality and regaling an audience with an attractive sonic rendering of pious words. In Pakistan, girls'
schools and colleges have a tradition of presenting impressive *na't* recitation during the Prophet's month of birth.

The *milad* normally contains a series of hymns embedded within a
clearly delineated performance sequence. Like all religious events, the
milad begins in the name of God. A lead reciter, supported by one or two
accompanists, presents a *ḥamd*, a hymn in His praise, sometimes preceded
by a passage recited from the Qur'ān. Then follows a series of *na't*, alternating with spoken prose passages that relate to the birth of the Prophet
and its significance. The transitions between chanted hymn and spoken
prose are marked with a brief litany for the Prophet in Arabic. Hymn
recitation concludes with the *Salām*, in which verses of praise alternate
with a verse of salutation in Arabic. Out of respect for the Prophet, everyone rises to a standing position and joins in reciting the refrain while the
reciters present the verses. The main reciter then intones a supplicatory
prayer, or *du'ā*, and finishes with a silent recitation of a Qur'ān passage that
concludes this and other religious assemblies (*Sūrat al-Fātiḥa*).

Na't are cherished, and are widely recited in private contexts and even
at Urdu poetry recitals. There are many poets who compose and recite
na't as acts of faith, in addition to their secular poetry. Musically, *milad*
hymns evoke feelings of both devotion and exultation; they convey an
experience of veneration and submission before the Prophet, the most
exalted personage in Islam, and they also convey a deep affection for his
humanity.

Majlis assembly and hymns commemorating the martyrdom at Karbalā: *Soz, Nauha*

Based on the same fundamental concept and performance structure, the *majlis* is a recitational assembly to commemorate the martyrdom of Imām Husain and the tragedy of his massacre at Karbalā. At the heart of religious practice for Shī'a Muslims, it is performed in homes and also in *imāmbāras* or *imāmbargahs*, meeting halls that serve as Shī'a religious centres. *Majlis* assemblies constitute the primary Shī'a religious observance during the month of *Muharram*, marking especially each of the first ten days that culminate in Husain's death on the tenth of *Muharram* (*ashura*), but they are also held on significant days throughout the year.

Diverse hymns that express all spiritual and emotional facets of mourning, devotion, and remembrance are gathered together in a sequence that takes the listener from hymns expressing introspective personal grief (*soz*) through dramatic narrative poetry (*marṣīya*), and a sermon about the events of struggle and death and suffering survivors. Then simple dirges of intense grief (*nauha*) build to a climax of participation, with everyone rising and beating their chest in mourning (*matam*). An Arabic salutation to the Prophet and his descendants concludes the *majlis* event.

Majlis recitation, in reinforcing the strongly emotional text, creates for listeners a deep involvement in suffering that is both universal and deeply personal. Through the coordinated movement of chest beating (*matam*), it also creates a participatory bond among Shī'as which other Muslims who attend may not share. That bond is publicly articulated in *matam* processions during Muharram. In the broadest sense, *majlis* hymns constitute a repository of Shī'a heritage, interpretation and sentiment which their recitation brings to life for the community.

Samā' assembly for spiritual advancement: *Qawwālī*

At least since the thirteenth century, Islamic mystics have been active reciters of mystical poetry across North Africa, the Middle East, Iran, and South Asia. Pursuing discipleship and spiritual training as well as ecstatic experience to achieve nearness to God, Sufis have established a practice of reciting and listening to mystical words.

Expressly designated as an "assembly for listening," *samā'* ("listening" in Arabic) or *qawwālī* employs mystical poetry set to music as an essential means to reach a state of ecstatic communion with God. To aid in achieving this effect, Sufis have added selected instruments to enhance the recitation of their hymns. Drum beats, together with handclapping, articulate the incessant repetition of divine names. Melodic instruments sustain the voice during extended recitation that can last all night; they also extend its reach. However, the use of instruments, as well as an unorthodox emphasis on cultivating emotion, has always rendered *qawwālī* hymns religiously controversial, and even some Sufi orders disapprove totally of *samā'* assemblies.

In South Asia, the musical delivery of Sufi poems is improvisational in style, in response to the listeners' spiritual needs of the moment. Performers are highly skilled hereditary professionals, often related to a classical musician. The lead singer accompanies himself on the harmonium, and one of the supporting reciters also plays the barrel drum (*dholak*).

Samā' is a very intimately spiritual experience among a brotherly circle of Sufi disciples; it is also the most public and institutionalized of the recitational assemblies. *Qawwālī* events are held throughout the year, both among exclusive spiritual groups in any location and at shrines before large public audiences. The principal occasion, however, is the anniversary of the numerous Sufi saints, especially the great Chishti and Qādirī founders of Indic Sufism.

Like all religious, and many non-religious, occasions, the Sufi assembly begins in the name of God, with recitation of a passage from the Qur'ān. Unique to Sufi recitation, the name of God is also uttered musically. As a prelude to singing hymns, the lead *qawwālī* performer intones the *dhikr* phrase *Allāhu* in a melodic sequence on the harmonium to focus the attention of the listeners on the purpose of the Sufi assembly: finding a connection with God. Then a succession of powerful and moving hymns are drawn from a diverse repertoire that includes venerable foundational poetry in classical Persian and Hindi, but also in contemporary Urdu. *Qawwālī* texts emphasize and evoke mystical love; they also extol the hierarchy of Sufi spiritual personages from living spiritual guides (sheikhs) to saints, to Hazrat Alī, and finally to the Prophet Muḥammad, who is the human being most closely connected with God.

The role of the specialist

The professional Qur'ān reciter is a highly trained specialist, but reciters can also be untutored amateurs. The range is wide, topped by highly trained reciters like Sheikh Abd al-Basit Abd al-Samad, the outstanding Egyptian Qur'ān reciter who, in the late 1960s, travelled through the Muslim world giving Qur'ān recitals and literally moving people to tears. His were perhaps the first sets of complete Qur'ān recordings on cassette; widely disseminated, they have induced non-Arab recitation to adapt more closely to the Egyptian model of recitation, or at least to improve the standard of pronunciation.

"Sufi Musicians." Watercolour by Kajal Beck. Courtesy of the artist.

Professional Qur'ān reciters are highly trained in textual articulation and all aspects of sonic interpretation. Such specialists fulfill a relatively prominent role, particularly in Egypt, where there is a tradition of public Qur'ān recitals that now extends to the media. They are also involved in government-sponsored teaching and competitions in Qur'ān recitation, which have further enhanced amateur interest in recitation across that country.

Sunnī *milad* and Shī'a *majlis* reciters are principally amateurs, though there is a tradition of professional musicians reciting Shī'a laments to classical Indian modes. Amateur reciters with good voices, especially women, are in great demand, even in the diaspora, and particularly both during the special month of the Prophet's birth and, for Shī'as, during the month of Husain's martyrdom. A majority of these amateur reciters are women because more of these events are held by women than men, and often are in domestic settings.

The Sufi reciter, or *qawwāl*, stands in a class apart. Because of the preoccupation of the Sufi with spiritual listening or *samā'*, and because of the need for musically skilled performers, most Sufi communities have traditionally employed hereditary professional musicians who specialize in the Sufi repertoire and the special style of its performance. As the only hereditary professional specialist, the Sufi reciter is most explicitly a service provider, but the fact is that all Islamic reciters are message bearers, not stars. Thus, the role of the reciter is spiritually subordinate and the effect of the words, no matter how well recited, is strictly God's work; reciters do not contribute to the religion—the religion does not need that.

Ritual context: Music in private devotions

The term "private" is challenging in relation to Islamic recitation, because it suggests ritual contexts that are variously "domestic," "individual," or "secluded." Furthermore, public recitation, discussed above as public ritual, can also be practiced in a domestic setting with invited guests, especially among women, and even Sufi *qawwālī* assemblies are held in homes, for instance, to commemorate the weekly or monthly death day of a saint. Women may pray together on a special day like *Īd-ul Fitr*, which marks completion of the month of Ramadān. They normally may pray singly at home, as do men, and they may recite alone as well, especially after *fajr* prayer before dawn. The implication that private devotion is more introspective is problematic, because witnessing the performance of a hymn or Qur'ānic passage with others can have a deep and profound impact on the listener. Even individuals praying or reciting in their home need not be "private," since others can be present, engaged in different activities; thus, private can also mean "nonformal."

Hymnal and songbook

There is a literal version of the Qur'ān designed for reciting the entire text in multiple or successive readings. For this purpose, the Qur'ān is divided into thirty segments that provide recitation for about two hours a day for one lunar month, or individual reading portions for people who assemble to complete the Qur'ān in one day, for blessing or spiritual benefit. But the text, substantively speaking, is the orally retained sequence of words. There exists a highly elaborated rule system to govern recitation of the Qur'ān, with techniques for memorization of the entire text.

Hymn texts are non-canonical, with the exception of a small number of classical poems and tunes that mark special ritual events, usually at their beginning. There are printed collections of hymns for use in all three ritual assemblies, but their use is optional and varies greatly. However, there are well-known and favourite hymns: examples 4, 5, and 7 belong to that category, while examples 3, 6, and 8 are sophisticated poems associated with individual poets whose stature and appreciation are more variable.

Six hymns have been selected to give the reader a taste of the words and sounds of Islamic hymn recitation: two illustrate hymns to the Prophet, two are hymns on Shī'a martyrdom, and the final two are hymns for Sufi *qawwālī*.

Hymns to celebrate the Prophet: *Na't*

The following two hymns encompass the range of devotional expression articulated by *na't*. The first is a hymn of praise by the Sufi poet Bedam Warsi. It is composed in a personal, yet sophisticated poetic language, and artfully incorporates as a refrain a blessing of the Prophet derived from the Qur'ān.

▪ EXAMPLE 3 (Track 17)
"*Ai Nasim-e-ku-e-Muḥammad*" ("A breeze flows from the abode of Muḥammad"). Text (Urdu); translation by the author.

Ai Nasim-e-ku-e-Muḥammad, salla Allāhu 'alaihi wasallam
Khinchne laga dil su-e-Muḥammad, salla Allāhu 'alaihi wasallam
Dekh khula ab bab-e-karam hai, rakh de jabin mehrab-e-haram hai
Dekh khame-abru-e-Muḥammad, salla Allāhu 'alaihi wasallam
Bhini bhini khushbu mahki, bedam dil ki dunya lahki
Khul gaye jab gesu-e-Muḥammad, salla Allāhu 'alaihi wasallam

〰

A breeze flows from the abode of Muḥammad;
May God's blessings and peace be upon Him.
My heartstrings are pulled toward Muḥammad;
May God's blessings and peace be upon Him.
Behold, the Gate of Mercy is open;
Prostrate in prayer at the threshold of the holy sanctuary.
Behold the countenance of Muḥammad;
May God's blessings and peace be upon Him.
Surrounded by a delightful fragrance,
Bedam says: my heart is leaping
When I see the beauty of Muḥammad revealed;
May God's blessings and peace be upon Him.

Example 4 celebrates the glorious moment of the Prophet's birth. It addresses Muḥammad's mother Āmina in the affectionate language associated with women, while extolling his spiritual qualities. The powerful Arabic refrain praises the one and only God with phrases closely resembling the opening of the Call to Prayer (see example 1).

▎ EXAMPLE 4 (Track 18)
"Allāh Allāh Allāhu." Text (Arabic and Urdu); translation by the author.

> Allāh Allāh Allāhu, Lā Ilāha Illah hu
> Āmina Bibi ke gulshan men ai hay taza bahar
> Parhte hain sallallaho alaihe wasallam dar-o-diwar Nabiji
> Allah Allah Allahu, La Ilaha Illah hu
>
> Bara Rabi-ul-Awwal ki who ae hain durr-e-yatim
> Awwalo-akhir, zahir-o-batin, ban kar ghafur-o-rahīm Nabiji
> Allāh Allāh Allāhu, Lā Ilāha Illah hu
>
> Jibrā'īl aen jhula jhulaen, lori de Rahmān
> So ja, so ja, ai rahmat-e-alam do jag ke sultan Nabiji
> Allāh Allāh Allāhu, Lā Ilāha Illah hu
>
> ⌁
>
> Allāh, Allāh Allāhu, there is no God but He.
> A new spring has come to the garden of Lady Āmina,
> The whole house is resounding: May God's blessing and
>   peace be upon you, Oh revered Prophet
> Allāh, Allāh Allāhu, there is no God but He.
>
> On the 123rd Rabī-ul-Awwāl the priceless jewel has arrived
> He who is first and last, apparent and concealed, forgiving and
>   merciful, has come, O revered Prophet
> Allāh, Allāh Allāhu, there is no God but He.
>
> Gabriel has come to rock the cradle and there are lullabies from God,
> Sleep, sleep, you who are a Blessing to the Universe and Ruler of both
>   this and the other world, O revered Prophet
> Allāh, Allāh Allāhu, there is no God but He.

Shī'ite hymns to mourn the martyrs: *Soz, Nauha*

The expressively ornate *soz* hymns have traditionally been the domain of professional reciters with musical training. The accompanists support the solo melody with a vocal drone that is clearly a vocal substitute for the drone instrument of art music. Example 5 is a moving lament of Zainab, sister of the martyred Imām Husain; it is recited in an ornate melody resembling *rāga kāfī*.

⸬ EXAMPLE 5 (Track 19)

Soz: "Mujrayi Shah ne Kaha" ("O Reciter, thus spoke Husain, the Exalted"). Text (Urdu); translation by the author.

> Mujrayi Shah ne kaha pani jo pana Zainab
> Tashnagi bhayi ki tum bhul na jana Zainab
>
> Raham kha kar koi beraham agar pani de
> Pahle tum meri Sakina ko pilana Zainab
>
> Mujrayi Shah ne kaha pani jo pana Zainab
> Qaid men chup ke chali jayio sar neorae
> Apni Awaz kisi ko na sunana, Zainab
> Mujrayi Shah ne kaha pani jo pana Zainab
>
> ∾

> O Reciter! Thus spoke Husain, the Exalted:
> Whenever you drink water, O Zainab,
> Forget not your brother's thirst, O Zainab.
>   O Reciter, thus Husain, the Exalted
>
> Should any of the merciless enemies have mercy and give you water,
> Then give it first to my daughter Sakina, O Zainab.
>   O Reciter, thus spoke Husain, the Exalted
>
> Walk into the prison without speaking and with bowed head
> Let no one hear your voice, O Zainab.
>   O Reciter, thus spoke Husain, the Exalted

Example 6, in contrast, is a simple dirge with a tune that emulates weeping and total despair. The poem of artful simplicity and childlike disbelief addresses the river that could not give water and save the martyr from death.

⸬ EXAMPLE 6 (Track 20)

Nauha: "Ai wa-e-nahr-e alqauman" ("Woe on You, River of Alqauman"). Text (Urdu); translation by the author.

> Pyasa raha jan-e-Nabi, ai wa-e-nahr-e-alqauman
> Uthti rahin maujen teri, ai wa-e-nahr-e-alqauman
>
> Woh khushk lab sukha gala, sher-e-khuda ki al ka
> Woh tere honton par tari, ai wa-e-nahr-e-alqauman
>
> Tufan uthana tha tujhe, ya sukh jana tha tujhe
> Kuchh tu ne khidmat hi na ki, ai wa-e-nahr-e-alqauman

Ata hai who yad jab, Woh karawan-e-tishnalab
Hai Najam ka nauha yehi, ai wa-e-nahr-e-alqauma

He remained thirsty, the beloved grandson of the Prophet;
woe on you, river of Alqauman
　　Even though you were full of water; woe on you, river of Alqauman

So dry were the lips and throat of the son of the Lion of God
　　While your lips were full of water; woe on you, river of Alqauman

You should have raised a storm or dried up in dismay
　　But you did nothing for him; woe on you, river of Alqauman

Sufi hymns to the saints: *Qawwālī*

The first hymn in a *qawwālī* assembly normally addresses the Prophet or his son-in-law, Alī; then follow hymns in praise and in search of saints, especially the saint to whom the listeners have a special spiritual connection. Example 7 is a hymn to India's greatest and most beloved saint, Muinuddin Chishti, who in the thirteenth century established the strongest Sufi lineage in South Asia. The simple devotional poem is in a folk-like Hindi, with a vocabulary typical of Hindu devotional poetry that speaks as a woman in search of her beloved lord. Notable is the repetition of the names of the saint and of his spiritual successors whose strength is ultimately their connection to Muinuddin; this is articulated in the ascending sequence of names, culminating in that of Muinuddin.

｜ EXAMPLE 7
"Kirpā karo Mahārāj" ("Have Mercy, My Lord Muinuddin").
Text (Hindi); translation by the author.

> Kirpā karo Mahārāj Muinuddin
> Tumrī dayā kī sun ke khabariyā
> An pari hun tori nagariyā
> Sar jhukaun tumrī dahaliyā
> Jahān karo tum rāj, Muinuddin
>
> Tum bin kaise ab nibhāun
> Tum bin kis ko hal sunāung
> Tumrī kahā par kis dar jāun
> Tumhi kaho Mahārāj Muinuddin
> 　　Khwaja Nijāmuddin
> 　　Khwaja Farīduddin

Khwaja Qutābuddin
Khwaja Muinuddin
Kirpā karo Mahārāj Muinuddin

Have mercy, my lord Muinuddin
I have heard the news of your powers
And I have come to your abode
Let me bow my head before your threshold
You rule over a vast realm

Without you, how can I cope?
Without you, whom can I tell my sorrow
Tell me, to which door should I go?
Only you can guide me, my lord

Have mercy, my lord Muinuddin,
my lord Nijāmuddin,
my lord Farīduddin,
my lord Qutābuddin
my lord Muinuddin
Have mercy, my lord Muinuddin.

The second *qawwālī* example is a sophisticated poem in veneration of Alī.
The poet, unknown, was also a spiritual guide and successor of a saintly
lineage in southern India.

| EXAMPLE 8

"Batufail-e-daman-e-Murtaza" ("My Attachment to Alī"). Text (Urdu);
translation by the author.

Batufail-e-daman-e-Murtaza, main batāun kyā mujhe kyā milā
Keh Alī mile to Nabi mile, jo Nabi mile to Khudā mile.
Tere naqsh-e-pa se qadam qadam, woh maqam-e-sabr-o-raza milā
Kahin khak-e-ahl-e-junun mili, kahīn khun-e-rang-e-wafa milā

Tu amir ibn-e-amir hai, tera faiz faiz-e-azim hai
Tere dar se jo bhi milā mujhe, mere hausla se siwa milā
Tere dar se jo, Mere Maula
Maula Mushkilkusha
Ya Sher-e-Khudā
Ya Hajat Nawa
Tere dar se jo bhi mila mujhe, mere hausla se siwa milā
Batufail-e-daaman-e-Murtaza

What blessing I have received through my attachment to Murtaza (Alī):
Once I reached Alī, I reached the Prophet; and when I reached the Prophet,
  I reached God.
Following your model, I strive to attain perseverance and submission.
You have shown me ecstatic faith, and constancy in belief.

You are a Lord of Lords, your beneficence is immense.
The gifts I have received at your door always exceed what I asked for.
The gifts I have received at your door, my Lord
      Solver of Difficulties
      Lion of God
      Helper in Need

Technical dimensions

The technical dimensions of recitation styles are best illustrated by examples. For Qur'ān recitation, *tajwīd* rules cover articulation, duration, and sectioning. Qur'ān recitation follows the pattern of the words, alternating the dynamic presentation of phrases with echoing silences; the "music" is subservient to the text and its meaning. An elaborate philological discipline governs pronunciation, textual variants, and delivery of holy words. However, there is no explicit technical regulation for the purely musical dimension, in particular the melody.

Hymns too are meant to be musically enhanced; in fact, that is their purpose. Since these are invariably poems with a set metric and rhyming scheme, there are equally set melodic settings that are composed to fit the particular poetic form. In other words, they are more like songs, but even here the musical setting is governed by textual features. The ideology is for the musical setting to make the hymn text better understood by underscoring the poetic form, by articulating the shape and rhythm of the words, and by enhancing the affective power of the words with appealing melody. This is a principle realized in all hymn genres. It can be done in a number of creative ways, but the important point is that the musical metre—that is, the rhythmic flow of the melody—corresponds with the textual metre, or the prosodic sequence of long and short syllables in the text.

Musical technical dimensions are more highly articulated in *qawwālī*. To begin with, the use of musical instruments means that playing skills are required, although instrumental performance is always subordinate to the vocal articulation of the poetic texts. Drum patterns provide forceful accents, but little else in elaboration. The same principle governs melodic instruments: they underscore the vocal melody in an inconspicuous way, and solo instrumentals are not appropriate, except for the *dhikr* prelude.

Music as spiritual discipline

Musical sound contributes to the emotional impact of the spiritual message of religious words in Islam. Starting with Qur'ān recitation, music's sound and meaning permeate the daily life of many individuals; musical sound frames activities and focuses the individual's attention through spiritual discipline, especially in the five daily calls to prayer and in prayer itself.

Sufism uses music explicitly as a tool for spiritual advancement and expansion of mystical experience. However, that goal is not shared by orthodox Islam precisely because, along with listening to music, it allows for release beyond the discipline of traditional structures of worship.

Musical sound, in Islam, remains subordinate to the divine word. Where a role for musical sound is acknowledged, it is strictly one of mediation: to transmit and enhance the experience of speaking and hearing the spiritual message. As a mediator, the reciter cannot be a central figure in Islam. Nevertheless, throughout the history of Islam there have been reciters who are remembered for their compelling voice and outstanding abilities. The following stand out for their special contribution to recitation in different times and places:

David (Daūd), the prophet common to Judaism, Christianity, and Islam, is named in the Qur'ān for the power and beauty of his voice in uttering the word of God.

Bilāl was the first muezzin of Islam, chosen and approved by the Prophet himself. He was famous for the beauty of his recitation of *adhān*.

Amir Khusrau, a great Sufi devotee, poet, and hymn composer of thirteenth century Iran and India, is the acknowledged founder of *qawwālī* singing. His spiritual poetry in Farsi and Hindi still form the core of South Asian Sufi ritual.

Sheikh Abd al-Basit Abd al-Samad is one of the outstanding Qur'ān reciters of Egypt, and perhaps the best-known reciter of the twentieth century; he was the first to record and disseminate tapes containing his recitation of the complete Qur'ān.

Nusrat Fateh Ali Khan spread Sufi devotional hymns across the world through his unique rhythmic virtuosity and a melodic appeal that carried the basic Sufi message to international audiences, always preserving the integrity of the texts regardless of sonic packaging.

Current trends and the future of music in Islam

The conceptual separation of text and music has kept recitation deliberately distinct and consistent within established norms of verbal articulation. Recordings of Qur'ān recitation (*qirā'a*) continue to have a preserving, as well as a standardizing, influence on *qirā'a* by disseminating highly renowned Egyptian performances across the Islamic world. The role of women in Qur'ān recitation is also gaining attention, especially in Indonesia.

An examination of trends in hymn recitation suggests that here, too, recordings of talented and seasoned *na't* and *nauha* performers have disseminated standards of melodic and tonal excellence. At the same time, live performances of *na't*, and especially of *soz* and *Salām* hymns, continue to be tied to their respective ritual assemblies and to be performed on their special ritual occasions.

Not surprisingly, *qawwālī*—the recitational genre least clearly separated from music—has been openly prone to some degree of direct musical influence. This is reflected both in the changes in preferred instrumental accompaniment—from the traditional barrel drum (*dholak*) to the sophisticated tabla, and from the simple plucked accompaniment of the sitar to the more intrusive sonic presence of one or more harmoniums, and in the trend toward larger vocal groups. In the Islamic state of Pakistan, *qawwālī* has developed into a concert genre, somewhat like concerts of religious compositions in the West. What is remarkable is that, whether on stage or on record, male *qawwālī* artists like the Sabri Brothers and Nusrat Fateh Ali Khan, as well as new female artists like Abida Parveen, have retained their spiritual repertoire and performance style. This can only be ascribed to the fact that even these international stars never stopped performing *qawwālī* in ritual assemblies for the spiritual goals of Sufism.

Notes

1 Kristina Nelson (1987), 3.
2 Michael Frishkopf (1999), 290.
3 Kristina Nelson (1987), 15.
4 Regula Burckhardt Qureshi (1981), 81.

Bibliography

Ali, Abdullah Yusuf. *The Holy Quran: Text, Translation and Commentary*. Washington, DC: American International Printing, 1946.

Esposito, John L. *Islam, the Straight Path*. New York: Oxford University Press, 1988.

Farmer, Henry George. "The Music of Islam." In *The New Oxford History of Music. Vol. 1, Ancient and Oriental Music*, ed. Egon Wellesz, 228–54. Oxford: Oxford University Press, 1968.

Frishkopf, Michael. "Sufism Ritual and Modernity in Egypt: Language Performance as an Adaptive Strategy." PhD dissertation, Department of Ethnomusicology, UCLA, 1999.

Graham, William A. "Qur'ān as Spoken Word: An Islamic Contribution to the Understanding of Scripture." In *Islam and the History of Religions: Perspectives on the Study of a Religious Tradition*, ed. Richard C. Martin, 23–40. Tucson, AZ: University of Arizona Press, 1982.

Grunebaum, G.E. von. *Muḥammadan Festivals*. New York: Olive Branch Press, 1988.

Nelson, Kristina. *The Art of Reciting the Qur'ān*. Austin, TX: University of Texas Press, 1987.

Neubauer, Eckard, and Veronica Doubleday. "Islamic Music." In *The New Grove Dictionary of Music and Musicians*, 2nd ed., ed. Stanley Sadie, 12: 599–610. New York: Macmillan, 2001.

Pinault, David. *The Shiites: Ritual and Popular Piety in a Muslim Community*. New York: St. Martin's Press, 1992.

Qureshi, Regula Burckhardt. "Islamic Music in an Indian Environment: The Shī'a Majlis." *Ethnomusicology* 25 (1981), 41–71.

———. *Sufi Music of India and Pakistan: Sound, Context and Meaning in Qawwālī*. Chicago: University of Chicago Press, 1995 (with accompanying CD). Originally published 1986 by Cambridge University Press.

———. "'Muslim Devotional': Popular Religious Music under British, Indian, and Pakistani Hegemony." *Asian Music* 25 (1992/93): 111–21.

———. "Recorded Sound and Religious Music: The Case of Qawwālī." In *Media and the Transformation of Religion in South Asia*, ed. Lawrence Babb and Susan Wadley (pp. 139–66). Philadelphia: University of Pennsylvania Press, 1995.

———. "Transcending Space: Recitation and Community Among South Asian Muslims in Canada." In *Making Muslim Space in North America and Europe*, ed. Barbara Daly Metcalf, 17–101. Berkeley and Los Angeles: University of California Press, 1996.

———. "50 Years of Building National Identity through Culture: The Sonic Arts in Pakistan." In *Pakistan at 50*, ed. Carl Ernst. Oxford: Oxford University Press, forthcoming.

Rahman, Fazlur. *Islam*. 2nd ed. University of Chicago Press, 1979.

Sakata, Hiromi Lorraine. "The Sacred and the Profane: *Qawwali* Represented in the Performances of Nusrat Fateh Ali Khan." *The World of Music* 36 (1994) 86–99.

Schimmel, Annemarie. *Mystical Dimensions of Islam*. Chapel Hill: University of North Carolina Press, 1975.

Schubel, Vernon James. *Religious Performance in Contemporary Islam: Shī'i Devotional Rituals in South Asia*. Columbia: University of South Carolina Press, 1993.

Shiloah, Amnon. *Music in the World of Islam: A Socio-Cultural Study*. Detroit, MI: Wayne State University Press, 1995.

Touma, Habib Hassan. *The Music of the Arabs*. Portland, OR: Amadeus Press, 1996.

Waugh, Earle H. *The Munshidin of Egypt: Their World and Their Song*. Columbia: University of South Carolina Press, 1989.

4

HINDUISM AND MUSIC

Guy L. Beck

Religious chant and music occupy a central position in the heritage of Hindu religion. Unlike some traditions that have considered music as a secular or profane art, the relationship between music and the sacred in Hinduism holds no ambiguity. Encompassing a broad spectrum from the chanting of ancient Vedic priests to the melodic *bhajans* of modern-day devotees, Hindu religious chant and music are firmly rooted in theological principles of sacred sound found throughout the Vedic and Hindu scriptures, and associated with spiritual power and ecstasy from the earliest times. While there was no single founder of Hinduism who was a musician, as for instance, in the case of Sikhism with Guru Nānak, all of the famous rishis or sages in ancient India, like Nārada Rishi and Vaśishta, were either exemplary musicians or chanters of the Vedic texts. Most of the founders of Hindu religious schools or lineages have also been patrons of music or musically adept and, conversely, all founders and teachers of Indian musical styles were directly associated with religious lineages.

This chapter will outline some of the basic theoretical concepts underlying the formation of Hindu chant and music, cite selected examples of important genres of chant and devotional music, and provide a historical framework for understanding music as a prominent form of religious practice and experience in the living traditions of Hinduism.

Basic teachings and primary sources

The ancient texts of the Vedas and the Upanishads, said to be eternal and authorless, are believed to embody the eternal and primeval sacred sound that generated the universe, represented by the syllable Oṁ (AUM). The original four Vedas, including the *Rig-Veda*, *Yajur-Veda*, *Sāma-Veda*, and *Atharva-Veda*, were comprised mainly of ritual hymns and incantations that depended on their power as intoned speech for their effective execution. The Supreme Absolute underlying all existence, mentioned in the Vedas and described more fully in the Upanishads as Brahman, is also exemplified by the syllable Oṁ. Oṁ is comprised of the elemental sound *śabda*, and therefore is also known as Śabda-Brahman, which manifests on earth through the power of sonic expression. In the evolving Vaishnava, Śaiva, and Śākta theistic traditions of worship, and especially in Tantrism, the concept of sacred sound as Śabda-Brahman was further developed and transformed into the idea of *Nāda-Brahman*, which included musical sounds and non-linguistic sounds heard in deep yogic meditation. Brahman also become personified, gradually, as either Lord Brahmā, the creator of the universe including sound, or as simply the male Īśvara ("Lord"), with sacred sound as his female energy (Nāda-Śakti). As Brahman pervaded the entire universe, including the human soul at its core, the notion of sacred sound as manifested through chant and music provided a veritable thread binding the human realm to the divine. Musicological treatises such as *Saṅgīta-Ratnākara* discussed *Nāda-Brahman* as the foundation of musical sound. Since music was believed to be linked with the realm of the gods, *Bhakti* devotional traditions continued to combine the theoretical notions of *Nāda-Brahman* with Hindu aesthetics in establishing the legitimacy of music in Hindu worship.

Considered to be of divine origin, music has always been closely identified with the Hindu gods and goddesses, and forms an integral part of the narrative mythology concerning them. The goddess Sarasvatī, depicted with the *vīṇā* (a musical instrument) in her hand, is believed to be the divine patroness of music and receives the veneration of all students and performers of Indian music. Brahmā, the creator god who, with Sarasvatī, fashioned Hindu music out of the ingredients of the *Sāma-Veda*, plays the hand cymbals. The supreme deity of the Vaishnava traditions blows the conch as Vishnu the Preserver, and plays the flute as Krishna. Krishna is viewed by Vaishnavas as the musical god par excellence, as he dazzles the universe with his enchanting melodies. Śiva, the god of Śaivism, plays the *damaru* drum during the dance of cosmic dissolution, and is the recognized source of all rhythm in the universe. The dancing Śiva, Naṭarāja, is central to most Indian classical dance traditions. Each instrument held by

"Sarasvati, Goddess of Music." Painting by Ravi Varma, 1890. Courtesy of H. Daniel Smith Collection 114.

the gods also symbolizes Nāda-Brahman, manifestations of sacred cos-mic sound. Divine appearances of these deities on earth have stimulated the cultivation of chant and music as integral parts of worship and service.

The major theistic branches of Hinduism, including Śaivism, Śaktism, and Vaishnavism, display remarkable continuity in the ways in which the standard concepts of sacred sound, such as Oṁ and *Nāda-Brahman*, are presented in the classical Sanskrit texts of their respective theological tra-ditions. In the tradition of Śiva worship known as Śaivism, the ancient texts of the Śaiva-Āgamas in South India discuss the syllable Oṁ and speculate on Nāda in terms of Śiva and his energy or Śakti, influencing Śaiva-Siddhānta philosophy and the Śiva Purāṇas. The gendered pairing of the male deity Śiva as *bindu* (seed) with the female consort Sakti as *ardha-candra* (half-moon or "womb") exists throughout both Śaivism and Śaktism.

The worship of Devī as the supreme goddess is the basis of Śaktism, a tradition also replete with esoteric notions of sacred sound. The *Śaradā-Tilaka-Tantra* and other Sanskrit texts known as Śākta Tantras abundantly discuss Oṁ, *Nāda-Brahman*, and the energies of mantra in relation to God-dess worship. Nāda-Śakti is identified with the potencies of the various let-ters of the Sanskrit alphabet believed to reside in the centres (*chakras*) of the human body, as in Kuṇḍalinī Yoga, a mystical discipline also present in Śaiva and Vaishnava traditions.

Vaishnavism, the largest body of traditions in Hinduism that includes the worship of Rāma and Krishna, contains extensive coverage of sacred sound and music that is similar in essence to that found in Śaivism and Śākta Tantra. The principal sources here are the *Pāñcarātra Saṁhitās*, Purāṇas such as the *Vishnu Purāṇa* and *Bhāgavata Purāṇa*, and the commentarial literature of the various sectarian lineages. Authoritative for nearly all Vaishnava theory and practice, the *Pāncarātra Saṁhitās* (earliest ca. 500 CE) discuss Nāda-Śakti in relation to Vishnu instead of Śiva, associating it with Lakshmī or Vishnu's wife. The *Śeṣa-Saṁhitā* enumerates up to nine components of Oṁ that correspond with names of Vishnu, like Nārāyaṇa, Vāsudeva, and Bhagavān Hari.

The major Vaishnava devotional lineages were established during the medieval period by famous saints who propagated service and devotion (*bhakti*) to Vishnu or Krishna as the Supreme Brahman. Following the directions given in the *Pāñcarātra* texts and the *Bhāgavata Purāṇa*, these sects and others acknowledged Nāda as the energy of Vishnu and prom-ulgated music in all their temples and shrines. Their founders wrote the-ological treatises in Sanskrit that have been handed down for generations. In addition, there are many Sanskrit prayers and recitations that are appro-priately rendered within their respective worship regimens.

The primary sources for theoretical presentations and discussions of sacred sound and music in Hinduism are in classical Sanskrit. These texts formulated a theoretical basis for music to be recognized as a sacred art that granted all four aims of human life, namely *dharma* (righteousness), *artha* (wealth), *kāma* (enjoyment), and *moksha* (liberation), to both the performer and the listener. In addition to the Sanskrit treatises and various prayers and hymns that were also in Sanskrit, vernacular songs came to prominence in liturgical and devotional contexts, both public and private, that have been found in the various regions of India. This chapter will include a few examples of these in the following sections. But, before discussing religious music in practice, we will consider Vedic chant in Sanskrit as the most important underlying basis for the establishment of Hindu religious music.

Chant and music in ancient India

The Hindu experience of scripture has been oral/aural from the beginning, with a strong emphasis on maintaining purity of transmission by means of disciplined memorization. The ancient Indian practice of formal recitation and chanting of sacred utterances in Sanskrit is traceable to the Vedic period (ca. 4000–1800 BCE), when verses from the Vedas were chanted by Brahmin priests during fire sacrifices. The term "Hinduism" was unknown in the ancient period. Instead, there was the wide network of language, culture, and religion that may be described as Ārya-Dharma, the dharma or "religious culture" of the ancient Aryans, and which was first known within the region from India to ancient Persia (Iran) in and about 4000–2000 BCE. The religion of the Aryans, closely bound up with sun worship, fire rituals, and solar phenomena, incorporated conceptions of sacred sound whereby the chanted word in combination with sacrificial activity was recognized as the requisite means to interact with the cosmos and obtain unseen spiritual merit. Vedic chant was comprised of metrical verses, whose syllables were measured according to a system of precise time duration. The powers of sound and speech found in the Vedas are said to be inherent in the pronunciation and metrical structure of the mantras, or ritual chants, themselves. In fact, each poetical metre was associated with a particular demigod or divine power, and accurate chanting by the priest meant some degree of control over a specific power or being. The accumulated powers of the mantras and metres were gradually condensed into the syllable Oṁ, symbolizing and representing the metaphysical Śabda-Brahman, or Sound-Absolute. Oṁ was also personified as Vāc, goddess of speech and "Mother of the Vedas," or the goddess Sarasvatī, patroness of music and learning. Vāc was later transformed into Nāda-Śakti, or female sound-energy.

In terms of practice, Vedic priests performed fire sacrifices called *yajña* that entailed various forms of mantra chant. Special priests known as *Hotrī* chanted verses from the *Rig-Veda* in a type of elongated monotone, reflecting an ancient Aryan, and indeed pan-Asian, belief in the magical power of tonal recitation. Early notations in manuscripts suggest at least three accents that most probably referred to three separate tones: *anudatta* (grave, "not raised"), *svarita* (circumflex, "sounded"), and *udatta* (acute, "raised"). The grammarian Panini (fourth century BCE), who knew the living tradition, has described these accents and tones. Modern scholars interpret this notation to mean that *udatta* was the tonic (middle C) and the principal note upon which the chants were generally intoned. The *anudatta* was a whole step below (B♭), while the *svarita* was a half step above (D♭). Example 1 below is the most famous Vedic chant in Sanskrit, known as the "Gāyatrī Mantra," and preceded by the sacred syllables of *Oṁ Bhūr Bhuvaḥ Svaḥ*.[1] These syllables refer to the *triloka* or three worlds of the ancient Aryans— earth, sky, and heaven. The chanting of the "Gāyatrī Mantra" follows the three-tone system above, and is in the Gāyatrī metre of three lines of eight syllables each, from which the mantra is named.

⊩ EXAMPLE 1 (Track 21)
Vedic Chant: *Rig-Veda* 3.62.10. "Gāyatrī Mantra" in Gāyatrī metre. Text (Sanskrit); translation by the author.

> Oṁ Bhūr Bhuvaḥ Svaḥ
> tat savitur vareṅyaṁ
> bhargo devasya dhīmahi
> dhiyo yo naḥ pracodayāt
>
> ᨆ
>
> Oṁ! Earth, Sky, Heaven.
> We meditate on the brilliant light of the Sun:
> May it illuminate our minds.

The thrice-daily chanting of the "Gāyatrī Mantra" is obligatory for all Brahmin priests and twice-born Hindus, and is performed roughly around sunrise, noon, and sunset, corresponding with the Aryan emphasis on sun worship and solar phenomena. The "Gāyatrī Mantra" continues to be an essential ingredient in almost all Hindu rituals.

The most famous complete "hymn" from the *Rig-Veda* is the *Purusha-Sūkta* (RV 10.90), in which a sacrifice of the Cosmic Man (Purusha) is described with reference to the creation of the universe. The Purusha is beyond time and space, yet manifests partially (that is, one fourth of it does) within the created universe. The pantheistic language is symbolic and figurative. As such, terms like "thousand-headed," and so on, refer to the multiplicity of living beings. *Virāj* refers to the splendour of the Deity in its feminine dimension. This is also the hymn in which the *varṇa* (caste) system is first articulated as a revelation from the gods. Portions of this hymn continue to be chanted during Hindu worship rituals known as *pūjā* in addition to strict Vedic rites. While the entire hymn contains fifteen stanzas, the first five stanzas are given below as example 2.

❙ EXAMPLE 2 (Track 22)
Purusha-Sūkta, Rig-Veda 10.90.1–5. Sanskrit text and English translation from Abinash Chandra Bose, *Hymns from the Vedas* (New York: Asia Publishing House, 1966), 284–85.

Hari Oṁ
1 sahasra-śīrshāḥ purushaḥ sahasrākshaḥ sahasra-pāt
 sa bhūmiṁ viśvato vritvā atyatishtad daśāngulam

2 purusha evedaṁ sarvam yad bhūtam yac ca bhavyam
 utāmritatvasyeśāno yad annenātirohati

3 etāvān asya mahima ato jyāyāṁś ca purushaḥ
 pādo'sya viśvā bhūtāni tripādasyāmritam divi

4 tripād ūrdhva udait purushaḥ pādo'syehābhavat punaḥ
 tato viśvad vyakrāmat sāśanānaśane abhi

5 tasmād virāll ajāyata virājo adhi purushaḥ
 sa jāto atyaricyata paścād bhūmim atho puraḥ
ᴧᴧ

O Lord Hari (Vishnu). Oṁ
1 Purusha is thousand-headed, thousand-eyed, thousand-footed;
 And, pervading the earth on all sides, he exists beyond the ten directions.
2 Purusha, indeed, is all this, what has been and what will be;
 And the Lord of immortality transcending by mortal nurture.
3 Such is his magnificence, but Purusha is greater than this;
 All beings are a fourth of him, three-fourths—his immortality—
 lie in heaven.
4 Three-fourths of Purusha ascended, the fourth part was here
 again and again,
 And, diversified in form, it moved to the animate and the
 inanimate world.
5 From him was Virāj born, and from Virāj was born Purusha;
 And, as soon as born, he spread over the earth from behind and in front.

For purposes of ritual application by the priests, many stanzas such as these from the *Rig-Veda* were selected and rearranged in the *Yajur-Veda* according to specific sacrificial formats. This included additional prose formulas to be uttered by *Adhvaryu* priests as they performed the material functions of the sacrifice, such as making oblations into the fire. The *Sāma-Veda* is also comprised of verses from the *Rig-Veda*, but these verses were set to music and sung by another group of priests known as *Udgātrī*. The *sāmans*, songs of the *Sāma-Veda*, were rendered especially during elaborate public Soma sacrifices involving the offering of the juice of the Soma plant, a still unidentified plant believed by some scholars to have hallucinogenic properties. Soma juice, sometimes mixed with milk and honey as an oblation, was particularly enjoyed by the god Indra, and the remainder was later imbibed by priests as a sacrament after the ritual. The *Sāma-Veda* was also connected with the worship of ancestors, whose abode was the moon. Great importance was given to the *Sāma-Veda* in the Upanishads, particularly in the *Chāndogya Upanishad*.

Unlike the *Rig-Veda* chant, which was a strict metrical cantillation limited to about three tones, the more flexible *sāmans* of the *Sāma-Veda* were more musical as they were rendered according to pre-existent melodies that contained from five to seven tones. Adjusting and enlarging the original tone system, the *sāmans* required an expansion of the original three tones of *Rig-Veda* chant up to seven distinct musical notes forming a new *Sāma-Veda* scale. These seven notes correspond roughly to the notes of the Western diatonic scale, yet were understood to be in a descending order beginning with F above middle C, down to G below. While all seven notes were sometimes applied, most *sāman* singing utilized five notes.

The chanted *Sāma-Veda* hymns were believed to possess supernatural qualities capable of petitioning and summoning the deities in charge of the forces of nature. Another unique feature of the *sāmans* was the insertion of a number of "meaningless" words or syllables (*stobhā*) for musical and lyrical effect, such as *o*, *hau*, *hoyī*, and *vā*. The *stobhās* were inserted according to the metrical format of the stanza, yet were extended vocally by the singers, who would give specific notes a longer duration. In this way, priests enhanced the function of *epiclesis*, or summoning the gods to the sacrifice, through extended vocal droning on these notes, all of which were believed to hold magical properties. Vedic scholar G.U. Thite has explained that "the poet-singers call, invoke, invite the gods with the help of musical elements. In so doing they seem to be aware of the magnetic power of music and therefore they seem to be using that power in calling the gods." The Vedic gods even seem to have had a sense of music appreciation: "Gods are fond of music. They like music and enjoy it. The poet-singers sing and praise the gods with the intention that the gods may be pleased thereby and having become pleased they may grant gifts." The singing of *sāmans* was so essential to the sacrifice that "without it no sacrifice can go to the gods."[2] The chanting and hearing of sustained musical notes was

"Woman playing the vina." Watercolour by Kajal Beck. Courtesy of the artist.

mysteriously linked, then, to the divine at this early stage of Hindu ritual practice.

Precise methods of singing the *sāmans* were established and preserved in three different schools, the oldest of which was the Jaiminīya. Each school has maintained a distinct style with regard to vowel prolongation, interpolation, and repetition of *stobhās*, metre, phonetics, and the number of notes in a scale. Accordingly, there has been a fervent regard for maintaining continuity in *Sāma-Veda* singing to avoid misuse or alteration over the years. Since written texts were not in use, and in fact were prohibited, the priests memorized the chants with the aid of accents, melodies, and hand gestures called *mudrās*, enabling them to pass down this tradition orally from one generation to the next for over three thousand years.

The tradition of *sāman* singing set the stage for the creation and development of the Indian classical music style known first as *Gandharva Saṅgīta*, and then simply as *Saṅgīta*. According to V. Raghavan, *Saṅgīta* was born from the *Sāma-Veda*: "Our music tradition in the North as well as in the South remembers and cherishes its origin in the *Sāma-Veda*, the musical version of the *Rig-Veda*."[3] Hinduism is one of the few traditions of religious music where the "transition" from religious cantillation or chant, normally comprising a minimum of notes, to music that utilizes the full gamut of notes has occurred directly within the same textual tradition.

Gandharva Saṅgīta ("celestial music"), the courtly counterpart to the Vedic *Sāma-Veda sāmans*, was considered to be similar in kind to the music performed and enjoyed in Lord Indra's court in heaven. Viewed as a replica of heavenly archetypes, this ancient religious music was primarily vocal but included instruments such as the *vīṇā*, flutes, drums, and cymbals, as mentioned in Vedic literature, and the *vīṇā* was, in fact, actually played during Vedic rites. The celestial performers of *Gandharva Saṅgīta* were the Gandharvas, a class of male singers and demigods led by Nārada Rishi, who resided in heaven. They were accompanied by their wives, the dancing Apsarās, and the Kinnaras on musical instruments. Each of these arts— vocal music, dance, and instrumental music—was thus considered divine, being performed by divine beings that were also connected with the Soma plant and sacrifice. The leader of the Gandharvas was Nārada Rishi, the son of Brahmā and author of seven hymns in the *Rig-Veda* (and the *Sāma-Veda*). He was also said to be the inventor of the *vīṇā* and the sage who instructed human beings in *Gandharva Saṅgīta*, having learned it from the Goddess Sarasvatī, who herself had received training from Lord Brahmā.

Indian music, known as *Saṅgīta* ("well-formed song"), has three divisions as understood from the musical texts: vocal music, instrumental music, and dance. All three have always been intertwined, whether in religious observances, in sacred dramas, or in courtly entertainment. *Saṅgīta* utilized a slightly different musical scale from that of the above *Sāma-Veda* scale mentioned earlier, which was gradually recast into a new seven note system, called the Gandharva scale, used first in *Gandharva Saṅgīta* and later in all other types of Indian music. Current today, the standardized notes are labelled in Sanskrit as *sa ri ga ma pa dha ni*, (C D E F G A B of the Western diatonic scale) and named, metaphorically, after the sounds of different birds and animals: *sa*—peacock, *ri*—bull, *ga*—ram, *ma*—crane, *pa*—cuckoo, *dha*—horse, and *ni*—elephant. This system first appears in the early text known as the *Nārada-Śikṣā* (first century CE), where the alleged author, Nārada Rishi, explained how these seven notes were directly determined from the original three Vedic accents: *udatta* into *ni* and *ga, anudatta* into *ri* and *dha,* and *svarita* into *sa, ma,* and *pa.* The notes D E F A B (*ri ga ma dha ni*) were also modified with raised or lowered half-notes (like the Western sharp and flat notes) to create multiple variations of parent-scales known as *rāgas* for use in musical expression. The tonic C (*sa*) and the dominant G (*pa*) however, generally remained fixed.

Complex rules and standards for scales, rhythms, and instrumental styles of Gandharva music were gradually codified in a number of texts that came to be known collectively as the *Gandharva-Veda*, an auxiliary text attached to the *Sāma-Veda*. While several of these much earlier musical works have been lost, the oldest surviving texts of Indian music, the *Nāṭya-Śāstra* by Bhārata Muni and the *Dattilam* by Dattila (both ca. 200 BCE), as well as the *Nārada-Śikṣā* (first century CE), provide glimpses of *Gandharva Saṅgīta*. These ancient texts provide evidence of the very sophisticated musical thought in ancient India. For example, Bhārata had classified musical instruments into four categories based on the Gandharva instruments: chordophones or stringed instruments (*vīṇā*), membranophones or skin-covered instruments (drum), aerophones or air-driven instruments (flute), and idiophones or self-sound instruments (cymbal). These four categories formed the basis of the later Sachs-Hornbostel system (1914) currently used in the relatively recent academic field of ethnomusicology. Also, the term *rāga* as a type of scale or melodic formula was derived from *jāti*, first mentioned in Bhārata's work. Dattila provides a close analysis of ancient musical scales and complex rhythms.

Gandharva music soon developed into the principal style of music performed in Hindu festivals, courtly ceremonies, and temple rituals in honour of the emerging great gods and goddesses like Śiva, Vishnu, Brahmā, Ganesha, and Devī. In the ancient epics like the *Mahābhārata* and *Rāmāyaṇa*, and mythic histories called Purāṇas, there are descriptions of temple musicians and dancers who performed for the pleasure of these deities, along with numerous other historical references to temple music since antiquity. Music was closely associated with sacred dramatic performances, as evidenced in Bhārata's *Nāṭya-Śāstra*. Herein, special songs called *dhruva* were used to propitiate the gods, and were rendered not in Sanskrit but in Prakrit, a derivative "vernacular" language with a less rigid grammatical construction. Their use gradually led to the predominance of vernacular dialects in Hindu liturgical and devotional music. The *dhruva* was the prototype of the medieval genres (like *prabandha*), which were the basis of classical devotional forms sung in vernacular, called *dhrupad* (*dhruvapad*) in the North and *kriti* in the South. The rapidly developing music of India also expanded to include materials from outside the original repertoire.

Music as a spiritual discipline and means of release

Sacred sound plays a major role in the spiritual disciplines of yoga. *Nāda-yoga* refers to the yogic discipline that aims at transcendental inner awareness of *Nāda-Brahman*, and is practiced by many diverse groups in India. It has also influenced Hindu traditions regarding chant and music. Philosophical yoga, including Patañjali's *Yoga Sūtra* and its commentaries, endorses the practice of meditation on the syllable Oṁ, and reflects the development of *Nāda-yoga* techniques as found in the *Yoga Upanishads* and the major *Haṭha-yoga* texts. Esoteric notions of male "seed" and female "container" associated with Tantrism indicate gender polarization such that Oṁ is viewed as the embodiment of Śiva with his consort Śakti in Śaivism, or Vishnu with Lakshmī in Vaishnavism. The actual musical sounds said to be heard during yogic meditation, such as the drum, cymbal, *vīṇā*, and flute, are discussed in the *Yoga Upanishads*. These sounds correspond with the musical instruments used since Vedic times, confirming an abiding connection between *Nāda-yoga* and Indian music that sustains its religious foundation.

By the period of the early *Bhakti* devotional movements in South India (seventh to tenth centuries CE), Indian musical texts such as Mataṅga's *Bṛhaddeśi* began to incorporate the theories of sacred sound as *Nāda-Brahman* and the speculations of *Nāda-yoga* and the Tantra traditions, interpreting all music as a direct manifestation of *Nāda-Brahman*. This integral connection of music with *Nāda* was "essential to Indian views of the soteriological significance of music, for music, as a manifestation of Nāda, is seen as a mode of access to the highest reality."[4] Music as such was viewed both as entertainment and as a personal vehicle toward *moksha*, or liberation from repeated birth and death. Authors influenced by Mataṅga discussed *Nāda-Brahman* in relation to the gods and as omnipresent in the cosmos, including all living beings. For example, the *Saṅgīta-Ratnākara* of Śārṅgadeva (ca. 1200–1250 CE), arguably the most important musical treatise of India, opens with the salutation: "We worship *Nāda-Brahman*, that incomparable bliss which is immanent in all the creatures as intelligence and is manifest in the phenomena of this universe. Indeed, through the worship of *Nāda-Brahman* are worshipped gods (like) Brahmā, Vishnu, and Śiva, since they essentially are one with it."[5] By this time, there is virtually a complete association of the tradition of sacred sound (i.e., *Nāda-Brahman* speculation) in India with the art of music in all its phases, including religious, secular, classical, and folk.

Bhakti is the concept of approaching God through love and devotion, as found in the literature of classical Hinduism, especially in the epics, the Purāṇas, and the *Bhagavad-Gītā*. The *Bhagavad-Gītā*, with its direct exposition of the principles of *bhakti* by the god Krishna, is a favourite text for recitation by Hindus in groups or in private. Hindus believe that regular chanting of a sacred text brings *moksha*. Many pious Hindus have memorized the entire *Bhagavad-Gītā* and chant it regularly. The chanting is normally done through simple repetition of melodic motifs, with verses in strophic form. Example 3 includes a standard stanza or *śloka* in *Anushtubh* metre, which has four lines of eight syllables each (8 × 4). In these verses, Krishna is telling his disciple Arjuna to surrender to him fully and receive all of God's blessings. The listening selection demonstrates a simple melodic motif in three notes that is commonly employed for lengthy chanting of this popular text.

▐ EXAMPLE 3 (Track 23)

Chant. *Bhagavad-Gītā* 18.65–66. Text (Sanskrit); translation by the author.

man-manā bhava mad-bhakto
mad-yājī mām namaskuru
mām ev'aishyasi satyam te
pratijāne priyo 'si me

sarva-dharmān parityajya
mām ekam śaraṇam vraja
aham tvām sarva-pāpebhyo
mokshayishyāmi mā śucaḥ

Think of me, love me, and worship Me.
Sacrifice and offer submission to Me:
Thus you will come to me;
I promise you in truth, for you are very dear to me.

Renounce all types of religious duties and
Simply surrender to Me.
You will thus achieve liberation from all sins.
Of this there is no doubt.

Celebrated as a distinct doctrine and mode of religious life superior to knowledge (*jñāna*) and works (*karma*), *Bhakti* (devotion to God) became the primary motivation for creating and performing religious music from the early medieval period. As early as the sixth century CE in southern India, *Bhakti* emerged as a powerful force that favoured a devotion-centred Hinduism, with some song-texts composed in Sanskrit but the majority in vernacular dialects. At the head of the movement were two main groups of poet singer-saints in the area that promulgated devotion to Śiva and Vishnu in the Tamil language: the Śaivite Nāyanārs and the Vaishnava Āḷvārs. The collections of their devotional poetry in Tamil represent the oldest surviving verses in Indian vernaculars, and became the first hymnals of devotional music.

Hindu religious music soon incorporated a simple aesthetic that reflects back to these emerging *Bhakti* movements, and their perspectives on music as a means toward communion with a chosen deity. Since the Upanishads describe Brahman, the Supreme Truth, as full of bliss and *rasa* ("emotional taste, pleasure"), the performing arts, like theater and music, were closely aligned with religion since their goal was to produce *rasa*. In theistic Vedanta, Brahman as Īśvara (personal deity, whether Vishnu, Śiva, or Śakti) was believed to be the fountainhead and source of all *rasa* and extremely fond of music. The emotional pleasure of music produced by the musicians in the minds of the listeners was thus also linked to God and Brahman.

The musical scales or melody formulas of Hindu music are known as *rāga* ("emotional mood"), and are said to be timeless and transcendental. They must be discovered, much like the Vedas. Each *rāga* possesses a particular mood or flavour (*rasa*) mysteriously embodied within it, and is capable of generating those same feelings within the minds of the listener and performer when properly invoked. When those feelings are directed to God as Brahman or Īśvara (Lord), the result is higher attachment (also called *rāga*). And, if the music is both understood as *Nāda-Brahman* and performed properly in the spirit of *Bhakti*, then the musician and the listener are said to gain momentum for eventual release and the association of God in both this life and the next. There is a clever saying among musicians in India, as the term *svara* itself means "musical notes": "Through *svara*, Īśvara [God] is realized."

Rhythm, or *tala*, is also vitally important in religious music. Vedic ritual chants were punctuated by metrical divisions that, besides being aids to memorization, generated distinct units of unseen merit which accrued to the patron of the sacrifice, and led to an afterlife in heaven. In Gandharva music, similar metrical units were marked by the playing of drums and of metal hand cymbals. The idea of punctuated units of rhythm in music carried the same liberating effect as the Vedic unseen merit, as was explained in classical Gandharva music texts such as the *Dattilam*. Therefore, since Vedic chant was metrical, religious music must have a distinct rhythm or division of musical time sequence for it to deposit these unseen benefits to the listener. This was provided by the rhythms of the hand cymbals and the beats of the drums. This ancient theory of music, based upon the system of ritual, explained how both musicians and audience were able to earn liberation through the accumulation of unseen merit as exemplified in the marking of ritual (musical) time. The developing notion of release (*moksha*) within most forms of *Bhakti* music retained this same idea, and also included the special emotional states and experiences of the practitioners as cultivated in their relationship with their chosen deity.

Bhakti literature accumulated as a rapidly expanding body of song-texts in regional vernacular languages. Composers of song-texts throughout India were strongly influenced by the *Gīta-Govinda* of Jayadeva, a Sanskrit work of twelfth-century CE Bengal. This work contained linguistic innovations in Sanskrit metre and poetics that would inform new patterns of vernacular musical composition. There was, in fact, a magnificent outpouring of devotional poetry from the fourteenth century that addressed nearly every deity in the Hindu pantheon, with almost every linguistic region of India represented by its own composer of songs to a favoured deity, though mostly towards Vishnu and his incarnations of Krishna and Rāma. For example, in the North, Sūr Dās wrote in Braj Bhāshā about Krishna; Tulasī Dās addressed Lord Rāma in Avadhi; Tukarām and Nāmdev in Marathi expressed devotion to Krishna; Mīra Bāi in Rajasthani addressed Krishna; Govinda Dās wrote about Krishna in Brajbuli; and Chandidās in Bengali expressed devotion to Rādhā and Krishna. In the South, Purandaradāsa wrote in Kannada expressing devotion to Vishnu; Śyāma Śāstrī in Telugu devoted to the Goddess; Annamāchārya in Telugu to Lord Vishnu; and Tyāgarāja in Telugu to Lord Rāma. These composers, among many others, are believed to have achieved eternal liberation through singing and music-making.

Ritual context: Liturgical music

In practical application, religious music that fulfills a liturgical function is the most conservative of forms, and very close attention is given to the text and its clear pronunciation, establishing patterns of performance that are maintained over many generations. Although melody and rhythm are important, musical virtuosity for its own sake is normally discouraged, in contrast with classical traditions that laud improvisation and technical mastery. Essentially monophonic and without Western harmony, Hindu religious singing normally abstains from the excessive vocal styling found in classical singing. Devotional music, whether part of temple liturgies or private observances, includes a wide variety of styles and forms such that no single formula has been mandated to the exclusion of others. And, within certain guidelines, religious and devotional songs continue to be composed or arranged by musicians and religious leaders.

As music in Christian churches and monasteries was a primary source for classical music in Western countries, so the various traditions of religious music in India described here provided source material for the development of what is known as Indian classical music. Similar to the West, classical music in India refers to art music performed in the ruling courts by professional, skilled artists that pursued its own course guided by the preferences of patrons, individual improvisation, and even foreign influences. This type of music tended to showcase virtuosity and creativity for its own sake. Sometime after the thirteenth century, the classical traditions separated into northern and southern, yet each drew inspiration from roots in the devotional liturgies established in regional temples. Southern Carnatic music is founded upon the *kritis*, or devotional songs that Vaishnava and Śaiva saints and musicians performed in the temples and shrines of Tamil Nadu, Karnataka, and Andhra Pradesh. What became known as Hindustani classical music in the northern regions of India stemmed from the temple songs or *dhrupads* that were performed by Vaishnava musicians in places like Mathura, Vrindaban, Jaipur, and Gwalior. The presence of Persian culture in the north also influenced the development of Hindustani music.

Hindu temple liturgy had evolved from the Vedic system of sacrifice, and the outdoor sacrificial altar in Vedic practice was eventually replaced by an indoor altar upon which were placed statues (*mūrti*) of deities requiring regular worship. Deity worship in temples and shrines gradually developed into a complicated daily service called *pūjā* that was enhanced during special monthly and seasonal observances. Chant and music were always integral parts of these services. *Pūjās* continued to include unaccompanied Sanskrit chants called *stūtī* ("hymns of praise"), but gradually came to embrace vernacular hymns and songs accompanied by musical instruments as well. *Dhrupad*, perfected during the medieval period, represents the most important from of liturgical music in the northern regions, and is still associated with several Vaishnava traditions. *Kritis* were and still are the principal forms of temple music in South Indian traditions. While the lyrics of these forms include devotional praise and the depiction of pastimes of chosen deities, musically they are based upon *rāgas* in the Indian music tradition that are believed to be derived from divine inspiration. Beside these two examples of liturgical music, there is also what may be termed paraliturgical music—devotional and worship-oriented music that is often, but not necessarily, linked with seasonal religious observances or temple worship. Examples of these include the forms of *Padāvali-kīrtan* in Bengal, and *bhajan* and *nām-kīrtan* throughout India.

Dhrupad

In the North, *dhrupad* is the most important music of Hindu temple worship, and is also an ideal vehicle for vernacular *Bhakti* lyrics, mostly in the Braj Bhāshā dialect of Hindi. As part of the temple liturgy of a religious lineage, compositions in different rāgas are typically sung in *dhrupad* style by trained singers and musicians at the appropriate times of the day and seasons of the year, according to the liturgical calendar. The lyrics of the songs describing the deity's divine pastimes (*līlā*) are also matched with the specific times of the day that these pastimes are believed to have taken place during the deity's earthly manifestation in antiquity. Deity worship

Bhajans performed by Guy Beck and musicians in Calcutta, 1980. Courtesy of Guy L. Beck.

is generally centred around pleasing the Lord in the temple with offerings of food, water, incense, fan, sweets, camphor, lampwick, unguents, and conch. Music and devotional songs (also known as *kīrtan*) are important parts of this arsenal of offerings, as it is believed that hymns of praise set to Indian *rāgas* are especially pleasing to the deity. *Dhrupad* is closely related to several other subgenres of liturgical music in Vaishnavism that includes *havelī sangīt* and *samāj gāyan*. Musically, *dhrupad* is linked to the earlier *prabandha* songs mentioned in medieval Sanskrit treatises, and refers to the formal, slow, four-section vocal rendition of a religious poem using the pure form of a *rāga,* along with the strict rhythms of Cautāl (twelve beats) and Dhamār (fourteen beats). Like many Hebrew psalms in the ancient Israelite religion, most *dhrupad* poems were written with the intention of cultic performance. And, as most of the devotional poems contained at least four lines, there was a natural division into the four parts of *dhrupad*. *Dhrupad* spread wherever it was patronized by the ruling elite, both in temples and in ruling courts, and developed into a high art form. Example 4 below is two parts of a *dhrupad* song in Cautāl rhythm that depicts, in the language of Braj Bhāshā, the pastime of Krishna playing his flute and calling the cowherd maidens for the circular Rāsa Dance held during autumn. This *rāga*, "Lalit," is reserved for early morning worship, and is based on a scale using the notes C D♭ E F F# A♭ B C. After an extended solo portion, called *ālāp*, that introduces the *rāga*, the composition begins, set to a specific rhythmic accompaniment on the *pākhvāj* (barrel-drum). The first two lines serve as a refrain (*sthāyī*), sung in the lower register, while the latter three lines as verse (*antara*) are sung in the upper register. One of the unique musical features of *dhrupad* is the various repetitions and permutations of the lyric that are resolved upon the first beat known as *sam* (on the syllable *Vrin*) of the twelve-beat Cautāl rhythm cycle.

ǀᵈ EXAMPLE 4 (Track 24)
Dhrupad in *Rāga* "Lalit"; Text (Braj Bhāshā) from Pandit Bidur Mallik, Vrindaban, India. Translation by the author.

Dekho sakhī Vrindābana meṅ
Mohana rāsa racāyo

Mora mukuṭa candra bhāla
Mukhate muralī dhara
Dhyāna dhare saba loga

~

Look, my dear friend, in Vrindāban Mohan (Krishna)
   has commenced the Rāsa Dance.
Wearing the peacock crown and with the moon on his forehead,
He is holding the flute to his mouth, and everybody is meditating on him.

Swami Haridās (ca. 1500–95 CE), said to have been an expert singer and musician of the *dhrupad* style and the "Father of Hindustani Music," was traditionally reputed to be the teacher of Tansen, who sang at the court of Emperor Akbar in the sixteenth century CE, and whose disciples were almost solely responsible for the transmission of Hindustani classical music through the Mughal period and thereafter. Swami Haridās composed many *dhrupad* songs and, due to his ardent singing for the pleasure of Krishna, is believed to have achieved eternal spiritual association with God.

The same is said for Sūr Dās (sixteenth century CE), a blind musician-poet who was associated with the Vallabha sect and early *havelī saṅgīt*. *Havelī saṅgīt* as a subgenre of *dhrupad* is identified with the Vallabha tradition and means, simply, "music performed in the havelis or palaces of Krishna worship." *Havelī saṅgīt* is close in style to *dhrupad* and some scholars have called it the "Mother of North Indian vocal music." Sūr Dās spent his entire life singing and composing *dhrupad* songs to Krishna, and, according to his work *Sūr-Sāgar* in the Braj Bhāshā language, singing was the most viable means of salvation: "If anything in the *Sūr-Sāgar* spells release and salvation, it is the act of singing itself. Song, for Sūr—singing to the Lord—is as close as one can come to salvation."[6] In fact, most of the songs in the Hindustani classical repertoire are adapted from the Braj Bhāshā literature of poets like Sūr Dās, Swami Haridās, Hita Harivaṁśa, Nanddās, and Paramānand Dās, that describe the pastimes of Krishna in Vrindāban. A closely related subgenre of temple music in Vrindāban is *samāj gāyan*, a more vocally interactive style of *dhrupad* that is associated mostly with the Rādhāvallabha tradition.

Kriti

In the South, Carnatic music included the devotional compositions of Purandaradāsa (1480–1564 CE), a Vaishnava musician who is said to have composed nearly half a million songs known as *kīrtanas*. Hailed as the "Father of Carnatic Music," he was one of the main inspirations of Tyāgarāja (1759–1847 CE), whose devotional *kritis* ("compositions," evolved from *kīrtanas*) in Telugu to Lord Rāma comprise the major portion of the current repertoire of South Indian music. Tyāgarāja is recognized as one of a trinity of great musician-poets from Tiruvarur that included Śyāma Śāstrī and Muṭṭuswami Dikshitār, composers of songs to the goddesses Kāmākshī and Mīnākshī.

The liturgical musical texts and traditions cited above provided a common base for the further development of both southern and northern styles of religious music and set standards of scale and rhythm systematization. Accordingly, religious music developed along very similar lines regardless of sectarian message or affiliation. For example, believers in Nirguṇa ("Absolute without qualities"), Saguṇa ("Absolute with qualities"), Vaishnava, Śaiva, or Śākta deities all drew from the evolving musical genres, patterns of *rāga* and *tāla* structures, and assortments of instruments. The following three forms, *Padāvali-kīrtan*, *bhajan*, and *nāmkīrtan*, while not strictly liturgical, are devotional and worship-oriented, and thus fit into the category paraliturgical.

Padāvali-kīrtan

Another very distinctive style of devotional music is found in eastern India, including Bengal and Orissa. *Padāvali-kīrtan* of Bengal is one of the most refined forms of devotional music in India, adapted and modified from *dhrupad* style by Narottama Dās, a seventeenth century follower of Caitanya (early sixteenth century CE). *Padāvali-kīrtan* combines recitation of religious narratives with songs composed by *bhakti* saints in Bengali, and is associated with seasonal festivals of the Bengal Vaishnavas. The songs include short improvisatory phrases called *ākhar* inserted into the lyrics of the original songs by the singers themselves for the purpose of interpreting or reiterating the meaning in colloquial language for the benefit of the audience. The performers usually include one or more vocalists, a drummer, a hand cymbal player, and sometimes a violinist or flautist. Example 6 presents a portion of a song in Brajbuli (a medieval dialect of Bengali) composed by Govinda Dās, which praises and describes Krishna and his incarnation as Caitanya. The *ākhar* section interrupts with the exclamation in colloquial Bengali, *sheito esheche* ("He has come! Caitanya has appeared on earth as a golden incarnation of Krishna who is normally black!"). This *ākhar* is followed by a continuation of the song with further *ākhars*. Today there are many skilled singers of *kīrtan*, both male and female, who have the ability to freely improvise *ākhars* on the spot.

┣ Example 5 (Track 25)

Padāvali-kīrtan. From Śri Rathin Ghosh, famed *kīrtan* singer of Calcutta. Text (Brajbuli); collected and translated by the author.

> śrī nanda nandana gopījana-vallabha
> jaya rādhā-nāyaka nāgara śyāma
> so śacī nandana naḍiyā purandara
> sūra nara muni mana mohana dhāma
> ᴡ

> All Glories to Krishna, the Son of Nanda,
>   beloved of the Gopī maidens,
>   Dark-colored urban sophisticate, hero of Rādhā.
> You are the same person who has appeared as
>   Caitanya in the town of Naḍiyā as the Son of Śacī,
>   in the holy place revered by gods, men, and sages.

Ākhar (Bengali)

> sheito esheche, kālo baron lukāiyāche,
>   shonār baron dhoreche
> ᴡ

> He has come, the one who previously
>   was black is now of golden hue.

Bhajan

Directly related to the word *bhakti* and a word for Vishnu as Supreme Being (Bhagavān) is the term *bhajan*, which means musical worship. *Bhajan* shares with them the common Sanskrit root *bhaj*, "to share, to partake of" (as in a ritual). Bhagavān means the Lord who possesses *bhaga*: good fortune, or opulence. *Bhajan*, as a kind of generic term for religious or devotional music apart from Vedic chant and *Gandharva Saṅgīta*, is directly linked to the rising medieval *Bhakti* movements, and is performed so that God, Bhagavān, is praised, worshipped, or otherwise appeased in a mutual exchange of loving affection, or *bhakti*. Within the *bhakti* traditions, as we have seen, there were a number of different styles of *bhajan* or *bhakti saṅgīta*, ranging from formal temple music to informal group or solo songs.

While almost every Hindu religious gathering includes chant or music, earlier types of formal devotional music (i.e., *dhrupad, kriti, havelī sangīt, samāj gāyan*) have become largely supplanted by the informal styles of *bhajan* that elicit more audience participation and which, consequently, have became more widespread in India and the Hindu diaspora. Just as the *Bhakti* movements stressed class egalitarianism, *bhajan* sessions continue to stress openness to people of all social strata, and frequently form part of congregational rites in which there is a sharing of *bhakti* experiences. Similar for male, female, or mixed gatherings, they are more flexible regarding attendance and may take place anytime. There are also occasions whereby they go on continuously for several days, a common occurrence in Bengal where intensive "unbroken" sessions of *nām-kīrtan* are regularly carried out. Distinct from other Hindu occasions, such as specialized *pūjās* or rites of passage, the atmosphere of the *bhajan* session, where all participants sit, sing and eat together regardless of caste, gender, or religious viewpoint, fosters intimate and informal social relationships.

Beginning with the chanting of Oṁ, a typical *bhajan* session proceeds with invocations in Sanskrit in honour of a guru, master, or deity, followed by sequences of *bhajan* songs that reflect the group's distinct or eclectic religious outlook; these are sometimes punctuated by short sermons or meditative recitations of Sanskrit verses from scripture. Toward the closing, a special ceremony called *āratī* is conducted as part of the *pūjā* ("worship service") which includes offerings of food, flowers, incense and lamps, and blowing of conches. The distribution of food, flowers, lampwicks, and holy water concludes the session.

Bhajan ensembles, like almost all types of Indian music, include musical instruments. Percussion instruments, membranophones and idiophones, include pairs of hand cymbals called *kartāl* or *jhāñjh*, drums such as the *tabla, pākhvāj, dholak,* or *khole,* and occasionally bells, clappers, or tambourines. Bowed chordophones such as the *sārangī* or *esrāj* may accompany the singing, but the harmonium often replaces these. A background drone may be provided by a *tānpura,* if not by the harmonium or by a *śruti* box, a small pumped instrument used in Carnatic music.

As musical compositions, *bhajan* songs currently range from complex structures to simple refrains or litanies containing divine names. Most have their own distinctive tune and rhythm that are easily followed by the audience, but some are based on classical *rāgas* and *tālas,* and require musical skill. The most common *tālas* are uptempo such as Kehervā, which has eight beats roughly corresponding to a Western cuttime in 4/4. The sixteen-beat Tintāl serves as a straight 4/4 time sequence with an accent on the first beat. Another common rhythm is Dādrā, a six-beat *tāla* corresponding to Western 3/4 or 6/8. Example 7 below presents a typical type of *bhajan* by the poet Sūr Dās in Hindi. It is in the more popular rhythm of Kehervā.

⊩ EXAMPLE 6 (Track 26)
   Bhajan of Sūr Dās. Text (Hindi). Collected and translated by the author.

   Aba merī rākho lāja Hari
   Tuma jānata saba antarajāmī
   Karaṇi kachu na karī
   Avaguṇa hamase bisarata nāhī
   Pala china gharī gharī
   Saba pāpana ki poṭa bāndha ke
   Apane sīsa dharī
   Dāṛā sūta dhana mohaliye hai
   Śuddha buddhi saba bisarī
   Sūr Dās Prabhu vega udhāro
   Aba merī nāva calī

   ∿

   Lord, unabashed and shameful,
   I implore you to uphold my dignity.
   You are the knower of everything,
   as you reside in the heart;
   you are the doer, although you do not act.
   I cannot forget my bad qualities,
   which affords me no rest, even for a second.
   I will tie all of my sins into a bundle
   and hold it on top of my head.
   Through my over-attachment for wife,
   children, and wealth, I have lost all of my clear intelligence.
   Sūr Dās implores, "Lord, please relieve me of this great load,
   for now my ship (this body) has set sail."

Nām-kīrtan or Nām-bhajan

The collective singing of the names of God, as in Sītā-Rām, Śrī Rām Jai Rām, Hare Krishna, Hare Rāma, Rādhe Shyām, Oṁ namaḥ Śivāya, Jai Mātā Dī, and so on, is very popular everywhere in India and is called *nām-kīrtan*, *nām-sankīrtan* or *nām-bhajan*. Sung to simple melodies accompanied by drums and cymbals, *nām-kīrtan* or *nām-bhajan* expresses fervent devotion and serves as an important means of spiritual release. As primarily a congregational practice, *nām-kīrtan* also enables persons not schooled in classical music traditions to experience a parallel sense of musical elation. In example 4, three popular chants are given. The first is "Hare Krishna," the chant known as the "Mahāmantra" ("Great Mantra for Deliverance"), which was propounded by Śrī Caitanya and other *bhakti* saints, and was continued in India by many pious Hindus and also worldwide by Indian and non-Indian members of the Hare Krishna movement (ISKCON). It is a petition to Rādhā ("Harā"), the energy of Krishna, and to Krishna who is also full of pleasure ("Rāma"). The second is the "Chant to Rāma and Sītā"; and the third is the "Chant to Śiva."

⁞ EXAMPLE 7
  Nām-kīrtan. Text (Sanskrit); translated by the author.

  1 Hare Krishna, Hare Krishna, Krishna Krishna, Hare Hare
    Hare Rāma, Hare Rāma, Rāma Rāma, Hare Hare

  2 Sītā Rām, Sītā Rām, Sītā Rām Jaya Sītā Rām
    All Glories to Lord Rāma and his consort Sītā.

  3 Oṁ namaḥ Śivāya
    I bow to Lord Śiva.

Most religious music, including the forms discussed here, is performed as a group enterprise, with participants seated on the floor in proximity to a lead singer; the exceptions are standing groups in temples or groups in processions. Generally, a separate area in the temple facing or adjacent to a deity or picture is designated for music. Reading from an anthology of verses, lead singers often accompany themselves on a harmonium, a floor version of the upright, portable reed organ used by nineteenth-century Christian missionaries. The metal reed used in the harmonium, however, is Asiatic in origin. Linked to mouth organs used on the subcontinent, it is the basis for the Western harmonica and accordion. Group members generally repeat the lines in unison after the leader in call and response format. However, the leader may also sing solo or with occasional refrains sung by the group. To facilitate the performance of religious music, there are a large number of published hymnals in use by various religious groups. The staggering number of hymnals that are available throughout India make it nearly impossible to identify a single text that would serve a majority of Hindu religious worshippers.

Music in private devotion

Besides the temple liturgies and paraliturgical group forms of *Padāvali-kīrtan, bhajan,* and *nām-kīrtan,* the term *bhajan* may also denote individual private practices of spiritually advanced devotees in their worship of a particular form of God in solitude. These invariably include use of rosary beads, singing, and chanting of scripture, as in the *Bhagavad-Gītā* in example 3. The rosary chanting of mantras, called *japa,* while not done in a singing style with a melody, is normally carried out in declamatory fashion in one or two monotones, or muttered in near silence. From Vedic chant to classical singing to *bhajan,* the power of the sustained musical tone or note cannot be underestimated within the Hindu consciousness. Hindus who prefer to engage their spiritual life in private *sādhana* (spiritual practice) generally customize their schedule of devotion according to the directions of a guru, in an admixture of *japa, nām-kīrtan,* scriptural readings, mantra incantations, prayers, *pūjā* (worship) of a personal or family deity employing a series of offerings (incense, food, water, sandalwood paste, collyrium, camphor, and flowers), ritual bathing, ablutions, and perhaps even short sermons to a few devoted followers. Since there are no public mandates about temple or festival attendance for Hindus, there are strong tendencies, with encouragement, for the devout to pursue private worship and devotion. All serious musicians set aside daily alone time for their practice, in a private space, and often in front of a deity like the goddess Sarasvati or a picture of a guru, so that musical practice itself has a sacred aura around it and is suitably referred to as *svara-sādhana* ("spiritual exercise involving musical notes").

Current trends and the future of Hindu music

In the first half of the twentieth century, some religious and devotional music in India became associated with the general anticipation of political independence, finally achieved in 1947. Many proponents of Indian classical music supported the freedom movement, and so several religious and patriotic songs were likely to be performed often at political rallies and broadcasts. While anthems like "Vande Mātaram," by Bankimchandra Chatterji, and "Jana Gaṇa Mana," by Rabindranath Tagore (eventually India's national anthem) expressed devotion to "Mother India," famous *bhajans* like "Raghupati Rāghava" prayed for an ideal peaceful world in which the gods of differing religions are reconciled with Rām, including the Muslim Allāh. Originally recorded and made popular by the singer D.V. Paluskar, this song was a favourite of Mahātma Gandhi, and was even used on the soundtrack of the Oscar-winning film *Gandhi* (1982). Modern versions sometimes employ electronic effects like those found in film music. Example 8 below includes the complete Hindi verses with translation.

‖ EXAMPLE 8 (Track 27)
"Raghupati Rāghava." Text (Hindi) from *Prārthanā Saṅgīt*, ed. Laxmi Narayan Garg (Hathras: Sangit Karyalaya, 1989), 94. Translation by the author.

Raghupati Rāghava Rāja Rām, patita pāvana Sītā Rām
Sītā Rām Sītā Rām, bhaja pyāre tū Sītā Rām
Īśvara Allāh tere nām, sabako sanmati de Bhagavān
Rāma rahīm karīm *sāman*, hama saba hai unakī santān
Saba mila māṅge yaha varadān, amara rahe mānava kā jñān

∿

O Lord Rāma, descendent of Raghu, Uplifter of the fallen.
You and your beloved consort Sītā are to be worshipped.
All names of God refer to the same Supreme Being,
    including Īśvara and the Muslim Allāh.
O Lord, Please give peace and brotherhood to everyone,
    as we are all your children.
We all request that this eternal wisdom of humankind prevail.

Religious and devotional music also permeate the modern movements that arose during the twentieth century. These were founded by famous Hindu saints, such as Swami Vivekānanda, Swami Śivānanda, Paramahaṁsa Yogānanda, Śrī Aurobindo, Maharishi Mahesh Yogī, Swami Muktānanda, Satya Sai Bābā, Ānandamāyī Mā, Swami Rāma, and A.C. Bhaktivedānta Swami Prabhupāda. Many of these movements spread to the West and brought with them a particular style of devotional music and chant. Hindu *bhajans* are also widely performed among various yogic and New Age groups, and by non-Indian Hindus and Buddhists. Also, while a new style of improvised solo *bhajan* has entered the classical concert repertoire, pop *bhajan* has achieved great success, along with devotional songs sung by male and female playback singers in Indian films. Film *āratīs* or worship songs, such as "Oṁ Jaya Jagadīsha Hari" (featured in the Hindi film *Purab aur Pacchim*) are now widely used by Hindus in home and temple worship practices all over the world. While the number of performers of serious religious music in India may not be on the rise, there has been a recent surge of interest in devotional music of all kinds that is fed, equally, by commercialism.

In conclusion, music is an extraordinarily significant component of Hindu religious practice, and it persists today throughout India and the

Diaspora by maintaining religious faith, cultural ties, and moral discipline within Hindu culture. Performed by skilled musicians or lay enthusiasts, Hindu music continues to serve as a vehicle for religious teachings and as a source of spiritual renewal and ecstasy. And, alongside the newer *bhajan* forms, traditional religious and devotional music endures in the multiple temples, shrines, and domestic chapels that exist in the villages and countryside of India.

Countering the traditional emphasis on textual studies in scholarship on India, Hinduism scholar Vasudha Narayanan reaffirms the perspective in this chapter in saying, "The performers of music and dance, the transmitters of the religious traditions, speak for Hinduism. We should listen to them."[7]

Notes

1 Apart from Example 2, translations of all selections are by the author.
2 G.U. Thite (1997), 87, 68, 71, 94.
3 V. Raghavan (1962), 127.
4 Donna M. Wulff (1983), 154.
5 R.K. Shringy and Prem Lata Sharma, ed. and trans. (1977), 108–109.
6 John Stratton Hawley (1984), 163.
7 Vasudha Narayanan (2000): 776.

Bibliography

Beck, Guy L. "Religious and Devotional Music: Northern Area." In *The Garland Encyclopedia of World Music*. Vol. 5, *South Asia*, ed. Alison Arnold, 246–58. New York and London: Garland, 2000.

———. *Sonic Theology: Hinduism and Sacred Sound*. Columbia: University of South Carolina Press, 1993.

———. "Vaiṣṇava Music in the Braj Region of North India." *Journal of Vaiṣṇava Studies* 4 (Spring 1996): 115–47.

Chakrabarty, Ramakanta. "Vaiṣṇava Kīrtan in Bengal." In *The Music of Bengal: Essays in Contemporary Perspective*, ed. Jayasri Banerjee, 12–30. Bombay and Baroda: Indian Musicological Society, 1988. Reprinted in *Journal of Vaiṣṇava Studies* 4 (Spring 1996): 179–99.

Gaston, Anne-Marie. *Krishna's Musicians: Musicians and Music Making in the Temples of Nathdvara, Rajasthan*. New Delhi: Manohar Publishers, 1997.

Hawley, John Stratton. *Sūr Dās: Poet, Singer, Saint*. Seattle: University of Washington Press, 1984.

Henry, Edward O. *Chant the Names of God: Musical Culture in Bhojpuri-Speaking India*. San Diego, CA: San Diego State University Press, 1988.

Manuel, Peter. *Cassette Culture: Popular Music and Technology in North India*. Chicago: University of Chicago Press, 1993.

Narayanan, Vasudha. "Diglossic Hinduism: Liberation and Lentils." *Journal of the American Academy of Religion* 68.4 (December 2000): 761–79.

Paul, Russill. *The Yoga of Sound: Healing & Enlightenment through the Sacred Practice of Mantra*. Novato, CA: New World Library, 2004.

Pesch, Ludwig. *The Illustrated Companion to South Indian Classical Music*. Delhi: Oxford University Press, 1999.

Prajnanananda, Swami. *The Historical Development of Indian Music: A Critical Study*. Calcutta: Firma KLM, 1973.

Raghavan, V. *The Great Integrators: The Saint-Singers of India*. Delhi: Ministry of Information, 1966.

———. "Sāmaveda and Music." *Journal of the Music Academy of Madras* 33 (1962): 127–33.

Ray, Sukumar. *Music of Eastern India*. Calcutta: Firma KLM, 1985.

Rowell, Lewis. *Music and Musical Thought in Early India*. Chicago and London: University of Chicago Press, 1992.

Shringy, R.K., and Prem Lata Sharma, eds. and trans. *Saṅgīta-Ratnākara of Śārṅgadeva*. Delhi: Motilal Banarsidass, 1977.

Thielemann, Selina. *The Music of South Asia*. New Delhi: A.P.H. Publishing, 1999.

Thite, G.U. *Music in the Vedas: Its Magico-Religious Significance*. Delhi: Sharada Publishing, 1997.

Wade, Bonnie C. *Music in India: The Classical Traditions*. Englewood Cliffs, NJ: Prentice-Hall, 1979.

Wulff, Donna M. "On Practicing Religiously: Music as Sacred in India." In *Sacred Sound: Music in Religious Thought and Practice*, ed. Joyce Irwin, 149–72. Chico, CA: Scholars Press, 1983.

5

SIKHISM AND MUSIC

Pashaura Singh

The sacred music of the Sikhs is the heart of their devotional experience. It is commonly referred to as *Gurmat Saṅgīt* or "music in the Guru's view." To understand the centrality of devotional singing (*kīrtan*) in the Sikh tradition, it is necessary to place the inquiry in the historical context of the sixteenth century. The term *kīrtan* is derived from a Sanskrit root, *kīrti*, which in Sikhism means singing a devotional song in praise of Akāl Purakh or "the Timeless One" (God). The form of the *kīrtan* was derived from the old *prabandha* (classical song) style of singing described in the Indian classical music treatises, a style that was characterized by rigorous rules, which left little place for improvisation. It was a rich and flourishing musical genre from the Gupta age, starting in the fourth century, up to the fourteenth century. These early classical songs led to the *dhrupad* (fixed word) style of music in vernacular languages like Braj Bhāshā, which became popular in North India during the fifteenth and sixteenth centuries. In this transition from the classical *prabandha* to the *dhrupad* style, the "devotional" (*bhakti*) concept of music (as distinguished from the contemporary court music) emerged in which "it is ultimately for God and not for an earthly audience that the devotee plays and sings."[1] Most of the songs of medieval poet-saints were sung in the *dhrupad* style by trained professional singers, and this was one of the styles that became the model for *shabad kīrtan* (hymn singing) in early Sikh tradition.

Shabad kīrtan has been an integral part of Sikh worship from the very beginning. The founder of the Sikh tradition, Guru Nānak (1469–1539), kept with him as his lifelong companion a Muslim musician, Mardānā, who used to play the *rabāb* (plucked rebec) while he sang the praises of God. All of the old murals and paintings show the two of them sitting together in musical performance. Bhai Gurdās (ca. 1558–1633) acknowledges Mardānā as the professional *rabābi* (rebec player) who accompanied the Guru on his missionary tours (1:35).[2] The *janam-sākhīs* (birth narratives) record that once, while sitting in meditation, Guru Nānak suddenly exclaimed: "Mardānā! Touch the chords, the Word is descending." "But Master," replied Mardānā, "the horse is grazing and my hands are occupied holding the reins, lest the animal run away." "Let go of the horse," commanded the Guru.[3] Indeed, spontaneity was the keynote of Guru Nānak's experience of divine inspiration. The verbal expression of that experience was in the form of poetic compositions of surpassing beauty, referred to as the *bānī* (divine utterance) of the Guru. Devotional singing of the *bānī* in many *rāgas* (musical modes based on specific scales), accompanied by particular rhythmic beats (*tālas*), was the medium through which Guru Nānak laid down the foundation of a new religious community. In that sense, Guru Nānak is unique as the only founder of a major world religion who was himself a performing musician.

Basic teachings and primary sources

The primary source of the Sikh teachings is the Ādi Granth (First Book), the sacred scripture of the Sikhs, which contains the writings of Guru Nānak and his successors along with the writings of fifteen medieval poet-saints (*bhagats*) of Sant, Sufi, and Bhakti origin. The compilation of the Ādi Granth evidently owes much to the enormous energies of the fifth Guru, Arjan (1563–1606). He prepared an authoritative text in 1604, primarily in response to the process of consolidation of the Sikh tradition that was taking place during this period. He organized the works of the Gurus, the *bhagats*, and other Sikh bards into a coherent pattern reflecting both theological and musicological perspectives. The formal aspects of texts of the Ādi Granth, including their metrical, poetic, melodic, and linguistic structures, are fully at one with their theological content, and all these aspects provide an internal unity to the Sikh scripture.[4]

The Ādi Granth repeatedly proclaims that God is One (Akāl Purakh) and that there is only one God in all religions. It conveys a consistent message that liberation can be achieved only through meditation on the divine name (*nām*) and the music of the divine word (*shabad*, Sanskrit *śabda*). These two key terms, *nām* and *shabad*, must be understood in the context of the teachings of the Sikh Gurus. Guru Nānak employs the word *nām* to express the nature of divine revelation in its totality. Accordingly, the *nām*

Golden Temple in Amritsar. Photograph courtesy of Guy L. Beck.

reflects the manifestation of divine presence everywhere, yet the people fail to perceive it due to their *haumai*, or self-centredness. The Punjabi term *haumai* (I, me) signifies the powerful impulse to succumb to personal gratification, with the result that a person is separated from Akāl Purakh and thus continues to suffer within the cycle of rebirth (*sansār*). However, Akāl Purakh, who is the sole creator of the entire universe, looks graciously upon the suffering of the people. He reveals himself through the Guru by uttering the *shabad* (divine word) which communicates a sufficient understanding of the *nām* (divine name) to those who are able to "hear" it. The Guru is thus the "voice" of Akāl Purakh, mystically uttered within the human heart, mind, and soul (*man*). The *shabad* is the actual "utterance," and in "hearing" it one awakens to the reality of the divine name, immanent in all that lies around and within one.[5]

In line with the metaphysical theory of ancient Indian music and Hindu tradition of sacred sound, Sikh doctrine maintains that the inspired "utterance of the Guru" (*gurbānī*) embodies the divine word (*śabda* or *nāda*). In his "Rāmakali" hymn, for instance, Guru Nānak proclaims: "*Gurbānī* embodies all the scriptural knowledge (Veda) and the eternally sounding melodious vibration (*nāda*) that permeates all space."[6] This "unstruck melody" (*anāhata nāda*) cannot be directly perceived or "heard," although it is the basis of the entire perceptible universe. The physical vibrations of musical sound are inextricably connected with the spiritual world of "unstruck melody." Likewise, all the *rāgas* exist eternally and some of them are merely discovered from time to time by inspired musicians. In this context, Guru Nānak remarks: "The jewel-like *rāgas*, along with their fairy families, are the source of the essence of the 'nectar of immortality' (*amrit*). This wealth belongs to the Creator—Few they be who realize this."[7] This reference clearly indicates Guru Nānak's familiarity with the gender-based "*rāga-rāginī* system" which was prevalent at that time. In a similar vein, Guru Rām Dās says: "The *rāga* and the melody (*nāda*) embody the divine Truth (*sach*), and their value is beyond description. Those who are ignorant of divine music cannot truly comprehend the divine Order (*hukam*)."[8]

Oral transmission: The role of chant and music in the early community

At the end of his travels, Guru Nānak settled at Kartārpur ("Creator's abode"), a religious commune that he founded on the right bank of the River Ravi in the Punjab in the 1520s. He lived there for the rest of his life as the spiritual head of a newly emerging religious community. During that period, he gave practical expression to the ideals that matured during his missionary tours, and combined "a life of disciplined devotion with worldly activities, set in the context of normal family life and a regular *satsaṅg* [true fellowship]."⁹ In particular, oral recitation of the *bāṇī* began there in individual and communal settings as a part of daily discipline. The first testimony about the Kartārpur period comes from Bhai Gurdās, who refers to the "devotional chanting of *Japjī* [Recitation] in the ambrosial hours of early morning and the singing of *So Dar* [That Gate, part of Rahirās prayers] and *Āratī* [Adoration] in the evening" (1:38). He further testifies that "every Sikh house had become a place of worship [*dharamsāl*] where *kīrtan* was regularly performed like the celebration of the Baisākhī festival" (1:27). Indeed, one could listen to the melodious "songs of Guru Nānak [*Bābā*] being sung to the accompaniment of the music of the *rabāb* [rebec] and the rhythm of the *mridaṅg* [drum]" (24:4).

Both chant and music played a significant role in the transmission of scripture in the early Sikh community. A bard named Gayand specifically refers to the well-established tradition of "chanting, listening and singing" of sacred hymns among the Sikhs during the period of Guru Rām Dās (1534–81).¹⁰ In fact, it was Guru Rām Dās who prescribed the daily routine of early morning devotion for his followers. In response to the question Who is a Sikh? he offered the following definition: "He who calls himself a Sikh, a follower of the true Guru, should meditate on the divine name after rising and bathing and recite *Jap*[*jī*] from memory, thus driving away all evil deeds and vices. As day unfolds he sings *gurbāṇī*; sitting or rising he meditates on the divine name. He who repeats the divine name with every breath and bite is indeed a true Sikh [*gursikh*] who gives pleasure to the Guru."¹¹ Interestingly, the name of the fourth Guru is particularly associated with the daily routine of oral recitation of liturgical prayers as part of the "code of conduct" (*rahit*) of the Khālsā. For instance, the *Chaupa Singh Rahit-nāmā* explicitly states: "According to Guru Rām Dās, he who recites *Japjī* five times will acquire the radiance of [true] enlightenment. Thereafter let him recite whatever *bāṇī* he may know by heart."¹²

Even in modern times Sikh parents make an effort to ensure that their children learn Guru Nānak's *Japjī* and other prayers by heart in childhood. A key principle here is the Sikh belief that the recitation of daily prayers by heart has transformative and purifying effects. In this context, Harold Coward perceptively remarks: "For the Sikh, as for the Hindu, participation in the divine word has the power to transform and unify one's consciousness. The purifying power of the sacred scripture is understood as a combing of negative thoughts from one's heart and mind that occurs as a regular part of one's daily discipline."¹³ Through this personalized experience one is able to understand the subtler levels of meaning of various scriptural passages.

Ritual context: Chant and music in private devotion

To follow the Sikh path of spirituality one must transcend the unregenerate condition created by the influence of self-centredness (*haumai*). One can achieve this objective by means of the strictly interior discipline of *nāmsimaran* or remembering the divine name. This threefold process ranges from the repetition of a sacred word (usually *Vāhigurū*, meaning "Praise to the eternal Guru"), through the devotional singing of hymns in the congregation to sophisticated meditation on the nature of Akāl Purakh (God). The first and third levels of this process involve private devotions, while the second is a communal practice. On the whole, the discipline of *nāmsimaran* is designed to bring a person into harmony with the divine order (*hukam*). In this way, a person gains the experience of ever-growing wonder (*vismad*) in spiritual life, and achieves the ultimate state of blissful equanimity (*sahaj*) when the spirit ascends to the "realm of Truth" (*sach khand*), the fifth and the last of the spiritual stages in which the soul finds mystical union with Akāl Purakh (God).

It is enjoined upon every Sikh to perform morning prayers, especially the *Japjī* of Guru Nānak. This individual prayer, while not set to music, is normally recited in a low monotone. The language is simple Punjabi, yet all of the basic Sikh principles are outlined in this prayer for purposes of meditation. Though there are nearly forty stanzas in the complete hymn, the first two stanzas, along with the invocation at the beginning, are given below in example 1.

⊩ EXAMPLE 1 (Track 28)

Japjī of Guru Nānak, including Invocation. Gurmukhī text is from *Sacred Nitnem: The Divine Hymns of the Daily Prayers by the Sikhs* 23rd ed., by Harbans Singh Doabia (Amritsar: Singh Brothers, 2002), 18–20. The translation is adapted from W.H. McLeod, *Sikhism* (London: Penguin Books, 1997), 271–72.

Invocation

Ik Oṅkār
Sat(i) nām(u) Kartā-purakh(u)
Nirbhau Nirvair(u)
Akāl-mūrat(i) Ajūnī
Saibhaṅg Gur-prasād(i)
Jap(u)
Ād(i) sach(u) Jugād(i) sach(u)
Hai bhī sach(u)
Nānak hosī bhī sach(u)

∿

There is only One God, the eternal Reality, the Creator,
without fear and devoid of enmity, immortal, never incarnated,
self-existent, known by grace through the Guru.

Recitation

The eternal One, from the beginning, through all time, present now,
Nānak, the everlasting Reality.

Japjī

1 Sochai soch(i) na hovaī je sochī lakh vār.
  Chupai chup na hovaī je lāe rahā liv-tār.
  Bhukhiā bhukh na utrī je bannā purīā bhār.
  Sahas siāṅpā lakh hoh(i) ta ik na chalai nāl(i).
  Kiv sachiārā hoīai kiv Kūrai tuṭai pāl(i).
  Hukam(i) rajāī chalṇā Nānak likhiā nāl(i).

2 Hukmī hovan(i) ākār hukam(u) na kahiā jāī.
  Hukmī hovan(i) jīa hukam(i) milai vadiāī.
  Hukmī utam(u) nīch(u) hukam(i) likh(i) dukh sukh pāīaih.
  Īkna hukmī bakhsīs ik(i) hukmī sadā bhavāīaih.
  Hukmai aṅdar(i) sabh(u) ko bāhar(i) hukam na koe.
  Nānak hukmai je bujhai ta haumai kahai na koe.

~

1 Never can You [O Lord!] be known through ritual purity though one
  cleanse oneself a hundred thousand times. Never can You be revealed by
  silent reflection though one dwell absorbed in the deepest meditation.
  Though one gather vast riches the hunger remains, no cunning will help
  in the hereafter. How then is truth to be attained, how the veil of false-
  hood torn aside? Nānak, thus it is written: submit to the divine Order
  (*Hukam*), walk in its way.

2 Though all that exists is its visible expression, the divine Order is far
  beyond all describing. All forms of life are created by it, and it alone can
  determine who is great. Some are exalted by the divine Order, some
  debased; some must suffer while others find joy. Some receive blessing,
  others are condemned, doomed by the divine Order to endless transmi-
  gration. All are within the sphere of the divine Order, none can evade it.
  They, Nānak, who truly comprehend the divine Order renounce their
  blind self-centred pride.

The process of meditation on the divine name begins with the recognition that the human body is a field in which the seed of the divine name
is to be sown. The simple repetition of the sacred word sanctifies the whole

life of the individual in much the same way as a seed sprouts with continual watering and grows into a beautiful tree in a garden. It involves the cultivation of virtues like patience, contentment, charity, humility, love, fear of God, purity, and truthful living. This process makes a person virtuous in thought, word, and deed. It results in experiences that develop progressively as meditation draws the individual nearer and nearer to God. At the highest stage, the process becomes internalized and *nām-simaran* continues automatically (*ajapa jāp*). This is where one listens to the music (*dhuni*) of the divine word within one's self. Guru Nānak describes this experience as a kind of musical mysticism: "There, the drum of the divine word resounds, with the accompaniment of the melody of five musical instruments. In that spiritual state shall be revealed wondrous continents, regions, lands and zones. The King of the Universe sits on the true throne, where the celestial strain resounds to the accompaniment of stringed instruments."[14]

In his celebrated hymn "Anand" ("Bliss"), Guru Amar Dās refers to the five types of "mystic sounds" (*pañch shabad*) that resound in the heart of the individual who feels the divine presence within and all around.[15] Although the Sikh Gurus' personal experience was not the inevitable result of any *Haṭha-yoga* (physical yoga) technique, the *Nāda-yoga* (sound yoga) texts offer description of five "mystic sounds." These are the sounds of "a kettledrum [*bheri*], a conch [*śaṅkha*], a *mridaṅg* [drum], a *vīṇā* [stringed instrument], or a flute [*vaṁśa*]."[16] Elsewhere, they are described as the sounds of the hum of the honey-intoxicated bee, a flute, a harp, ringing bells, and the roar of thunder.[17] Accordingly, the musical sounds heard in meditation correspond to musical instruments used to accompany devotional singing. As Guy Beck aptly puts it: "The divine sounds of the drum, cymbal, *vīṇā*, and flute ... exhibit marked correspondences with the instruments employed in devotional music."[18]

In personal religious experience, therefore, music plays a threefold role. First, it satisfies one's aesthetic sensibilities. Second, its dominant "sentiment" (*rasa*) delights one's inner consciousness and offers spiritual nourishment. Third, it transports one's soul into a realm of ecstasy.[19] On the topic of the paramount importance of devotional music, Guru Arjan proclaims "The true aim of my life lies in absorption in religious discourse, *kīrtan* and vibration of the divine word through singing and music."[20] It is no wonder that Sikhs frequently play musical recordings of *kīrtan* in their households. Even while driving to work, they attune themselves to the sacred sound by listening to a CD of *kīrtan*. Thus, they experience the "eternal Guru" as "an intimate companion of [their] soul."[21]

Ritual context: Music in public liturgy ·

Sikh congregational worship consists mainly of devotional singing of scriptural hymns set to melodic modes with the accompaniment of musical instruments. Through such *kīrtan*, devout Sikhs attune themselves to vibrate in harmony with the divine word and thereby immerse themselves in the deeper levels of its meaning. It is based upon the assumption that the melody in the singing of hymns evokes the divine word, and is an earthly resonance of it. As Harold Coward observes: "A direct correspondence is seen as existing between the physical vibration of the phenomenal chant and the noumenal vibration of the transcendent. The more the physical vibrations of the uttered chant are repeated, the more transcendent power is evoked in experience until one's consciousness is purified and put into a harmonious relationship or even identity with the Divine."[22]

The morning and evening services of the Sikh liturgy were first established by Guru Nānak at Kartārpur. He employed nineteen major *rāgas* for his 974 hymns. The early Sikh community had already started using these compositions in devotional singing as a part of congregational worship. Bhai Mardānā and his son Shahzada were the forerunners of the *rabābi* tradition within the Sikh community. At present, Bhai Lāl (Ashik Ali), a seventeenth-generation descendant of Bhai Mardānā, performs *kīrtan* at Gurdwara Janam Asthan at Nanakana Sahib (Pakistan), when Sikhs gather there on special occasions.[23] Tradition records that Guru Nānak instructed his successor, Guru Angad (1504–52), to start the practice of devotional singing of "Āsā di Vār" ("Ballad in the Āsā mode") before dawn.

Guru Amar Dās (1479–1574) composed 907 hymns in seventeen different *rāgas*. At times, the Guru himself recited his own compositions to a gathering. He frequently exhorted his audience to "Come, dear Sikhs of the true Guru, sing the true *bānī* of the Guru, the best *bānī* of all *bānīs*."[24] In particular, his forty-verse composition "Anand" ("Bliss") in the Rāmakali mode has acquired a liturgical role in the Sikh tradition. Bhai Gurdās gives the names of Bula and Pandha as the singer and scribe "who knew *gurbānī* well and sang it beautifully" (11:16). Before his passing, Guru Amar Dās gave specific instructions to the Sikhs: "No one should lament at my departure. Instead of resorting to the customary rituals you should perform only *kīrtan* in my memory."[25]

Guru Rām Dās contributed a total of 679 hymns and expanded the range of available musical modes by adding eleven new *rāgas*. He was an accomplished musicologist, composed a wedding hymn ("Lāvan") in the Suhī mode, and he used to sing hymns in classical *rāgas*. In the following verse he expresses the joy of having performed in the Bilāval mode: "I have lauded the exalted Lord in the tune of Bilāval. I have faithfully followed the Guru's teachings, by great fortune, ordained from the Beginning.

All recite the Lord's praises day and night with constant devotion in their hearts."[26] Notably, in his praise of the ecstatic performance of the Bilāval *rāga*, it is devotion to the Guru that takes precedence over the music.

Guru Arjan composed 2,218 hymns in thirty major *rāgas*, which made him by far the most prolific contributor to Sikh scripture. Having installed the Ādi Granth in the newly built *Harimandir* ("House of the Lord," the present-day Golden Temple) in 1604, he established eight *chauṅkīs* (sittings) to sing *kīrtan* as part of the daily routine at Amritsar. These are: (1) *Āsā di Vār di chauṅkī* (early morning); (2) *Bilāval di chauṅkī* (after sunrise); (3) *Anand di chauṅkī* (before noon); (4) *Sārang di chauṅkī* (noon); (5) *Charan Kanwal di chauṅkī* (afternoon); (6) *So Dar di chauṅkī* (sunset); (7) *Kīrtan Sohile di chauṅkī* (night); and (8) *Kanare di chauṅkī* (late night). The establishment of these eight "sittings" may have been influenced by the "eight orders" of *darśanas* (the acts of seeing the divine), performed by the Pushtimarg sect of Vaishnavas at each *pahar* (an Indian unit of time equal to three hours) of every day and night at the Govardhan Temple.[27] Five of these "sittings" (1, 3, 5, 6, and 7) are regarded as permanent sessions of *kīrtan*, which conclude with the recitation of the Sikh Prayer (*Ardās*) and the distribution of sacramentally offered food (*karah prashād*) to the congregation (*saṅgat*). They may have been inspired by the contemporary fivefold imperial *naubat* (periodic musical performance) at the court of Emperor Akbar.[28] These five "sittings" are still observed at the Golden Temple in Amritsar.

In a *gurdwārā* or Sikh temple, public worship is normally led by a group of three or four Sikh musicians (*rāgīs*), who are often joined in the singing by the congregation. Both specialists and non-specialists join in musical religious worship. Lay people are normally encouraged to participate in devotional singing; when the *rāgīs* are singing in classical *rāgas*, however, they simply listen to their performance and focus on the meaning of the hymn. Devotional singing has the power to inspire every member of the congregation, although its effect may be different for different people.

The standard devotional song in Sikhism is called a *shabad*. The following is an example of a *shabad* composed by Guru Arjan.

| EXAMPLE 2 (Track 29)

Shabad of Guru Arjan. Gauḍī Mahalā 5. Gurmukhī text is from *Amrit Kīrtan* (2003), 952. AG, 90. Gauḍī 121. Translation by the author.

Hari kīrtanu suṇai hari kīrtanu gāvai, tisu jana dūhkha nikaṭi nahī āvai
Jā kau apanī kirapā dhārai, so janu rasanā nāmu ucārai
Hari kī ṭahala karata janu sohai, tā kau māiyā agani na pohai
Hari bisarata sahasā dukhu bilāpai, simarata nāmu bharamu bhau bhāgai
Mani tani mukhi hari nāmu dayāla, Nānaka tajīale avari janjāla

Suffering can never approach the person who listens and
    performs devotional singing.
To whomsoever God shows his grace, he utters the Divine Name
    with his tongue.
To be forgetful of the Lord is to be assailed by doubts and suffering.
By contemplating the Divine Name doubt and fear are banished.
One is ennobled by performing the service of the Lord.
The fire of worldly attachment (*māyā*) cannot touch such a one.
Contemplate the Name of the Compassionate One with your mind, body,
    and tongue, says Nānak (Guru Arjan): Discard all other entanglements.

The appropriation of the meaning of the divine word depends to a
large extent upon the capacity, preparation, and interest of the hearer.

Many poems of the famous Sant Kabīr, who preceded Guru Nānak
by several centuries, are also included in the Ādi Granth, since his teachings bear a striking similarity to those of Nānak. The following is an example of a *shabad* by Kabir.

‖ EXAMPLE 3 (Track 30)
Shabad of Kabīr. "Āsā Srī Kabīr Jīu." Gurmukhī text is from *Amrit
Kīrtan* (2003), 340. Āsā 10, AG, 478. Translation by the author.

Hari kā bilovanā bilova mere bhāi, sahaji bilova jaise tatu na jāi,
Sanaka sananda antu nahī pāiyā, beda paḍe paḍi brahame janamu gavāiyā
Tanu kari maṭuki mana māhi biloī, isu maṭukī mahi sabadu sanjoī
Hari kā bilovanā mana kā bīcāra, gur prasādi pāvai amrita dhārā
Kahu Kabīra nadari kare je mīrā, rāma nāma lagi uttare tīrā

~

My brother! Churn the milk of devotion to God.
Churn it with poised mind, lest its essence is lost.
Sanak and Sanandan, Brahmin sons,
have not realized the extent of the Creator.
Brahmā himself has made his life waste in the study of the Vedas.
Make your body a churning pot, do the churning in
your heart, mind and soul (man).
Gather the Holy Word into this pot.
Divine churning consists of contemplation in heart, mind, and soul.
One obtains the stream of divine nectar (*amrit*)
through the grace of the Guru.
Says Kabīr: Should the Lord cast his glance of grace,
One gets across the other shore through the Divine Name.

Hymnals and songbooks

In the standard manual of the Sikh code of conduct, *Sikh Rahit Maryādā*, under the section headed *Kīrtan*, it explicitly states: "Within a Sikh congregation the only works which may be sung as *kīrtan* are those which are recorded in the sacred scriptures or the commentaries on sacred scripture composed by Bhai Gurdās and Bhai Nand Lāl."[29] The sacred scriptures include the Ādi Granth and the *Dasam Granth*, which contains the works attributed to the tenth (*dasam*) Guru, Gobind Singh (1666–1708). In Sikh usage, the Ādi Granth is normally referred to as the Guru Granth Sāhib. As the manifest body of the Guru, it carries the same status and authority as the ten Gurus did in person, and the ultimate authority within the Sikh community for a wide range of personal and public conduct lies in the Guru Granth Sāhib. As such, it provides the principal repertoire for *shabad kīrtan* (hymn singing).

The *Dasam Granth*, which enjoyed equal status with the Ādi Granth in the eighteenth and nineteenth centuries, has been relegated to a secondary position as a result of the Tat Khālsā reforms within the Singh Sabhā movement of the late nineteenth and early twentieth centuries. It was compiled by Bhai Mani Singh (d. 1734) in the early eighteenth century. Its modern standard version consists of 1,428 pages, containing such works as *Jāp Sāhib* (Master Recitation), *Akāl Ustat* (Praise to the Timeless One), and *Bachittar Nāṭak* (Wondrous Drama), and a collection of mythical narrative and popular anecdotes. Recently, Sikh scholars have questioned the inclusion of a large section of Hindu mythology and traditional romance tales in the *Dasam Granth*. Nevertheless, the authentic compositions of the tenth Guru are always used in *kīrtan* sessions.

The tertiary position in the authorized Sikh canon of musical compositions is occupied by the works of two early Sikhs, Bhai Gurdās Bhalla (d. 1633) and Bhai Nand Lāl Goya (1633–1715). As the amanuensis of the fifth Guru, Bhai Gurdās played a major role in the compilation of Sikh scripture in 1604. He was a poet and a theologian whose works are generally regarded as "the key to the Guru Granth Sāhib." The most influential among his works are the thirty-nine *Vārs* (Ballads), which provide an extensive commentary on the teachings of the Gurus. In addition, he wrote a series of 675 poems in Braj Bhāshā in "a four-line poetic metre" (*kabitt*) style. Bhai Nand Lāl was both a disciple of Guru Gobind Singh and a celebrated poet in the Persian language. His most famous Persian works are *Divan-i-Goya* (a collection of sixty-one *ghazals*, or odes) and the *Zindagināmā* ("Life-manual," a series of 510 couplets). The works of Bhai Gurdās and Bhai Nand Lāl are approved for singing in the *gurdwārās*, along with the sacred compositions of the Gurus.

Certain key hymns from the Ādi Granth have become an integral part of Sikh liturgy. Three examples are provided here. First is Guru Nānak's *Āratī*, which is normally sung in *rāga* Dhanāsarī as part of the afternoon "sitting" (*Charan Kanwal di chaunkī*) at the Golden Temple in Amritsar.

‖ EXAMPLE 4 (Track 31)
"Āratī." Text (Gurmukhī). From *Sacred Nitnem*, 264–66. Translation by the author. (M1, *Rāga* Dhanāsarī 3, AG, 13)

Refrain
Kaisī āratī hoe. Bhava-khaṇḍanā terī āratī.

1 Gagana mai thāl(u) rav(i) chand(u) dīpaka bane,
    tārikā maṇḍala janaka motī.
    Dhūp(u) mala-ānalo pavaṇ(u) chavaro kare,
    sagala banarāe phūlanta jotī.

2 Sahasa tava naina, nana naina hah(i) tohe kau,
    sahasa mūrat(i), nanā eka to(u)hī.
    Sahasa pada bimala, nana eka pada, gandha bin(u),
    sahasa tava gandha, iva chalata mohī.

3 Sabha maiha jot(i) jot(i) hai soe.
    Tisa dai chānan(i) sabha maiha chānan(u) hoe?
    Guru sākhī jot(i) pargat(u) hoe.
    Jo tis(u) bhāvai su āratī hoe.

4 Har(i) charana kavala makaranda,
    lobhita mano andino(u) mohe āhī piāsā.
    Kripā jal(u) deh(i) Nānaka sāringa kau,
    hoe jā te terai nāe vāsā.

∿

Refrain
Thus we offer worship to the One who stills our longings; thus we raise our lamps to offer praise. The mystic word within us is the drum we beat in praising you, that soundless word which faith alone can hear.

1 The sky shall be our salver with its lamps the sun and moon, its pearls the host of stars which shine above. Sweet sandalwood our incense, gently wafted by the breeze, and the plants which clothe the earth shall be our flowers.

2 Your mystery must baffle us, a thousand eyes yet none; a thousand forms, yet you can have no form. A thousand feet of purest forms, though you must footless be; no fragrance, yet a host of sweet perfumes.

3 A splendour shines in every place, its light the light of you; a light which lightens every living soul. Yet, only by the Guru's grace can that light stand revealed, and godly lives alone can give you joy.

4 The dust your lotus feet lets fall is sweetness to our souls; each day I seek
the joy my spirit craves. As cuckoos thirst for drops of rain I long to sip
your grace, and find the joy your name alone can bring.[30]

The "Āratī" hymn is also recited as part of the night "sitting" (*Kīrtan Sohile
di chaunkī*) when one is retiring to bed.

The second example, Guru Nānak's "So Dar" hymn, presents his personal experience of heavenly joys in the company of all the liberated ones,
who sing in eternity the praises of Akāl Purakh's glory at the door of his
ineffable court. There is divine music everywhere and in everything.

‖ EXAMPLE 5 (Track 32)
"So Dar." Text (Gurmukhī). From *Sacred Nitnem*, 206–210. Translated
by the author. (M1, So Dar *rāga* Āsā, AG, 6, 8–9 and 347–48)

So dar(u) terā kehā so ghar(u) kehā, jit(u) baih saraba samāle.
Vāje tere nād aneka asankhā, kete tere vāvana-hāre.
Kete tere rāg parī sio kahīah(i), kete tere gāvana-hāre.
Gāvan(i) tudh-no pavan(u) pānī baisantar(u), gāvai rājā dharam(u) duāre.
Gāvan(i) tudh-no chit(u) gupat(u) likh(i) janan(i), likh(i) likh(i)
    dharam(u) bichare.
Gāvan(i) tudh no Īsar(u) Brahmā Devī, sohan(i) tere sadā savāre.
Gāvan(i) tudh no Indr Indrāsan(i) baithe, devtiā dar(i) nāle.
Gāvan(i) tudh no sidh samādhi andar(i), gāvan(i) tudh no sādh bīchāre.
Gāvan(i) tudh no jatī satī santokhī, gāvan(i) tudh no vīra karāre.
Gāvan(i) tudh no pandit paran(i) rakhīsur, jug(u) jug(u) vedā nāle.
Gāvan(i) tudh no mohañiā man(u) mohan(i), surag(u) machh(u) pae-āle.
Gāvan(i) tudh no ratana upāe tere, ath-sath(i) tīrath nāle.
Gāvan(i) tudh no jodh mahābala sūrā, gāvan(i) tudh no khāni chāre.
Gāvan(i) tudh no khanda mandala brahmandā, kar(i) kar(i)
    rakhe tere dhāre.
Seī tudh no gāvan(i) jo tudh(u) bhāvan(i), rate tere bhagata rasāle.
Hor(i) kete tudh no gāvan(i) se mai chit(i) na āvan(i),
    Nānak(u) kiā bīchāre.
Soī soī sadā sach(u), sāhib(u) sāchā, sāchī nāī.
Hai bhī hosī jāe na jāsī, rachnā jin(i) rachāī.
Rangī rangī bhātī kar(i) kar(i) jinasī, māiā jin(i) upāī.
Kar(i) kar(i) dekhai kītā āpanā, jio tis dī wadiāī.
Jo tis(u) bhāvai soī karsī, phir(i) hukam(u) na karnā jāī.
So pātisāh(u) sāhā pat(i) sāhib(u), Nānaka rahan(u) rajāī.
    ⁓

Where is the place where you view your creation, with its gate where you
sit keeping watch over all? There, the music resounds to your glory, with

the heavenly strains of a host without number. Countless are the *rāgas* and their harmonies, infinite they who unite in your praise. The wind, the waters, and the fire sing your praises; so does your scribe, Dharamrāja, at your doorstep. His tireless attendants, Chitar and Gupat, join in the song while recording every deed of human beings for his consideration. Śiva, Brahmā, and the Goddess, radiant with splendour bestowed by you, sing hymns of your praise. Indra, seated upon his throne in the company of gods, sings your praises. Siddhas in their deep meditation and sages in contemplation sing hymns to your glory. Celibates, saints, and the serene sing your praises; so too do invincible heroes. Scholars and great seers with their texts in every age sing your praise. Ravishing beauties add joy to the harmony, music in heaven, on earth, and below. Spirits most precious give voice to their gladness, their music resounding at sixty-eight sacred sites. Heroes and warriors, famed for their victories, sing with the four sources of creation one vast song of praise. Continents, constellations, and universes sustained by you, all sing in wondrous ecstasy. Your devotees who are enraptured lend voice to this harmony; all win your love for the praises they sing. How many other singers and players sing of you, I cannot even conceive. How, then, can Nānak think of them? Assuredly you are the one true Lord, with Truth as your Name.

You are the Creator of the universe, the Eternal One, present now, the Everlasting Reality. All that exists in its various forms and colorful diversity is your own handiwork. You watch over all and sustain your creation; all glory belongs to you.

Whatever pleases you comes to pass; no one has any authority to challenge your purposes. You are the Sovereign, the Emperor above us, Nānak, before you all creatures must bow.

The appearance of this hymn three times is unique in the Ādi Granth. Also noteworthy is the presence of additional vocatives (*terā* [Yours, O Lord!] and *tudh no* [To You, O Lord!]) in the "So Dar" hymn and the opening hymn in Āsā mode, which are absent from the morning prayer (*Japjī*). The vocatives are considered musical devices that form part of a singing tradition. Since *Japjī* is a contemplative composition and is meant for recitation during the hours before dawn, vocatives are unnecessary.

The evening prayer, on the other hand, is meant for congregational worship. The "So Dar" hymn, therefore, is sung at the evening "sitting" (*So Dar di chauṅkī*) in Āsā mode at the Golden Temple.

Finally, Guru Amar Dās's hymn "Anand" in the Rāmakali mode enjoys particular prominence in Sikh ritual and liturgy. Though the complete hymn has forty stanzas, its short version (the first five and last stanzas) has become a part of the regular evening prayer. It is also sung at the conclusion of every Sikh service or ceremony. The first stanza is given below.

‖ EXAMPLE 6 (Track 33)
"Anand." Text (Gurmukhi). From *Sacred Nitnem*, 164. Translated by the author. (M3, Rāmakali Anand 1, AG, 917)

> Shabada gāvana āiā parīā, rāg ratana paravār parīā
> Anaṅd(u) bhaiā merī māe, Satigurū mai pāiā.
> Satigur(u) ta pāiā sahaj setī, man(i) vajīā vādhāiā.
> Rāg ratana paravār parīā, shabada gāvana āiā.
> Shabado ta gāvoh Harī kerā, man(i) jinī vasāiā.
> Kahai Nānak(u) anaṅd(u) hoā, Satigurū mai pāiā.
>
> ∿
>
> Jewel-like *rāgas* with their fairy families have come
>   to sing the divine word, filling my heart with joy.
> Joyous bliss is mine, O mother, I have found the True Guru.
> Boundless blessing, mystic rapture, spontaneously rise within my soul,
>   with the coming of the True Guru.
> Jewel-like *rāgas* with their fairy families have come
>   to sing the divine word, filling my heart with joy.
> They who realize the Lord within sing the divine songs of gladness.
> Joyous bliss is mine, Nānak, I have found the True Guru.

Technical dimensions

The Ādi Granth is divided into three major sections. It begins with an introductory section containing liturgical texts, and concludes with an epilogue consisting of a group of miscellaneous works. The bulk of the material, however, is arranged in the middle section and is based, in the standard version of the Ādi Granth, on thirty-one *rāgas*. Each *rāga* has further subdivisions based on poetic metre, ranging from the shorter *pad* (verse) through other poetic forms (*aṣṭapadi, chhant,* and other longer works such as Guru Arjan's *Sukhmanī*), to the longer *vār,* or ballad. Since *chaupadas* (four-verse hymns) and *aṣṭapadīs* (eight-verse compositions) are sung in the classical *rāgas*, they are put together at the beginning of the *rāga* section. In the last part of each *rāga* section, which is connected to the folk tradition, *chhants* (lyrical songs) and *vārs* are put together along with longer works that are meant to be recited. In this final sequence, a theological and musicological coherence is achieved by balancing the classical and folk traditions.

The names of the *rāga* and the rhythm to be used in singing are stated at the beginning of each section of hymns in the Ādi Granth. The hymns are also classified according to the *gharu*, or clef, in which each hymn is to be sung. In the Indian method of singing, the accent falls, and the voice rises and falls, in different positions, according to the *gharu* in which a hymn is sung.[31] There are seventeen different positions of *gharu* employed in the Ādi Granth. For instance, the musical direction for Guru Nānak's composition "Lunar Dates" is given as *"Bilāvalu Thitin Gharu 10 Jāti,"* which refers to the music that is scored in Bilāval mode and also in a particular rhythm of the drum.[32] These musical instructions in the written text fulfill the same function as that of a musical score in relation to performed music. Like the written music, the written text of the Ādi Granth has spiritual power only as it is sung devotionally. Guru Arjan, for instance, stresses the spiritual power of *kīrtan* in saying: "The false thinking of both performers and hearers is destroyed when they participate in devotional singing."[33]

Guru Rām Dās employed technical terms to provide direction in the musical performance of his hymns. For instance, the use of the word *sudhaṅg* (pure note) in the title of the Āsāvari mode clearly indicates that his hymns must be sung by using the "pure notes" of that *rāga*.[34] In the Naṭnārāyan *rāga*, Guru Rām Dās prescribes the changing of drum rhythms (*partāl*) after each verse in the singing of those particular hymns.[35] The bracing throb of changing rhythms in this style evokes a ready response in the hearts of the listeners. There are fifty-five hymns of both Guru Rām Dās and Guru Arjan in eleven *rāgas* that must be sung in *partāl* style. In this style, different parts of the same hymn are sung in different *tālas* (rhythmic beats) such as *tintāl, rūpak, dhamar, sulphakte, jhaptāl, chanchal, kaheravā, dādrā,* and so on. In this context, Ajit Singh Paintal observes: "While singing *partāl* composition, *rāgīs* enjoyed complete freedom to create variety by employing different *tālas* for various parts of the *shabad*. Such composition can only be rendered by well-versed *rāgīs*."[36] The ministry of Guru Rām Dās and Guru Arjan occurred during the reign of Emperor Akbar, which was certainly the peak time of North Indian music. It is no wonder that professional musicians frequently performed in the court of the Gurus.

According to the "time theory" of the Indian musical tradition, the most important points in a twenty-four-hour period are sunrise and sunset. It is not difficult to understand why Guru Arjan placed the Siri *rāga* (performed at sunset) at the beginning of the Ādi Granth and the Prabhāti *rāga* (performed at sunrise) at the end of the original compilation. The performance of the Siri *rāga* in the evening prepares one for the dark night of the Soraṭhi *rāga*, representing the worldly powers in life, whereas the Prabhāti *rāga* brings promise of light. The organization of the Ādi Granth reflects the spirit of optimism that is described as the "end" or final goal of the Sikh scripture. All other *rāgas* are assigned time intervals between sunrise and sunset. The division of the first canonical text into thirty major *rāgas* by Guru Arjan may have been inspired by the system of thirty *grāma-*

rāgas (parent scales) developed in the musical treatise *Bṛhaddeśī* (late first millennium), attributed to sage Mataṅga.[37] It should, however, be noted that the final version of the Ādi Granth ends with the Jaijavantī *rāga*, which is an added contribution of the ninth Guru, Tegh Bahādur (1621–75), and which is a highly majestic *rāga* assigned to the night hours. Its performance is associated with the feeling of victory (*jai jai*) over worldly temptations. With it placed at the end of the *rāga* sequence of the Ādi Granth, the cycle of time is complete. In addition to these thirty-one major *rāgas*, there is an equal number of regional varieties of "mixed form" (Śaṅkar *rāgas*) used in the Ādi Granth. Interestingly, five major *rāgas* (namely the Mājh, Āsā, Vadahans, Māru, and Tukhari *rāgas*) and seventeen regional varieties are to be found only in the Ādi Granth.

In musical theory, *rāgas* are suited to various moods, intervals of time, and specific seasons, and each *rāga* has acquired its own particular spiritual significance on the basis of tradition and usage. Guru Nānak and the succeeding Gurus selected the *rāgas* very carefully. They explicitly stated that only those *rāgas* should be used which produce a peaceful effect in the minds of both listeners and performers. Any *rāga* that arouses passion of any kind must, ipso facto, be omitted. For instance, it is believed that the Dīpak *rāga* generates fire if correctly performed by an inspired musician. This *rāga* is not used on its own in the Ādi Granth; it is, however, used as Gauṛī-dīpakī in a mixed form so that its extreme effect is toned down. The result is most suitable for the creation of a reflective mood. Similarly, the Hiṇḍol *rāga*, which is thought to create a mood of amorous love, is not used independently in the Ādi Granth; it is employed in the mixed form as Basant-hiṇḍol to create a gentle tonal effect. In their choice of *rāgas*, the Gurus' aim was to create a mood of sobriety and to avoid extremes.

In addition to the classical *rāgas*, there are many folk traditions that maintain independent styles. The sociological significance of this medium and its message should never be underestimated. For instance, there are twenty-two *vārs*, or ballads, in the Ādi Granth. They are sung by performing groups of three or four *dhadhis* (minstrels) to popular folk tunes, and are accompanied by *dhadhs* (small two-faced drums held in one hand and played with the fingers of the other), and a *sārangī* (bowed-lute). There are also popular folk genres like *chhants* (lyrical songs), *ghorian* (wedding songs), *alahanian* (laments), *birahare* (songs of separation), *āratī* (prayers), *saddu* (calls), *sohilā* (songs of happiness), *karahale* (camel tunes), *vanajara* (songs of traders), *pahare* (songs of the times of the day), *maṅgal* (songs of celebration), and so on.[38] Interestingly, Abu'l Fazal records in the *Ain-i-Akbari* that members of the Indian *dhadhi* community "chiefly play on the ḍaf and the *duhul*, and sing the *dhrupad* and the *sohilā* on occasions of nuptial and birthday festivities in a very accomplished manner."[39]

Bhai Abdulla and Nātha Māl were the renowned *dhadhis* who performed heroic ballads at the court of the sixth Guru, Hargobind (1595–1644). Evidently, classical and folk music developed side by side within the Sikh tradition, interacting with each other during the process of their evolution. They were both employed in *kīrtan* sessions, since the primary intention of the Gurus was to reach out to various audiences. If they wanted to address a Sufi audience, they would employ the Kāfī class of *rāgas* in singing. Similarly, they would employ folk tunes to address the rural people. While the performance of the Rāmakali *rāga* was best suited for an audience of Nāth yogīs, the Siri *rāga* was mostly addressed to Vaishnava audiences. In these and other ways, the Gurus employed all the popular styles of singing for their compositions to achieve a balance between classical and folk traditions.

In actual *kīrtan* performance it is of the utmost importance that the music always be subservient to the divine word. It must be simple, sublime, and dignified so that "the listener does not get unduly enraptured in its embellishments, and lose the bearings of the Word."[40] Ultimately, it is the transforming power of the divine word that uplifts every soul. The lyrical effect of the poetry and music serves to magnify the emotional appeal and to enliven the performance. Music should be neither sombre nor exuberant, but should produce a feeling of divine bliss. In keeping with the required mood of tranquility, dancing and clapping are totally prohibited in Sikh *kīrtan*. In this context, Ajit Singh Paintal aptly observes, "The Sikh Gurus adopted only the more vital elements of music in their *kīrtan*, but they completely eschewed the dance performed by Vaishnava and Śaiva devotees and by the Sufis in their *samā* gatherings. The Sikh Gurus also rejected the rhythmical clapping with hands with which the Sufis accompanied their singing."[41]

The acceptable musical instruments for Sikh *kīrtan* that are mentioned in the scriptures and the traditional texts are drawn from the standard instruments used in Hindu musical traditions, both classical and folk. The first category of chordophones (stringed instruments) include the following: (1) *rabāb* (the plucked lute, with six main strings and twenty-two metallic strings below for resonance); (2) *sarinda* (an instrument with three main strings); (3) *taus* (peacock-shaped instrument with stretched wires and frets); (4) *sārangī* (bowed lute with an extremely wide neck); (5) sitar (an instrument with seven main strings); (6) *dilruba* (bowed lute); (7) *tānpura* (drone instrument); and (8) violin. The second category of membranophones (drums) include the following: (1) *mridaṅg* (barrel-shaped drum); (2) *pākhvāj* (large barrel drum); (3) *dholak* (small barrel drum); (4) tabla (a pair of small kettledrums); and (5) *dhadh* (small two-headed drums). The third category, idiophones ("self-sounding"), includes *chimata* (a pair of long steel tongs), and *kartāl* (hand cymbals). Instruments in the fourth cat-egory, aerophones (wind instruments), are used sparingly since the mouth is needed for singing the divine word. However, this category includes the keyboard instrument known as the harmonium, a hand-pumped portable organ that employs the resonance of air made by free-sounding metal reeds. The harmonium was introduced in the nineteenth century from Europe, where it was invented in Paris in 1840 by Alexandre Debain.[42] The Sikh Gurus avoided the use of the *kingri* (harp) and *bin* (snake-charmer's flute) because of their association with the Nāth yogīs. Although the use of the *shahnai* (oboe-like reed instrument) and flute is not accept-able in the *gurdwārās*, the blowing of huge conches is a well-established tra-dition at Takhat Śrī Hazur Sāhib in Nander to maintain the "military atmosphere of the temple."[43]

Much like the musical tradition of North India, Sikh religious music was transmitted orally through a singing tradition. In this context, Lewis Row-ell rightly points out that early Indian musicians placed musical notation in a more realistic perspective: "preserve the music in skeletal form as a spur to the memory, but impart its full details in face-to-face instruction, by demonstration and imitation, teacher seated across from student."[44] The *rāgas* of the Ādi Granth were passed on to different generations of *rāgīs* belonging to old family traditions (*gharāṇās*) and Sikh institutions of learning (*takasāls*). The musical notational system of these *rāgas* was com-mitted to writing only in the late nineteenth and early twentieth centuries during the Singh Sabha period. M.A. Macauliffe was the first Western writer to study the music of the Gurus in some detail. In the fifth volume of his celebrated *The Sikh Religion* (1909), he gives the compositions of all the thirty-one *rāgas* of the Ādi Granth in the section on international staff notation. He was assisted by Mahant Gajja Singh, whom he complimented as "the greatest minstrel of the Sikhs." Macauliffe claimed that these *rāgas* were sung differently in different provinces of India, which is why he gives at least two different versions of eight *rāgas* in his book. Comparing the *rāgas* of the Ādi Granth with Rāja Sir S.M. Tagore's "collection of Indian airs," he remarks, "The Rāja's music is in high pitch adapted for musical instruments; the Gurus' Rāg[a]s are in low pitch adapted for voice,"[45] underlining the fact that the low pitch of the *rāgas* in Sikh *kīrtan* is to enhance the meaning of *gurbānī*. A recent analysis of the intonation of sev-eral performers of North Indian *rāgas* using oscillograms has revealed that "within each performance the intonation does vary."[46] It is not surpris-ing, then, if the same divergence in intonation is found among the perform-ers of the *rāgas* of the Ādi Granth.

Music as a spiritual discipline

A careful analysis of Guru Nānak's works reveals that he stressed devotional singing as the only efficacious means of liberation. "It is through singing of divine praises that we find a place in the Lord's court."[47] For him, the ethical aspects of devotional music must always take precedence over its technical performance; merely singing devotional songs in melodic modes is of no use if one's heart is full of hypocrisy (*kapat*).[48] That is why devotional music must always be seen as a means of spiritual development rather than as a source of entertainment. Moreover, Guru Nānak offered strong criticism of the voluptuous indulgence in secular music popular among the upper classes at that time:

> False are those songs, musical modes and reverberating accompaniments, which arouse the three qualities (of Māyā) and, destroying devotion, draw people away from the Divine. Suffering cannot be removed by duality and evil thinking. Liberation is achieved through the teachings of the Guru, and the singing of the divine praises is the true remedy for life's ills. —(M1, *Bilāvalu Aṣṭapadian* 2, AG, 832)

Clearly, any musical performance that takes people away from God is not endorsed in Guru Nānak's teachings. However, singing of the divine praises is acknowledged as the panacea for all the sufferings of the world, and a distinction must be made between the secular and sacred contexts in which particular musical performances take place.

The primary objective of Sikh *kīrtan* is spiritual discipline, which is why it is kept free of secular characteristics that may be in vogue at any given time. Any kind of music that might contribute to the arousal of sensuality has no place in the Sikh tradition. In fact, devotional music "gradually washes the inner consciousness" and one becomes "holy and spotless through the power of *kīrtan*."[49] In this context, Guru Arjan proclaims: "Blessed are the notes of those *rāgas* which put the mind in a tranquil mood."[50] As in the Hindu tradition, music is a divine gift which finds an echo in the hearts and minds of the people. In Sikhism it is used with the divine Word as an aid to ethical and spiritual development.

According to Guru Rām Dās, the transforming power of *kīrtan* purifies the mind of all evil inclinations and leads to a life of spirituality: "Truly blessed is the destiny of those saintly people who become virtuous by performing *kīrtan*."[51] There are indeed some outstanding musical personages in Sikh history who achieved spiritual liberation in their lifetime, and who made a seminal contribution to the preservation of the original styles of devotional singing. One such personage, during the reign of Mahārāja Ranjit Singh (b. 1780, ruled 1799–1839), was Bhai Mansa Singh, a gifted and pious musician who used to perform *kīrtan* at the early morning "sitting" (*Āsā di Vār di chauṅki*) at the Golden Temple in Amritsar. The Mahārāja was a great admirer of his devotional singing, and travelled with his courtiers from Lahore to offer a handsome reward to the devout *rāgī* at Amritsar. As he approached the house with a bag full of gold coins, Bhai Mansa Singh bolted the door from inside and addressed the Mahārāja in all humility from the window of his balcony: "It is gracious of your Majesty, but I realise that as Wealth will come in, Art of music and learning will go out."[52] This anecdote truly exemplifies Guru Arjan's remark that *kīrtan* itself is a "priceless jewel" for which there is no worldly compensation.[53]

Sant Sham Singh (1803–1926) was an accomplished musician who belonged to the Sevapanthī ("followers of the ideal of service") sect within the Sikh community. He received his training in music from Bābā Naudh Singh, and became an eminent player of the *sarinda*. He regularly performed *kīrtan* at the early morning "sitting" (*Āsā di Vār di chauṅkī*) at the Golden Temple in Amritsar for more than five decades. He led a simple life of humility and service, and enjoyed a reputation for great spirituality among his contemporaries. Impressed by his piety, two Singh Sabha stalwarts, Bhai Vir Singh and Sundar Singh Majithia, received the Khālsā initiation at his hands when he was one of the "Cherished Five" (*pañj piāre*) for the ceremony. Sant Sham Singh was the author of *Hari Bhagati Premākār Granth* (1913), in which he specifically mentions the tradition of eight "sittings"of *rāgīs* and several "sittings" of *rabābis* (rebec players, usually Muslim bards) at the Golden Temple. He died on April 23, 1926, at the advanced age of 123.[54]

Bhai Javala Singh (1872–1952) belonged to a family (*gharāṇā*) of Sikh musicians. In their day, his father, Bhai Deva Singh, and grandfather, Panjab Singh, were celebrated *rāgīs* who performed *kīrtan* to the accompaniment of the *sarinda*. Javala Singh excelled at playing the *taus* and inherited an abundance of traditional and classical tunes, which could be traced back to the times of the Gurus. In fact, the family has kept alive the memory of their ancestor Sahib Singh, who received the Khālsā initiation directly from Guru Gobind Singh. Javala Singh performed *kīrtan* for sixty years, and he presided over the first all-India Rāgīs Conference, held at Amritsar in 1942. He died on May 29, 1952.[55] Fortunately, his two sons, Bhai Avtar Singh and Bhai Gurcharan Singh, have been performing *kīrtan* for the last fifty years. They have written down all the musical notations of ancient *dhunis* (tunes), *partāls* (musical styles based on the changing of drum rhythms), and *rītīs* (musical styles) in a two-volume work, *Gurbānī Saṅgīt Prāchin Rīt Ratanāvali* (1979), published by Punjabi University Press in Patiala. They have also recorded all these musical styles.

Current trends and the future of music in Sikhism

A few years ago, some scholars raised the concern that the Sikhs do not "seem to have devoted much attention to preserving a fixed form or character for their music, being open to the influence of what was popular or current at different times."[56] That concern is being addressed now with great enthusiasm, and an attempt in this direction was made at the first *Aduti Gurmat Saṅgīt Samelan* (Unique Gathering of the Performers of Sikh Sacred Music), held in 1991 at Gurdwara Gur Gian Prakash in Ludhiana, when all the classical *rāgas* of the Ādi Granth were performed by various professional musicians. The ancient tunes of various *rāgas* were discussed by a panel of judges, who tried to identify the original tradition of singing. There were, of course, some disagreements, with one in particular arising over the character of the Māru mode. Nevertheless, the performance of the *rāgas* of the Ādi Granth, along with ancient folk tunes, has been given a new lease of life within Sikhism.

Another effort is underway in the form of the Rabāb Revival Project, a plan to revive the use of stringed instruments for *kīrtan*. Historically, the *rabāb* was the original musical instrument adopted by Guru Nānak to accompany devotional singing, and thus has deep cultural significance within the Sikh tradition. The project received further impetus when Chris Mooney Singh, an Australian-born convert to Sikhism, performed *kīrtan* in 1999 in the Golden Temple with an Afghani-style *rabāb* to mark the tricentennial celebration of the Khālsā. He claims: "I have decided to convey Guru Nānak's message to the Westerners by singing it on the *rabāb*."[57] He wants to start a movement for singing scriptural hymns to the accompaniment of stringed instruments, so that *"gurbānī* should be sung to the world in its original, pure and pristine form, in which it was handed down to us by the great Gurus, and thus freed from the stranglehold of the harmonium that has given birth to film music only."[58]

In contrast to Chris Mooney Singh's efforts to revive the original *rabāb* tradition, a Sikh musician from Australia, Dya Singh, sings Sikh hymns in the original Punjabi (with occasional English explanations), and blends traditional Sikh spiritual music with modern and contemporary genres. In the last seven years, he has produced six albums in which he has blended Sikh religious music with blues, jazz, folk, Australian indigenous, bush, and country and Western music. In his opinion, Sikh *kīrtan* within the narrow confines of the *gurdwārās* has become "static music," and reached a creative dead end. To him, Sikh music needs radical "evolution" toward universality and greater acceptability, especially among the younger generation of Sikhs born in the diasporic community. Not surprisingly, the Dya Singh World Music Group travels widely in different countries and is acclaimed by both Sikhs and alternative mainstream audiences.

In addition to these two contrasting trends, Sikh parents encourage their children to learn *kīrtan* at the *gurdwārās*, and one recent study of Sikh children's perceptions of the transmission of Sikh culture and religion through religious music classes revealed the following.[59] First, the children were motivated by their goal of performing *kīrtan* on the stage at the *gurdwārā* to develop musical skills. They were fully aware of the key role of *kīrtan* in Sikh worship. Second, many of the children valued learning an instrument as a factor in their identity as Sikhs, and for some it increased, or at least complemented, their commitment to Sikhism. The *kīrtan* classes thus equipped Sikh children, both male and female, with the skills to take an active part in worship, as well as making a positive contribution to their view of themselves as Sikhs. Religious music has thus played a central role in Sikh life in the past and it will continue to do so in the future.

Notes

1 Donna M. Wulff (1983), 157.
2 The reference here occurs in the thirty-fifth stanza of the first *Vār* of Bhai Gurdās. All subsequent references in the main text may be found in *Varan Bhai Gurdās Steek*, 1977.
3 Cited in *Sikh Sacred Music* (1967), 12.
4 See Pashaura Singh (2000), 283–85, particularly chapter 4, "*Rāga* Organization of the Ādi Granth."
5 For details, see W.H. McLeod (1989), 50.
6 M1, Rāmakali 10, AG, 879. This reference means that the passage is from hymn number 10, in the Rāmakali mode, by Guru Nānak, on page 879 of the Ādi Granth. The word *Mahalā* (or simply, M) with the appropriate number identifies the composition of each Guru. The works by Guru Nānak, Guru Angad, Guru Amar Dās, Guru Rām Dās, and Guru Arjan are indicated by M 1, 2, 3, 4, and 5, respectively. All the Gurus sign their compositions "Nānak" in the Ādi Granth. There are a total of ten Sikh Gurus, as follows: Guru Nānak, Guru Angad, Guru Amar Dās, Guru Rām Dās, Guru Arjan, Guru Hargobind, Guru Har Rai, Guru Harikrishan, Guru Tegh Bahādur, and Guru Gobind Singh.
7 M1, Āsā 9, AG, 351.
8 M4, *Salok Varan te Vadhik 24*, AG, 1423.
9 W.H. McLeod (1968), 228.
10 Bhat Gayand, *Savayye Mahale Chauthe Ke 4*, AG, P. 1402.
11 M4, Vār Gaurī 2 (11), AG, 305–306.
12 W.H. McLeod (1987), 149.
13 Harold G. Coward (1988), 133.
14 M1, Vār Malēr 1 (27), AG, 1290–91.
15 M3, Rāmakali Anand 5, AG, 917.
16 For details, see Guy L. Beck (1993), 99.
17 Guy L. Beck (1993), 103.
18 Guy L. Beck (1993), 110.
19 G.S. Mansukhani (1982), 80–81.
20 M5, Bilāval 6, AG, 818.

21 M5, Dhanāsarī 32, AG, 679.

22 Harold G. Coward (1988), 175.

23 I have witnessed a celebration of Guru Nānak's birthday (November 2000) at which Bhai Lal performed *kīrtan* at Nanakana Sahib.

24 M3, Rāmakali Anand 23, AG, 920.

25 Sundar, Rāmakali Saddu 4–5, AG, 923.

26 M4, Var Bilāval 1 (1), AG, 849.

27 I owe this suggestion to Prof. Guy L. Beck.

28 See Bonnie C. Wade (1998), 6–7, 30.

29 *Sikh Rahit Maryādā* (1995; originally published in 1950), 13.

30 Translation is taken from W.H. McLeod (1997), 297.

31 See Frederic Pincott (1885), 443.

32 M1, *Bilāvalu Thitin Gharu 10 Jāti*, AG, 838.

33 M5, Kanara 1, AG, 1300.

34 M4, Āsāvari Sudhaṅg 1415, AG, 36970. For more details on *Sudh Āsāvari*, see N.A. Jairazbhoy (1971), 16566.

35 M4, Naṭ-nārāyan *Partal 7–9*, AG, 977–978.

36 See Ajit Singh Paintal (1991), 51.

37 See Richard Widdess (1995), 10–12.

38 On camel tunes, see Ravi Shankar (1968), 33: "Among the other types of singing is the *tappā*, originally a Muslim folk form sung by the camel-cart drivers from Punjab and later developed to a classical level by the famous musician Mian Shori."

39 Cited in Bonnie C. Wade (1998), 95–96, 144, 191.

40 *Sikh Sacred Music* (1967), 39.

41 Ajit Singh Paintal (1991), 50.

42 See *The Encyclopaedia of Sikhism*, ed. Harbans Singh (1996), 2: 165.

43 Ethel Rosenthal (1928), 39.

44 Lewis Rowell (1992), 141.

45 See M.A. Macauliffe (1985; originally published in 1909), 333–51.

46 N.A. Jairazbhoy and A.W. Stone (1983), 96.

47 M1, Vār Mājh, 2 (12), AG, 143.

48 M1, Prabhāti *Aṣṭapadian 1*, AG, 1342.

49 G.S. Mansukhani (1982), 78.

50 M5, Rāmakali Ki Vār, 1 (4), AG, 958.

51 M4, Rāgu Sorathi Vār (18), AG, 649.

52 *Sikh Sacred Music* (1967), 71.

53 M5, Rāmakali 35, AG, 893.

54 See *The Encyclopaedia of Sikhism*, ed. Harbans Singh (1998), 4: 103.

55 *The Encyclopedia of Sikhism*, 2: 367.

56 Winand M. Callewaert and Mukund Lath (1989), 97.

57 Chris Mooney Singh (July 1999): 24. Also see his interview with Nirupama Dutt in *Indian Express Magazine*, (August 23, 1998).

58 Ibid., 25. For information on the Rabāb Revival Project, see the website ⟨http://www .4.50megs.com/gurfateh/Rabab/music.html⟩.

59 Sarah Davies (1997), 1–8.

Bibliography

Beck, Guy L. *Sonic Theology: Hinduism and Sacred Sound*. Columbia: University of South Carolina Press, 1993.

Callewaert, Winand M., and Mukund Lath. *The Hindi Padāvali of Nāmdev*. Delhi: Motilal Banarasidass, 1989.

Coward, Harold G. *Sacred Word and Sacred Text: Scripture in World Religions*. Maryknoll, NY: Orbis, 1988.

Dass, Nirmal, trans. *Songs of the Saints from the Ādi Granth*. Albany, NY: SUNY Press, 2000.

Davies, Sarah. "Children's Perceptions of the Transmission of Sikh Culture/Religion That Takes Place Through Religious Music Classes." *Sikh Bulletin* 14 (1997): 1–8.

Jairazbhoy, N.A. *The Rāgas of North Indian Music: Their Structure and Evolution*. London: Faber and Faber, 1971.

Jairazbhoy, N.A., and A.W. Stone."Intonation in Present-Day North Indian Classical Music." In *Essays in Musicology*, ed. R.C. Mehta, 84–98. Baroda: Indian Musicological Society, 1983.

Macauliffe, M.A. *The Sikh Religion: Its Gurus, Sacred Writings and Authors*. Vol. 5. Reprint, New Delhi: S. Chand, 1985. Originally published 1909 by Oxford University Press.

Mansukhani, G.S. *Indian Classical Music and Sikh Kīrtan*. New Delhi: Oxford University Press and IBH, 1982.

McLeod, W.H. *Guru Nānak and the Sikh Religion*. Oxford: Oxford University Press, 1968.

———, ed. and trans. *Textual Sources for the Study of Sikhism*. Manchester: Manchester University Press, 1984.

———. *The Chaupa Singh Rahit-nāmā*. Dunedin: University of Otago Press, 1987.

———. *The Sikhs: History, Religion and Society*. New York: Columbia University Press, 1989.

———. *Sikhism*. London: Penguin, 1997.

Paintal, Ajit Singh."The Traditions of Sikh Devotional Music." In *Simriti Granth: Aduti Gurmat Saṅgīt Samelan—1991*, ed. Satbir Singh and Gurnam Singh, 48–52. Ludhiana: Gurdwara Gur Gian Prakash, 1991.

Pincott, Frederic. "The Arrangement of the Hymns of the Ādi Granth." *Journal of the Royal Asiatic Society* (1885): 443.

Rosenthal, Ethel. *The Story of Indian Music and Its Instruments: A Study of the Present and a Record of the Past*. London: W. Reeves, 1928.

Rowell, Lewis. *Music and Musical Thought in Early India*. Chicago: University of Chicago Press, 1992.

Shankar, Ravi. *My Music, My Life*. New Delhi: Vikas, 1968.

Sikh Rahit Maryādā. Amritsar: SGPC, 1995; originally published in 1950.

Sikh Sacred Music. New Delhi: Sikh Sacred Music Society, 1967.

Singh, Avtar, and Gurcharan Singh. *Gurbānī Saṅgīt Prāchin Rīt Ratanāvali*. 2 vols. Patiala: Punjabi University Press, 1979.

Singh, Chris Mooney. Interview. *The Spokesman Weekly* 48:7 (July 1999): 25.

Singh, Harbans. *Guru Nānak and Origins of the Sikh Faith*. Bombay: Asia Publishing, 1969.

Singh, Harbans, ed. *The Encyclopaedia of Sikhism*. 4 vols. Patiala: Punjabi University Press, 1992–98.

Singh, Pashaura. *The Guru Granth Sāhib: Canon, Meaning, and Authority*. Delhi: Oxford University Press, 2001.

Singh, Satbir, Gurnam Singh, and Jasbir Kaur Khalsa, eds. *Simriti Granth: Aduti Gurmat Sangīt Samelan 1991–1997*. Ludhiana: Gurdwara Gur Gian Prakash, 1991–97.

Varan Bhai Gurdās Steek. 9th ed. Ed. Hazara Singh and Vir Singh. Amritsar: Khalsa Samachar, 1977. Originally published in 1911.

Wade, Bonnie C. *Imaging Sound: An Ethnomusicological Study of Music, Art, and Culture in Mughal India*. Chicago: University of Chicago Press, 1998.

Widdess, Richard. *The Rāgas of Early Indian Music: Modes, Melodies, and Musical Notations from the Gupta Period to c. 1250*. Oxford: Clarendon Press, 1995.

Wulff, Donna M. "On Practicing Religiously: Music as Sacred in India." In *Sacred Sound: Music in Religious Thought and Practice*, ed. Joyce Irwin, 149–72. Chico, CA: Scholars Press, 1983.

6
BUDDHISM AND MUSIC

Sean Williams

The term "Buddhism" describes a set of religious traditions that have developed across Asia and parts of the rest of the world over the past 2,500 years, originating with Siddhārtha Gautama (ca. 563 to 483 BCE), who was revered as the Buddha—the enlightened or awakened one—by his disciples. Buddhism has spread through many Asian cultures and has been altered and adapted according to local custom; as a result, its diversity is one of its hallmarks. This diversity makes it difficult sometimes to recognize similarities from one extreme of Buddhist practice to another, but all practices and practitioners share some points in common.

Basic teachings and primary sources

In spite of Buddhism's regional diversity, the primary figure of all Buddhist practice is the Buddha himself. Siddhārtha Gautama was an Indian prince who, in his twenties, chose to renounce his aristocratic life of luxury and seek enlightenment.[1] After a period of severe self-denial, he developed a more moderate approach, realizing that neither indulgence nor denial could be effective in realizing his goals: this philosophy of moderation is sometimes referred to as the Middle Path. He journeyed to a place called Bodh Gayā in northeast India, and meditated under a large tree that came to be known as the Bodhi Tree or the "tree of awakening." In spite of temptations and assaults by personifications of worldliness and desire, Siddhārtha became aware of the Dharma (Truth or Law) of human existence:

it was the beginning of his enlightenment. The Buddha meditated for several more weeks before beginning to pass on his newly acquired knowledge to others. The lessons and sermons that he delivered throughout his long missionary life are called *sūtra* (in Pali, *sutta*), and his early companions and disciples became the basis for the early community known as the Sangha, which eventually included hundreds of separate Buddhist groups. The sermons of the Buddha, along with monastic codes, wisdom narratives, and philosophical discourses, were collected after his demise into the Pali Canon, otherwise known as the *Tripiṭaka* (Three Baskets). This voluminous work, written in Pali, is the primary source for understanding the role of chant and music in early Buddhism.

Among the Buddha's teachings in the Pali Canon were the Four Noble Truths. Not every later text refers to them, but they are generally held up as central to the set of Buddhist beliefs. The Four Noble Truths are:

1. The truth of suffering or *dukkha* [that all life is filled with suffering].
2. The truth of the origin of suffering [that desire, or *tāṅhā*, causes suffering].
3. The truth of the cessation of suffering [that it is necessity to let go of desire].
4. The truth of the Path [that there is a way to achieve enlightenment or nirvana].

The fourth of the Noble Truths, the Path, has eight ways called the Noble Eightfold Path. The eight ways a Buddhist tries to follow to achieve enlightenment are right views, right intent, right speech, right action, right livelihood, right effort, right mindfulness, and right concentration. Each of these ways is context specific, and examples of them abound from the Buddha's life and teachings. However, Buddhists within different cultures behave appropriately according to their own cultural norms.

All of these ways to achieve enlightenment, or nirvana, are related to the laws of karma, in which right action will result in a quicker path to nirvana, but harmful action will lead to future suffering. Nirvana itself is the result of the extinction of desire and the "letting go" of the self. Huston Smith notes that "the Buddha listed impermanence (*anicca*) as the first of his Three Marks of Existence—characteristics that apply to everything in the natural order—the other two being suffering (*dukkha*) and the absence of permanent identity or a soul (*anatta*)."[2] As will be shown later on, the importance of impermanence in Buddhism makes the performance of music an effective metaphor for Buddhist practices. The practice of Buddhism has a very strong emphasis on discipline, ritual, and meditation, whether monastic or among the laity. Life-cycle rituals, including funerals, are also celebrated in Buddhist traditions.

The Buddha at a monastery in China. Photograph courtesy of Guy L. Beck.

The role of chant and music in early Buddhism

Shortly after the Buddha's death at the age of eighty, the first Buddhist council was formed to try to consolidate the essential canon of the Buddha's teaching. Some of the earliest Buddhist communities used chant to remember the teachings of the Buddha, and for hundreds of years after his death, all of his teachings were recalled solely through the use of chant—one can reasonably claim, then, that the use of musical chant is one of the earliest forms of information technology. Specialists in all the early Buddhist cultures were relied on to remember and recite the Pali Canon, and many of these specialists were drawn from the ranks of another cultural specialist: the bard. In many areas of the world, the bards have been the ones who have borne the cultural memory of a place, kept account records, and remembered the genealogies and the epic tales, and Buddhist tradition is no exception. Within Buddhism, those people who functioned as bards were the monks. It is important to recognize that, while musical chant was (and still remains) one of the most significant and effective ways to keep track of Buddhist teachings, it also plays a major role in Buddhist worship today.

A number of factions developed in the early years after the Buddha's death, but all falling loosely within the boundaries of what is now called the *Hīnayāna* (Small Vehicle) school. Hīnayāna splintered within a hundred years, and one of its major subsets, Theravāda, has since become virtually synonymous with Hīnayāna to many Westerners.[3] By approximately 100 CE, a second "school," called *Mahāyāna* (Great Vehicle), developed. Theravāda Buddhism is most closely linked with the areas of Sri Lanka and Southeast Asia (including, especially, Burma and Thailand), while Mahāyāna Buddhism is associated with Central and East Asia. The two traditions are markedly different, not only in terms of the cultural areas to which they belong but also in their fundamental beliefs and practices.

One of the biggest differences between Theravāda and Mahāyāna Buddhism is that Theravāda Buddhism relies heavily on the earliest scriptural sources only, meaning that new compositions or new additions to the early *sūtras* are not allowed. Mahāyāna Buddhism uses new texts, revelations, and teachings, rather than relying exclusively on the oldest *sūtras* or scriptures. For example, new *sūtras* based on the teachings of the Buddha's own disciples were developed by later writers, and were viewed within the Mahāyāna tradition as having come through the living memory of the Buddha.[4]

Theravāda Buddhism differs from Mahāyāna Buddhism in more than its exclusive focus on original source materials. Individual effort is seen as more important than the support of the divine; wisdom is seen as a key virtue rather than compassion; monks and nuns are seen as better positioned for committing themselves to regular practice than lay people; the Buddha is considered a supreme teacher rather than a savior; metaphysics and ritual are minimized rather than emphasized; and meditation is considered more important than petitionary prayer.[5] Most of these differences are reflected in ritual and musical practice as well.

Theravāda Buddhists regard music as a type of sensual luxury, and their tradition notes that music should be approached only with great caution. Among the Ten Precepts accepted upon entering monastic life, the seventh requires the monk to avoid dancing, singing, music, and entertainments, and to abstain from wearing garlands, perfume, or cosmetics. The risk regarding music and singing is that one might focus on the musical quality of the voice rather than on the teachings enunciated in the song or chant. The Buddha himself is said to have avoided attending musical performances, and cautions his disciples about musical chant: "O monks, there are five disadvantages for one singing the teaching in an extended sung intonation. (1) He is attached to himself regarding that sound; (2) and others are attached to that sound; (3) and even householders are irritated. (4) There is dissolution of concentration on the part of one straining to lock in on the sound; and (5) people who follow after [this procedure] undergo an adherence to opinions."[6]

The voice, however, is revered as essential for the performance of Buddhist ritual not only in Mahāyāna traditions, which emphasize mystical practices, but also in Theravāda traditions.

The literature of early Buddhism includes frequent references to the "Three Jewels" of Buddhism: the Buddha himself, the *Dhamma* (Sanskrit, *dharma*), or the Teachings, and the *Saṅgha*, or community of practitioners. The "Three Jewels" as a formula (*Trisaranam*, or Three Refuges) became the most important concise statement of Buddhist belief, and is chanted frequently as part of the early ritual services. Its recitation is also required among new candidates for admission into the Saṅgha, along with the Five or Ten Precepts. Theravāda chanting, including the chanting of the Three Refuges, is generally conservative and limited to a few basic notes that resemble in principle the Vedic cantillation from which it was primarily derived. The principal chanter is followed line by line in response by the other monks. Chanting of the Three Refuges is normally preceded by a short drum sequence and an invocation (*Mangalacharanam*), or an auspicious formula for revering the Buddha. Example 1 includes the drumming, the invocation, and the complete three-part *Trisaranam*.

| Example 1 (Track 34, 35)
Mangalacharanam and The Three Refuges (*Trisaranam*). Text (Pali). From *Puja: The FWBO Book of Buddhist Devotional Texts*, by Friends of the Western Buddhist Order (Birmingham, UK: Windhorse, 1999), 14–15.

1 Introductory Drum Sequence (Track 34)

2 *Mangalacharanam* (Track 35)

Namo tassa bhagavato arahato sammā-sambuddhasa (3×)

~

Homage to Him (Buddha), the Blessed One, the Worthy One,
the Perfectly Enlightened One!

3 The Three Refuges (*Trisaranam*). Text (Pali)

Buddhaṁ saraṇaṁ gacchāmi
Dhammaṁ saraṇaṁ gacchāmi
Saṅghaṁ saraṇaṁ gacchāmi

Dutiyampi Buddhaṁ saraṇaṁ gacchāmi
Dutiyampi Dhammaṁ saraṇaṁ gacchāmi
Dutiyampi Saṅghaṁ saraṇaṁ gacchāmi

Tatiyampi Buddhaṁ saraṇaṁ gacchāmi
Tatiyampi Dhammaṁ saraṇaṁ gacchāmi
Tatiyampi Saṅghaṁ saraṇaṁ gacchāmi

~

To the Buddha for refuge I go
To the Dharma for refuge I go
To the Saṅgha for refuge I go

For the second time to the Buddha for refuge I go
For the second time to the Dharma for refuge I go
For the second time to the Saṅgha for refuge I go

For the third time to the Buddha for refuge I go
For the third time to the Dharma for refuge I go
For the third time to the Saṅgha for refuge I go

In addition to the Three Refuges, all Buddhists are required to recite the Five Precepts, which enumerate the basic vows that Buddhists must honour. However, Buddhists who have accepted monastic vows recite the Ten Precepts, one of which abjures association with music and entertainment. Example 2 below provides the text and translation for the Five Precepts.

∥ Example 2 (Track 36)
The Five Precepts (*Pañchaśīlā*). Text (Pali). From *Puja* (1999), 16–17.

Pāṇātipātā veramaṇī sikkhāpadaṁ samādiyāmi
Adinnādānā veramaṇī sikkhāpadaṁ samādiyāmi
Kāmesu micchācārā veramaṇī sikkhāpadaṁ samādiyāmi

Musāvādā veramaṇī sikkhāpadaṁ samādiyāmi
Surāmeraya majja pamādaṭṭhānā veramaṇī sikkhāpadaṁ samādiyāmi

∿

I undertake to abstain from taking life
I undertake to abstain from taking the not-given
I undertake to abstain from sexual misconduct
I undertake to abstain from false speech
I undertake to abstain from taking intoxicants

In Theravāda Buddhism, music is appropriate only when it is subordinated to the message. Music has little actual liturgical function, yet chanting continues to be central to the preservation of the Pali Canon. The Buddha's First Sermon, including the Four Noble Truths and the Noble Eightfold Path, is regularly chanted in the form of the *Dhamma Chakka Sutta* (The Wheel of Dhamma/Truth). Example 3 below includes the Pali text and translation of verse 9 describing the Second Noble Truth of craving as the cause of suffering (*dukkha*). This is a unison chant without call and response.

∥ Example 3 (Track 37)
Dhamma Chakka Sutta, Verse 9. Text (Pali). From *Saddharma Ratnamālā*, by Dharmapāla Mahāthera. (Kolkata; Bauddha Dharmāṅkura Sabhā, 2002), 143.

Idaṁ dukkha-samudayam ariya-saccanti me bhikkave, pubbe ananussutesu dhammesu cakkhuṁ udapādi, ñānaṁ udapādi, paññā udapādi, vijjā udapādi, āloko udapādi.

∿

This craving, which should be eliminated, is the Noble Truth of the origin of suffering, which monks should know. Concerning things unheard of before, there arose in me vision, knowledge, understanding; there arose in me wisdom; there arose in me penetrative insight and light.

Rather than functioning as *epiclesis* (invoking the presence of deity), Theravāda chant is either didactic (teaching), as in the above, or *apotropeic* (warding off evil spirits and influences). Special protective chants known as *paritta* in Pali (Singhalese, *piritha*) form a surprisingly significant dimension of Theravāda practice in Southeast Asia. The *Mahā Piritha* (Great Book of Protection), which is comprised of different parts from the Pali Canon, is frequently chanted in Sri Lanka on many occasions. Example 4 provides three verses of blessings from a widely popular protective chant used at many festivals and other auspicious occasions. The chanting style is similar to the above examples. The complete chant in nineteen verses is known as the *Mahā Jayamaṅgala Gāthā*.

∤ EXAMPLE 4
Blessing from the *Mahā Jayamaṅgala Gāthā*, verses 13–15. Text (Pali). From *Puja* (1999), 44–45.

> Bhavatu sabbamaṅgalaṁ rakkhantu sabbadevatā
> Sabbabuddhānubhāvena sadā sotthī bhavantu te
> Bhavatu sabbamaṅgalaṁ rakkhantu sabbadevatā
> Sabbadhammānubhāvena sadā sotthī bhavantu te
> Bhavatu sabbamaṅglaṁ rakkhantu sabbadevatā
> Sabbasaṅghānubhāvena sadā sotthī bhavantu te
>
> ⌁
>
> May all blessings be yours;
> May all gods protect you.
> By the power of all Buddhas
> May all happiness be yours.
>
> May all blessings be yours;
> May all gods protect you.
> By the power of all Dharmas
> May all happiness be yours.
>
> May all blessings be yours;
> May all gods protect you.
> By the power of all the Saṅgha
> May all happiness be yours.

While there may be debate regarding the actual role of music in Theravāda Buddhism, since music-making as such is prohibited for most monks, John Ross Carter recently has summarized their position: "Music whether in liturgical or non-liturgical settings has a place in the Theravāda Buddhist tradition. Although it has no formal place in long established ritual procedures, except for drums and horana to inaugurate auspicious moments, its presence appears to have been long assured insofar as its legitimization derives from the religious themes on which it focuses. Music is accepted in this tradition as an authentic form of religious expression insofar as it points beyond itself as an art form."[7]

Technical dimensions of Buddhist music: Vocal and instrumental

Chant is, of course, the best-known aspect of Buddhist music in the Western world. The perusal of any music store will reveal at least a dozen different CDs of chant, and particularly Tibetan Buddhist chant. In Tibetan monastic communities, learning to chant is so important and universal that it is the one thing that almost all the communities have in common; it is written explicitly into the constitution of nearly every monastery. Young monks have to take specific examinations on chant, and if they do not memorize or perform the chants correctly, they may be dismissed from the monastery.

All Buddhists do not rely on a single text, like the Bible or the Qur'ān.[8] Instead, new revelations were added for centuries after the death of the Buddha, and many Buddhists disagree about the canonical relevance of scripture from different cultures. There are variations in the *sūtras* (literally, "thread") or teachings of the Buddha between Theravāda and Mahāyāna. Theravāda Buddhism relies primarily on the non-musical chanting of scriptures in the Pali language, which few lay people understand, and Theravāda Buddhist chanting does not follow a melody. Instead, because the words are considered of paramount importance, this type of chant is sung in a monotone. Placing a liturgical text over a complex melodic figure would cloud the articulation of the text, and potentially alter the meaning and the message of the words. In many areas of the world, the melodic content decreases when the textual content is more important, as in, for example, rap or opera. When it is less important to hear and understand the words, musicians are often freer to expand musical—especially melodic—material.

Mahāyāna Buddhist scriptures were originally developed in Sanskrit, but they have since appeared in every vernacular language in which Buddhism is practised. Buddhist services are essentially readings of doctrine, not occasions for worship in the Western sense. Their chant texts include words attributed to the Buddha himself, commentaries, statements of vows and of faith, dedications, mantras (recitation formulas), and hymns of praise.[9] One of the most important texts in the Mahāyāna tradition is the *Lotus sūtra*. Based on the sermons of the Buddha, it forms the basis for all the major Japanese sects of Buddhism, including the Pure Land and Nichiren sects.[10] Chinese, Tibetan, Korean, and non-Asian Buddhists use other texts specific to their cultures or translations of texts. Most importantly, the recitation of these texts is itself an act of worship.[11]

Instrumental music is most often used to demarcate aspects of Buddhist ritual. While Theravāda Buddhism relies more on non-musical chant,

Mahāyāna Buddhism uses a wide variety of wind as well as percussion instruments. These wind instruments include horns, double-reed oboe-type instruments, end-blown flutes, and conches. Drums are very common in Mahāyāna Buddhist ritual performance practice, and are associated metaphorically with the earliest days of the Buddha's teaching. "The act of proclaiming the Buddhist teaching is traditionally known as 'sounding the drum of the Dharma,'"[12] and the drum appears frequently in reference to Buddhist iconography.

Another important aspect of instrumental music in worship is its use in clockwise circumambulation around a *stūpa*, or funerary building. In walking around a *stūpa*—particularly if musicians are playing oboe-type instruments that employ circular breathing—the worshippers not only honour the Buddha and his teachings, but physically enact the movement of the sun around the cosmic mountain, as it is represented by the *stūpa*.[13] Circular breathing—the act of inhaling through the nose while expelling air through the lips—can in itself be a meditative practice that leads to tremendous focus and breath control. Musical performance is only one aspect that parallels circumambulation, however, as the latter is deeply associated with Buddhist devotional practice.

Mahāyāna Buddhist tradition includes a major offshoot, Mantrayāna Buddhism, and the Mahāyāna examples in this chapter come from the Mantrayāna traditions of Tibet and Japan.[14] This branch gives primacy to ritual and the transformation of consciousness through mantra, or sacred sound formulas. Mahāyāna Buddhism predominates in Central and East Asia and, since it is better known in the West, most studies of Buddhism and music are centred on those areas. From an intellectual and spiritual point of view, Mantrayāna Buddhism is represented by an epistemologically oriented approach to the human situation, codified in the Sūtras, and an experiential approach, codified in the Tantras. The Indian word *tantra* means, literally, "loom." In its expanded sense, the term may also refer to "living one's possibilities."[15]

Mantrayāna Buddhism developed by the eighth century CE, at least partly as a reaction to the excessively scholarly emphasis of earlier Mahāyāna. A discussion of music in the context of Mantrayāna (Sacred Sounds Vehicle) requires consideration of the many functions of music, and the ways in which sacred sounds work closely with other aspects of expression. In this context, one of the most important aspects of Mantrayāna Buddhism is that it relies on three forms of expression to symbolize the truth: mantras, which are spoken and chanted formulas; maṇḍalas, which are the representation through diagrams of cosmology (primarily visual); and *mudrās*, which are ritual gestures symbolic of religious truth.

Mantrayāna Buddhism is sometimes called Vajrayāna (Diamond Vehicle), Tantric Buddhism, or Esoteric Buddhism. Its essential approach is that one can accomplish enlightenment much more quickly than by expending effort stretched over the course of many lifetimes; one may even become enlightened in a single lifetime. Mantrayāna Buddhists pay special attention to ritual practices and intellectual discipline, and the emphasis on symbolic gesture, practice, and movement is crucial to proper performance of the rituals.

The next section focuses on two particular Buddhist traditions that derive from Mantrayāna: Tibetan Buddhism and Japanese Shingon Buddhism. As offshoots of Mahāyāna Buddhism, both use chant and instruments extensively, although the sounds are quite different. Both traditions also use basic monotone chanting of texts in addition to chants that include significant variation in melody or tone color.

Tibetan Buddhist Chant: *Dbyangs*

Buddhism in Tibet is characterized by adherence to Mantrayāna; however, four major schools have developed within Tibet, each with its own set of practices and important scriptural texts. Buddhism came to Tibet in the early eighth century CE, blending locally with Bön, an older religious practice that significantly influenced Buddhism's development. Herbert Guenther calls Tibetan Buddhism "a joint enterprise of philosophy, psychology, and the arts and sciences, as well as religion."[16] Prior to the Chinese invasion of Tibet in 1959, there were approximately thirteen thousand monasteries and nearly 20 per cent of the population belonged to a religious order. Tibetan Buddhism is present in Nepal and India, and can be found in any place where there are Tibetan refugees, including the Americas and Europe. Tibetan Buddhist music includes distinct regional differences in style, but each monastery is in contact with central mainstream traditions, and even the smallest monasteries have specialized roles for each person.

The use of sacred sound as a formula for the transformation of human consciousness is most apparent in the chanting of the Maṇi prayer to the Bodhisattva of Compassion, Avalokiteśvara (Tibetan, Chenrezig). All of the teachings of the Buddha are believed to be contained in this short, six-syllable mantra, which does not require initiation by a lāma and is the most widely used of all Buddhist prayers. As the Buddha taught that suffering was unnecessary, he offered various methods to root out the causes of suffering. The Mahāyāna school (Great Vehicle) believes that the practice of compassion is the surest means to remove all suffering from oneself as well as others. According to the Mantrayāna tradition of Tibet, the quickest and most powerful way to do this was by linking one's mind to the mind of Avalokiteśvara, the Bodhisattva of Compassion, through chanting of the Maṇi mantra. The act of chanting, which may be repeated indefinitely, enlarges the circle of compassion beyond oneself to all sentient beings, and completely removes attention from the desires of the individual ego. This chanting is often accompanied by rotating a Tibetan prayer wheel in one of various sizes. Though there are multiple meanings to this enigmatic formula, a literal translation and interpretation follows the text in both Sanskrit and Tibetan.

∤ EXAMPLE 5 (Track 38)
Maṇi Mantra to Avalokiteśvara. Collected and translated by the author.

Oṁ Maṇi Padme Hūṁ (*Sanskrit*).

Om Mani Peme Hung (*Tibetan*).

～

Behold! The Jewel is in the Lotus:
The practice of Compassion is united with Wisdom
to achieve the Buddha nature.

In considering Tibetan Buddhist chant, it is essential to rethink the entire concept of melody and rhythm. Many outside Tibetan culture are accustomed to think of melody as a sequence of rising or falling pitches. In Tibetan Tantric chanting, however, the melodic content occurs in terms of vowel modification and the careful contouring of tones. In other words, it is in the shift of timbre or tone color that the melodic content and forward movement occur. Because of the proliferation of CDs of Tibetan music, some Europeans and North Americans have come to recognize the very deep sounds and resonance of Tibetan Buddhist chanting, but few listeners follow the sounds much further beyond their superficial exoticism. In terms of rhythm, it is necessary to go beyond the idea of grouping notes in beats of twos and threes to dealing with extremely complicated, logorhythmic formulas that extend into the hundreds of beats. These rhythms not only form a link between song, ritual, dance, and drama, but also serve to enact or manifest aspects of Buddhist cosmology. The performance practice of Tibetan Buddhist chant occurs in multiple daily services, in which monks sit facing each other in rows. The leader, or *dbu mdzad*, not only leads the singing but also plays percussion. Tibetan chant falls into three categories: *'don* (recitation chant), *rta* (melodic chant), and *dbyangs* (tone contour chant). Of these three, *dbyangs* is the sound with which outsiders are most familiar. It is produced in such a way that listeners can perceive a very deep tone, a mid-level tone, and an upper harmonic tone, and this is referred to as a "chordal" chant. This multi-tone technique is related to the style of *khoomei* singing found in Mongolia and Tuva, and actually sounds as if one singer is producing two or three pitches simultaneously.[17] Some outsiders hear it only as a drone or as a single pitch, but it embodies the important technique of tonal contour chanting, which serves as a "note melody." An appropriate perception of it depends upon a willingness to train the ears to hear beyond the most obvious melodic feature of rising and falling pitch.

Dbyangs contour chanting, or Tibetan Tantric chant, is often performed in association with instrumental music, or *rol mo*, including cymbals (*sil snyan*), oboes (*ryga gling*) and long trumpets (*dung chen*). The cymbals symbolically create the mandala diagram through the way in which they are played: an imaginary line is drawn clockwise by the right cymbal around the rim of the left cymbal while accelerating pulses are played. Then the pattern goes from left to bottom centre, to upper right, and then from the lower right to top centre to lower left, crossing again. The cymbals are also played in decreasing mathematical formulas of even-numbered beats 180, 170, 160, 150, etc., and increasing by odd numbers. The trumpet players do their own contour playing as well, including trilling the tongue against the palate and buzzing the lips, shaping the cavity of their mouths to create overtones. The trumpets are six feet long and vibrate so powerfully against the players' skulls that only young people can play them; over a period of a year the teeth begin to loosen and can fall out. As in Japanese *shōmyō* chant, Tibetan Buddhist performance practice often includes an accelerating pattern (referred to as a "fall"); this pattern appears in the sound of the large cymbals.

⌐ EXAMPLE 6 (Track 39)
   Dbyangs: Tone Contour Chanting

Japanese Shingon Buddhism: *Shōmyō* chant

Buddhism came to Japan from Korea in the sixth century CE, and was essentially a part of the Mahāyāna tradition. Japanese Buddhists were in repeated contact with Chinese scholars over the next several hundred years, and Japan's location meant that it also came into contact with aspects of Theravāda Buddhism. All of the most important schools of Japanese Buddhism (including Zen, Nichiren, and Pure Land) arose during the Kamakura period (1185–1333 CE) and continue today. The most important text in the Japanese Buddhist tradition is the *Lotus Sūtra*, based on sermons preached by the Buddha. Its central thesis is that all life contains "buddha nature," or the capacity for compassion and the renunciation of desire. Acting on one's buddha nature through prayer, chant, and meditation brings one closer to nirvana and the goal of being released from the cycle of death and rebirth.

Japanese Buddhism is highly sectarian, but its initial form as a purveyor of Chinese culture and ideas included the theory and practice of chanting known as *shōmyō*. *Shōmyō* is believed to have originated with Vedic chanting in India, but the actual theory of notes, scales, melodies, and rhythms is believed to be more Chinese than Indian.[18] *Shōmyō* is sung in multiple languages, reflecting its origins in India (using the name *bonsan* for songs in Sanskrit) and its move through China (*kansan*) to Japan (*wasan*). The spread of Buddhist chant in Japan led to the adaptation of local musical styles, the use of local scales, and the evolution of local and sectarian performance of the tradition.

As in many other religious traditions, *shōmyō* performance occurs in a sacred space—in this case, a temple—and is preceded by a soloist performing the opening phrase. The soloist normally establishes a pitch for the other chanting monks to match, although they do not always choose to enter at the same pitch. Once the chanting has begun, it does not require a leader to sustain its momentum.

Different Buddhist sects in Japan, such as Shingon, Zen, and Nichiren, use varying amounts and types of percussion, including bells and chimes made of wood and/or metal. Percussion appears here as a means not only to establish the opening and closing of each section of the service, but also to mark out the sections of each day in the monastery. Two particular instruments appear frequently in Japanese Buddhist services: the *mokugyo* and the *uchiwa-daiko*. The *mokugyo* is a wooden slit gong with a handle. The *uchiwa-daiko*, or fan drum, used especially in the Nichiren sect, is a single-headed drum on a wooden handle, beaten with a stick. However, diversity in Japanese Buddhism means significant diversity in its use of percussion.

The esoteric branch of Japanese Buddhism is called Shingon, brought from China by Kūkai in the early ninth century CE. The word "Shingon" comes from the Chinese word for mantra (*chen-yen*), meaning "the word embodying a mysterious power that can bring about unusual effects, both spiritual and material."[19] This form of Buddhism stems from Indian Tantrism, which is also encountered in Tibet. Many *shōmyō* chant performances use a technique called "earthquake rhythm," a series of accelerating beats in the voice. These "beats" are one of the most characteristic rhythmic figures in Mantrayāna Buddhist musical practice.

While the *shōmyō* chant is probably the most important form of Buddhist vocal music in Japan, other kinds of Buddhist influence are dis-

Buddhist monk in meditative chant. Photograph courtesy of Guy L. Beck.

cernible throughout Japanese music and culture. For example, the classic Buddhist concept of emptiness (*śūnyatā*) is conveyed through *shakuhachi* performance. The *shakuhachi* bamboo flute, played by mendicant beggar-priests, has been widely recorded and features virtuosic playing techniques. One of the hallmarks of the *shakuhachi* performance is the skilful use of silence.[20] With a single instrument, judicious use of the "emptiness" of silence contributes tremendously to the overall "Buddhist" musicality of performance, just as absence is used to similar effect in Japanese art and architecture.

William Malm points out that Japanese Buddhist music functions as a means of appropriately symbolizing many important concepts of religious practice. In the following passage, he refers to the *o-gane*, or large hanging bell, that appears not only in temple grounds but also in representations of Japanese Buddhist culture by outsiders. The great Japanese classic, *Heike Monogatari* (The Tale of the Heike), begins and ends with the solemn tolling of such a bell, for it amply symbolizes the Buddhist concept of the impermanence of this world and the inextricable unity of life, death, and time. One might say that *shōmyō* destroys time in the sense that any deep religious meditation seems to escape temporality, but the *o-gane* symbolically restores a sequential regularity to life. The Buddhist tradition is rich with such ritualistic and artistic abstractions of its various religious precepts.[21]

In the Mahāyāna offshoot in Japan known as Zen, there is a strong monastic emphasis on the attainment of the nonverbal Buddhist experience of satori. Satori is similar to nirvana, except that it arrives suddenly and unexpectedly. Monks practise severe austerities in the monastery for many years in order to prepare their mind for satori. As there is a de-emphasis on texts and language, there are fewer chances for vocal music. While some instruments are used to punctuate the daily schedule, especially the bell, art music as such does not exist, reflecting some of the early Theravāda attitudes. However, there are Zen chants that, as with *shōmyō*, serve to focus attention and remove distractions for meditation. The following *Great Wisdom-Perfection Heart Sūtra* is often chanted in unison by groups of Zen monks and Jōdō nuns in Japan before or after a meditation sitting. With less than three hundred syllables, it is easy to memorize, and captures the essential elements of Buddhist teaching. However, it is believed that the benefits of the chant, concentration, and spiritual immersion are easily obtained without even understanding the meaning of the words. Approximately one-half of the complete chant is presented below in Example 7.

| EXAMPLE 7 (Track 40)
Hannya Shingyo. Prajñā Pāramitā Sūtra or "Great Wisdom-Perfection Heart Sūtra." Text (originally in Sanskrit) in Japanese as *Hannya Shingyo*, translated by Allen Ginsberg. From the website http://www.rockument.com/Prajna.html.

MA KA HAN NYA HA RA MIT TA SHIN GYO

KAN JI ZAI BO SATSU GYO JIN HAN NYA HA RA MIT TA JI SHO KEN
GO UN KAI KU DO ISSAI KU YAKU
SHA RI SHI SHIKI FU I KU KU FU I SHIKI SHIKI SOKU ZE KU KU
SOKU ZE SHIKE JU SO GYO SHIKI JU SO GYO SHIKI YAKU BU NYO
ZE SHA RI SHI ZE SHO HO KU SO FU SHO FU METSU FU KU FU JO
FU ZO FU GEN ZE KO KU CHU MU SHIKI MU JU SO GYO
SHIKI MU GEN NI BI ZETS SHIN NI MU SHIKI SHO KO MI SOKU HO
MU GEN KAI NAI SHI MU I SHIKI KAI MU MU MYO YAKU MU MU MYO
JIN NAI SHI MU RO SHI YAKU MU RO SHI JIN MU KU SHU

Great Prajñā Pāramitā Sūtra

Avalokiteśvara bodhisattva practices deep prajñā pāramitā.
When perceive five skandhas
all empty, relieve every suffering.
Sāriputra, form not different (from) emptiness.
Emptiness not different (from) form.
Form is the emptiness. Emptiness is the form.
Sensation, thought, active substance,
consciousness, also like this.
Sāriputra, this everything original character;
not born, not annihilated not tainted, not
pure, (does) not increase, (does) not decrease.
Therefore in emptiness no form, no
sensation, thought, active substance, consciousness.
No eye, ear, nose, tongue, body,
mind; no color, sound, smell, taste, touch, object; no eye,
World of eyes until we come to also no world of consciousness;
no ignorance, also no ignorance
Annihilation, until we come to no old age, death, also no old age, death,
also no old age, death, annihilation of no suffering, cause of suffering.

The Japanese traditions of Mahāyāna Buddhism, some relying heavily on ritual and symbolism, developed in tandem with Shintoism and blended with it in some areas until the nineteenth century, when the government stepped in to break the two practices apart once more. In twenty-first century Japan, Buddhism is an important aspect of Japanese culture, and its many sects, including Shingon, Jōdō (Pure Land), and Zen, have continued to flourish.

Music as a spiritual discipline

All the major Buddhist schools deal directly with the concept of change and impermanence. Part of human suffering is that people desire to hold on to something permanent when, in fact, all of reality is transient in nature. Music, because it is constantly shifting in time and space so obviously, teaches performers and listeners about the material world, which is also constantly shifting in time and space around them. Since they cannot really possess something so transient, listening to music serves to assist them in letting go of both desire and the individual sense of self. As Ter Ellingson points out, "the Buddhist concept of an impermanent music resulting from temporary combinations of causes and conditions reflects basic Buddhist religious beliefs."[22]

In many aspects of Buddhist practice, chant and instrumental music are responsible for making manifest an important segment of belief. Chanting requires great control over one's breathing as well as over one's vocal cords, and that intense control sustained over long periods of time can lead one to a meditative state. Chanting certainly is capable of assisting in the creation of a heightened state of consciousness in the performer. When a person performs Buddhist music as part of a crowd of chanters, the individual self disappears into the Saṅgha, or community, eliminating the problem noted by the Buddha himself of attaching importance to one's individual voice. Group chanting, mostly in unison, causes the self to become absorbed into the community.

Instrumental and vocal music are assigned differing degrees of spiritual weight, depending on local traditions. Buddhism's syncretic nature allows its practitioners considerable freedom to adapt and adopt local practices, depending on how important the voice is to spiritual communication or to the maintenance of community. Because song and chant generally contain lyrical meaning, the voice may be used to teach, to proselytize, and to enact prayer in the body of the practitioner. In the case of repetitively chanted mantras, specific sounds create physiologically appropriate reactions in the body of the chanter as well as in those of the listeners. Furthermore, Buddhists believe that "music consists not only of the 'actually present music' produced by sound-making voices and instruments but also the 'mentally produced music' perceived and imagined by each listener."[23] The combination of the two locations for music—the voice and the mind—leads to greater intensification of worshipful action.

Buddhist music also offers a ritual framework for performance, just as being involved in monastic life offers a ritual framework for each day. The musical marking of beginnings and endings of ritual segments, the performance of chant, and the logical progression from one piece to the next all serve to move rituals through time. Through the participatory nature of listening, being within hearing distance of Buddhist chant or instrumental music also helps to create a sense of ritual space. It is not simply hearing the sound that makes one a Buddhist; it is the years of training and conditioning in understanding the texts, the rituals, and the sounds that lead one to attain the appropriate state of mind.

In addition to helping practitioners to memorize and teach, musical chant also has a number of essential functions in religious practice. Although some Buddhist traditions use notation, the musical sound itself serves as a form of mental notation on which practitioners may draw. Ian Mabbett points out the importance of Buddhist music for evangelical purposes, as cosmological symbolism, as ritual framework, as ritual offering, as a means to dissolve the individual into a larger religious body, and as a means of inducing an altered state of consciousness.²⁴ Each of these functions is crucial not only in binding religious communities together, but particularly in building a spiritual foundation for the individual practitioner.

Current trends and the future of Buddhist music

In recent years, various forms of Buddhism have become fixtures in the religious life of the Americas and Europe, where Buddhism has seen increasing popularity. Major immigrant communities in the United States, Canada, and Europe have established temples of worship, and an increasing number of non-Asians have turned to Buddhism.

The production of three popular Hollywood films about Tibet—*Little Buddha* (1993), *Seven Years in Tibet* (1997), and *Kundun* (1997)—has increased outside contact with Buddhist music, but exclusively with only Tibetan Buddhist chant. His Holiness the Dalai Lama attracts huge crowds of Westerners to his lectures but, again, the message is that of Tibetan Buddhism. The Buddhist music of China, Japan, and Korea is far less well known outside Asia,²⁵ even though North America and Europe include communities of practising East Asian Buddhists. The use of Tibetan Buddhist chant in popular music and in advertising has led to the impression among outsiders that the "drone" of chant best serves as an underpinning for newly composed "melodies." It should be understood, however, that Tibetan *dbyangs* already contains "melody" in the form of tonal contours—if one knows what to listen for—and its depth and richness need no enhancement.

It is in Mahāyāna Buddhism that sacred sound in performance is fully realized, and where the cosmological significance of Buddhism is physically enacted through musical concepts and behaviors. Whether it appears in the highlighting of silence and emptiness through the sounds of a bamboo flute in Japan or in the constantly moving progression of sound through time as a reminder of life's impermanence, Buddhist music represents an enactment of Buddhist ideals and practices.

Notes

1 Having been sheltered from disease, poverty, and death during his early life, the Buddha became aware of those aspects of existence only as a young adult. It was this awareness that led to his renunciation of his life of luxury, which included his own wife and child.

2 Huston Smith (1991), 117.

3 Hīnayāna and Theravāda are not interchangeable terms, however. Theravāda should be considered a subset of Hīnayāna.

4 Peter Harvey (1990), 90.

5 Huston Smith (1991), 126.

6 The *Vinaya Piṭakam* II, 108/31.

7 John Ross Carter (1983), 137.

8 Many Christians and Muslims also rely on more than one text, although the Bible and the Qur'ān are absolutely central to their religious practice.

9 Peter Crossley-Holland (1980), 410.

10 Malcolm David Eckel (1998), 251.

11 The term "recitation" is perhaps too limiting. Tibetan prayer wheels, which are covered with lines from the *sūtras*, are "activated" (the prayer is considered to have been performed) when they are spun. Copying out lines from the sūtras also "counts" as an act of worship.

12 Ter Ellingson (1987a), 497.

13 These *stūpa* were often placed at pre-Buddhist sacred sites, blending together the pre-Buddhist with the Buddhist. The symbolism of the *stūpa* is pervasive in Buddhist cultures, from the importance of mountains to the significance of the Bodhi Tree. Peter Harvey (1990: 78) notes that "The Buddhist stūpa probably developed from pre-Buddhist burial mounds for kings, heroes and saints, which go back into prehistory in many cultures. They became important in Buddhism due to the holy relics they contained, their symbolizing the Buddha…, and in some cases their location at significant sites."

14 Although the word Tibet is used freely in this chapter, the reader should note that Tibet refers also to Tibet-in-exile, including especially the cultural practices of those Tibetans living in Nepal and India.

15 Herbert Guenther (1987), 406.

16 Ibid.

17 Producing two of the three tones is less difficult for outsiders than it may seem. The singer first makes a groaning sound without exhaling or voicing the sound, and then very gently lets out a relatively low-pitched tone. With practice, the two sounds will combine to trick the ear into hearing the low sound two octaves down…much lower than the person can actually "sing." To create the upper harmonic, the singer says "oh," and shifts the internal contours of the mouth, lips, and nose, as if playing a jaw harp, without exhaling. Combining both techniques brings a close approximation of what Tibetan Buddhists spend decades of their lives perfecting.

18 William P. Malm (1959), 65.

19 Tamaru Noriyoshi (1987), 430.

20 Ian W. Mabbett (1993–94), 19.

21 William P. Malm (1959), 71.

22 Ter Ellingson (1987b), 165.

23 Ibid.

24 Ian W. Mabbett (1993–94).

25 Tian Oing (1994), 63.

Bibliography

Bercholz, Samuel, and Sherab Chödzin Kohn, eds. *Entering the Stream: An Introduction to the Buddha and His Teachings*. Boston, MA: Shambhala Press, 1993.

Carter, John Ross. "Music in the Theravāda Buddhist Heritage: In Chant, in Song, in Sri Lanka." In *Sacred Sound: Music in Religious Thought and Practice,* ed. Joyce Irwin, 127–47. Chico, CA: Scholars Press, 1983.

Crossley-Holland, Peter. "Buddhist Music." In *The New Grove Dictionary of Music and Musicians,* ed. Stanley Sadie, 3: 417–21. New York: Macmillan, 1980.

Eckel, Malcolm David. "Buddhism." In *The Illustrated Guide to World Religions,* ed. Michael David Coogan, 163–97. New York and London: Oxford University Press, 1998.

Ellingson, Ter. "Drums." In *The Encyclopedia of Religion,* ed. Mircea Eliade, 4: 494–503. New York: Macmillan, 1987a.

———. "Music and Religion." In *The Encyclopedia of Religion,* ed. Mircea Eliade, 10: 163–72. New York: Macmillan, 1987b.

Guenther, Herbert V. "Buddhism in Tibet." In *The Encyclopedia of Religion,* ed. Mircea Eliade, 2: 406–14. New York: Macmillan, 1987.

———. *Tibetan Buddhism in Western Perspective.* Berkeley, CA: Dharma Publications, 1989 (1977).

Harvey, Peter. *An Introduction to Buddhism: Teachings, History, and Practices.* Cambridge: Cambridge University Press, 1990.

Mabbett, Ian W. "Buddhism and Music." *Asian Music Journal* 25 (1993–94): 9–28.

Malm, William P. *Japanese Music and Musical Instruments.* Rutland, VT: Charles E. Tuttle, 1959.

Noriyoshi, Tamaru. "Buddhism in Japan." In *The Encyclopedia of Religion,* ed. Mircea Eliade, 2: 426–35. New York: Macmillan, 1987.

Smith, Huston. *The World's Religions: Our Great Wisdom Traditions.* New York: Harper Collins, 1991.

Tarocco, Francesca. "Buddhist Music." In *The New Grove Dictionary of Music and Musicians,* 2nd ed., ed. Stanley Sadie, 4: 549–53. New York: Macmillan, 2001.

Tian Qing. "Recent Trends in Buddhist Music Research in China." *British Journal of Ethnomusicology* 3 (1994): 63–72.

GLOSSARY

Ādi Granth—"Original Book." The sacred scripture of the Sikhs compiled by Guru Arjan in 1603-4. It is commonly known as the Guru Granth Sahib.

Adonai Malach—laudatory Hebrew prayer mode that roughly parallels the Arabic Siga or Ecclesiastical Mixolydian modes.

Ahavah Rabah—supplicatory Hebrew prayer mode that resembles the Arabic Hijaz-Kar or Ecclesiastical Phrygian modes, with 3rd and 7th degrees raised a half-step.

Akāl Purakh—"The One beyond Time." Sikh concept of the divine Being, analogous to God.

Anāhata Nāda—"Unstruck Melody." The eternally sounding melodious vibration that permeates all space. Found in Hindu and Sikh traditions.

Antiphon—sacred song from antiquity involving call and response. A compositional form in which two separate choir groups alternate, found today mostly in Gregorian chant.

Apotropaia—the act of "chasing away" evil spirits or demons from a rite or community, as in the Theravāda rituals of *paritta*.

AUM (Oṁ)—the primal syllable used as a prefix in nearly all Vedic and Hindu mantras or chants. This phoneme, also known as *Pranava*, is said to contain the entire Sanskrit alphabet in seed form. It plays a critical role in Hindu rites and also prefaces concerts of vocal classical music.

Bhajan—devotional song in praise of a deity; also refers to *kīrtana*, usually a separate genre from classical music. Also called *nam-bhajan* or *nam-kīrtan* when utilizing names of a deity primarily.

Bhakti—devotion to god. This refers to the emotional dimension of Hindu worship that is best served through music. Other dimensions are knowledge (*jñana*) and action (*karma*).

Chasidim—devout eighteenth-century Polish/Jewish adherents of saintly religious leaders known as *Tzaddikim*.

Chaunkī—a division of each day in the larger *gurdwārās* (particularly, in the Golden Temple at Amritsar) in which a particular selection of *bānī* is sung. There are five to eight *chaunkīs* for each day.

Chazzan—a cantor who leads the prayer chant in a synagogue.

Dbyangs—Tibetan Buddhist tone contour chants.

Dhrupad—the original form of Hindustani music (from the older *dhruva* songs of antiquity), which was made up mostly of vocal stanzas in the Braj Bhasha language (a dialect of Hindi), and sung in the Hindu and Moghul courts in the medieval period. This music was formal in structure (four parts) with strict adherence to the purity of the *rāga* (melodic scale) and *tāla* (rhythmic cycle) with regulated improvisation around the texts, which were mostly devotional and Vaishnava (devoted to Krishna) in character.

Dukkha—suffering (in all Indian traditions).

Epiclesis—the act of "calling down" or invoking the presence of God or gods at a rite, as in calling down the Holy Spirit in the Roman Catholic Mass.

Ethos—mood of a prayer mode, created by inventive rearrangement of seemingly unrelated phrases into unexpected sequences, tempos, rhythms, and voice qualities.

Gurbānī kīrtan—devotional singing of the Sikh Gurus' compositions. It is also called *shabad kīrtan*.

Gurmat Sangīt—"Music in the Guru's view." Sacred music of the Sikhs.

Hīnayāna—"Lesser Vehicle." One of the major approaches to Buddhism.

Inshād—non-canonical Islamic hymns expressing devotion to the Prophet Muhammad and other religious figures.

Japa—the act of repeating mantras or divine names, counted normally on rosary beads of the joints of the fingers. These mantras are often intoned. Also called *nāma-japa*.

Kar—ecclesiastical Phrygian mode with 3rd and 7th degrees raised a half-step.

Kinnor—a lyre in the Hebrew Bible, akin to the Greek *kithara*.

Kīrtan—"Singing of hymns of praise." Hindu and Sikh traditions.

Kriti—a vocal genre of South Indian Karnatic music, pioneered by many of the famous saints associated with temples. The genre consists of three parts with some improvisation, with songs which were devotional in character in honour of Hindu deities and saints performed in Tamil, Telugu, Kannada, and Malayalam.

Magein Avot—didactic Hebrew prayer mode that approximates the Arabic Bayat-Nava, or Ecclesiastical Dorian modes.

Mahāyāna—"Great Vehicle." One of the major approaches to Buddhism.

Majlis—Shī'a religious assemblies during Muharram with hymns that express grief (*soz* and *nanha*) over the deaths at Karbalā.

Maṇḍala—an expression of cosmology, often visual, in Buddhism.

Mantra—spoken and chanted formulas.

Mantrayāna—"Sacred Sounds Vehicle." Part of Mahāyāna Buddhism.

Milad—Sunnī religious assemblies that include recitation of *na't* poems in praise of the Prophet Muhammad.

Mudrā—ritual gestures symbolic of religious truth in Hindu and Buddhist traditions.

Nāda-Brahman—sacred sound, including both the concept of *Sabda-Brahman* (linguistic word) and non-linguistic, or non-verbal, sound, such as music. *Nāda* as causal or unmanifest sound is called *Anāhata* or "unstruck" sound; when manifest, it is called *Āhata*, or "struck" sound.

Nām Simaran—"Remembrance of the Name." The devotional practice of meditating on the Divine Name in Sikhism.

Nām—"The Divine Name." A summary expression of the total being of Akal Purakh in Sikhism. Also refers to Hindu names of God.

Piyyut—Hebrew religious poem written in metrical form.

Purāṇa—early Hindu literatures containing mythologies and detailing religious rites and practices. The early history of music is described here involving gods and goddesses like Brahmā, Sarasvatī, Śiva, and Krishna, and divine beings like the Gandharvas, including Nārada Rishi.

Rāga—"musical mode or melodic organization." A series of five or more notes on which a melody is based. In the modal system of Indian music, a number of different modes or combinations of notes are identified for their individual emotive "flavour," and set to a fixed structure that includes a starting note, a final note, between five and seven notes ascending and descending, the use of accidentals, flats, and sharps, and unique phrasing.

Samā—Sufi assemblies of "divine listening" that include devotional music (*qawwālī*) and special hymns (*ḥamd*).

Sāman—Vedic verses set to music, primarily from the Sāma-Veda, the musical Veda. *Sāmans* are sung by priests called *udgātrīs* at Vedic rituals (*yajñas*) and *soma* sacrifices to the god Indra and others.

Saṅgha—Buddhist communities.

Saṅgīta—the term in Sanskrit for music, but which consists of three parts: vocal, instrumental, and dance.

Sarasvatī—Goddess of learning and music in Hinduism. She is the patron of the arts, and all students of Indian music recognize her as the matrix of melody and rhythm. She plays the *vīṇā*, one of the oldest instruments in the world, and is said to be the ancestor of all stringed instruments, including the piano and guitar.

Shabad Kīrtan—hymn singing in the Sikh tradition.

Shofar—ram's horn in the Hebrew Bible, used as a signaling instrument.

Shōmyō—Japanese Buddhist chant.

Stūpa—a round, usually domed building, used to house a Buddhist shrine.

Sūtra—the teachings of the Buddha.

Ta'am—Hebrew term for neume, a symbol indicating relative pitch and contour of a note grouping to be sung to the biblical word where it appears.

Tajwīd—the elaborate rule system governing the recitation of the Qur'ān (*qir'āt*).

Tāla—rhythm system in Indian music that is based on the notion of time cycles, rather than time signatures. Each particular rhythm pattern or *Tāla* contains a number of *tālas* (claps), *khālīs* (open hands), and other blank beats called *mātrās*, which add up to a total that is repeated indefinitely but variable in tempo.

Tānhā—desire, in Pali.

Tantra—the experiential approach to Buddhism and Hinduism.

Tefillat Haregesh—emotional, free-wheeling style of synagogue prayer.

Tefillat Haseider—orderly, predictable style of synagogue prayer.

Theravāda—part of Hīnayāna Buddhism.

Threnody—song of lamentation for the dead.

Tzaddikim—saintly religious leaders of eighteenth-century Polish Jewry, who lifted the yoke of ritual requirements so that their devout adherents—*Chasidim*—might have easier access to God.

Ugav—pipe in the Hebrew Bible, similar to the Greek *aulos*.

Vaishnava—the majority branch of Hinduism, containing the worship of Vishnu, Nārāyaṇa, Krishna, and Rāma. These deities are important objects of musical devotion. Śaivism denotes the worship of the deity of Śiva in his many forms, and Śāktā (and/or Tantra) refers to the worship of goddesses like Durgā and Kālī. All of the deities in Hindu traditions are worshipped with mantras and musical compositions.

Vedas—the oldest religious texts in the world and the basis for Hindu revelation, the Vedas are a large body of Sanskrit hymns and verse that lay the foundation of Hindu rites and practices, going back nearly six thousand years. These texts were memorized for millennia by priests known as *brahmins*, and contain the seeds of Indian musical thought. The Upanishads are the later philosophical portions of the Vedic literature.

CD TRACK LISTING

Recording, engineering, and mastering of CD by
Sanford Hinderlie of the College of Music,
Loyola University, New Orleans.

Judaism

1 **1st Question of Passover** (ex 1)
Sung by Joseph A. Levine.
From the accompanying CD 2, track 11, to Joseph A. Levine, *Synagogue Song in America* (Northvale, NJ: Jason Aronson, 2000), Ex 6.6a.
All tracks courtesy of Jason Aronson.

2 **High Holiday Prayer** (ex 4)
Sung by Joseph A. Levine.
From the accompanying CD 2, track 7, to Joseph A. Levine (2000),
Ex 6.2d.

3 **Shema** (ex 5)
Sung by Joseph A. Levine.
From the accompanying CD 1, track 20, to Joseph A. Levine (2000),
Ex 2.12a, b.

4 **Torah** (ex 6)
Sung by Joseph A. Levine.
From the accompanying CD 1, track 27, to Joseph A. Levine (2000),
Ex 3.10.

5 **Passover Haggadah** (ex 7)
Sung by Joseph A. Levine.
From the accompanying CD 3, track 6, to Joseph A. Levine (2000),
Ex 7.6c.

6 **Night Prayer** (ex 8)
Sung by Joseph A. Levine.
From the accompanying CD 3, track 13, to Joseph A. Levine (2000),
Ex 8.4.

7 **Priestly Blessing** (ex 9)
Sung by Joseph A. Levine.
From the accompanying CD 2, track 5, to Joseph A. Levine (2000),
Ex 5.12c.

Christianity

TRACK

8 **Kyrie, Sanctus, Agnus Dei** (ex 1)
Sung by Richard L. Crocker.
From the accompanying CD to Richard L. Crocker, *Introduction to
Gregorian Chant* (New Haven, CT: Yale University Press, 2000),
tracks 16, 18, 19. Courtesy of Yale University Press.

9 **A Mighty Fortress** (ex 2)
From the CD *Best Loved Hymns* HCP2 2894 (Nashville, TN: Madacy
Entertainment Group, 2001), track 5. Courtesy of Countdown Media
GmbH.

10 **Salve Regina** (ex 3)
Sung by Richard Crocker.
From *A Gregorian Archive*. (Berkeley, CA: Emeritus Press, 2004).
Courtesy of Richard L. Crocker.

11 **I'll Praise My Maker** (ex 4)
Sung by Gerald Hobbs, 2001.

12 **Holy Holy Holy** (ex 5)
From the CD *Best Loved Hymns* HCP2 2894 (Nashville, TN: Madacy
Entertainment Group, 2001), track 2. Courtesy of Countdown Media
GmbH.

13 **All Things Bright and Beautiful** (ex 6)
Sung by Gerald Hobbs, 2001.

14 **Amazing Grace** (ex 7)
From the CD *Best Loved Hymns* HCP2 2893 (Nashville, TN: Madacy
Entertainment Group, 2001), track 1. Courtesy of Countdown Media
GmbH.

Islam

TRACK

15 **Call to Prayer: Adhān** (ex 1)
Collected by the editor from old recordings.

16 **Qur'ān:** Al-Fātiḥa (ex 2)
Recited by Hafiz Kani Karaca.
From the CD, *The Music of Islam*, Volume 10, Qur'ān Recitation (Tucson,
AZ: Celestial Harmonies, 1997), track 2. Courtesy of Celestial
Harmonies.

17 **Ai Nasim e-ku-e** (ex 3)
Sung by Regula Qureshi, 2001.

18 **Allāh Allāh Allāhu** (ex 4)
Sung by Regula Qureshi, 2001.

19 **Mujrayi Shah** (ex 5)
Sung by Regula Qureshi, 2001.

20 **Ai wa-e-nahr-e alquaman** (ex 6)
Sung by Regula Qureshi, 2001.

Hinduism

TRACK

21 **Gāyatrī Mantra** (ex 1)
Chanted by Guy L. Beck, 2005

22 **Rig Veda:** Purusha Sūktam (ex 2)
Chanted by Sri Hariswamy and Vedaparayanar.
Excerpted from track 1 of the CD *Vedic Chanting/Sanskrit* (New Delhi:
Super Cassettes, 1995), SSKNCD 01/13. Courtesy of Super Cassettes.

23 **Bhagavad Gītā** 18.65–66 (ex 3)
Chanted by Guy L. Beck, 2005.

24 **Dhrupad:** Dekho Sakhī Vrindābana (ex 4)
Sung by Pandit Bidur Mallik and Family.
Excerpted from track 7 of the CD *India: Dhrupad of Darbhanga/
The Mallik Family* (Geneva: Archives Internationales de Musique
Populaire, 2000). VDE CD 1006. Courtesy of Archives Internationales
de Musique Populaire.

25 **Padāvali Kīrtan:** Śrī Nanda Nandana (ex 5)
Sung by Guy L. Beck, 1979.

26 **Bhajan of Sūr Dās:** Aba Merī Rākho Lāja Hari (ex 6)
Sung by Guy L. Beck.
Excerpted from track 6 of the CD *Sacred Rāga* (New Orleans: STR Digital,
1999), STR-9901, by Guy L. Beck. Courtesy of STR Digital Records.

27 Raghupati Rāghava (ex 8)
Sung by Sonu Nigam.
Excerpted from track 11 of the CD *Aarties & Bhajans from Films* (New Delhi: Super Cassettes, 1997). SVCD 1305. Courtesy of Super Cassettes.

Sikhism

TRACK

28 Japjī Prayer (ex 1)
Chanted by Ragi Bhai Tirlochan Singh Ji.
Excerpted from track 1 of the CD *Jap Jī Sāhib Raehraas Sāhib* (*Punjabi Devotional*) (New Delhi: Super Cassettes, 1996), SNCD 01/144. Courtesy of Super Cassettes.

29 Shabad of Guru Arjan: Har Kirtan Sune (ex 2)
Sung by Bhai Nirmal Singh Ji.
Excerpted from track 3 of the CD *Har Kirtan Sune, Har Kirtan Gaavai* (New Delhi: Super Cassettes, 1999). SNCD 01/1436. Courtesy of Super Cassettes.

30 Shabad of Kabīr: Har Kā Bilovanā (ex 3)
Sung by Bhai Harjinder Singh Ji.
Excerpted from track 1 of the CD *Satgur Bachan Tumhare* (New Delhi: Super Cassettes, 1998). SNCD 01/1295. Courtesy of Super Cassettes.

31 Kaisī Āratī Hoye (ex 4)
Sung by Bhai Harbans Singh Ji.
Excerpted from track 2 of the CD *Gur Kā Darshan* (New Delhi: Living Media, 2003). CD-D02106. Courtesy of Living Media Productions.

32 So Dar (ex 5)
Sung by Pashaura Singh, 2001.

33 Anand (ex 6)
Sung by Pashaura Singh, 2001.

Buddhism

TRACK

34 Drum Invocation
From the audiotape *Santi Pirit* (Kolkata: Mahābodhi Book Agency, n.d.), track 1. Courtesy of Mahābodhi Society.

35 Invocation: Mangalacharanam, Three Gems: Trisaraṇam (ex 1)
Chanted by Theravāda monks from the Mahābodhi Society, Calcutta.
From the audiotape *Santi Pirit*, track 2. Courtesy of Mahābodhi Society.

36 Five Precepts: Pañchaśīlā (ex 2)
Chanted by Theravāda monks from the Mahābodhi Society, Calcutta.
From the audiotape *Santi Pirit*, track 3. Courtesy of Mahābodhi Society.

37 Four Noble Truths: Dhamma Chakka Sutta (ex 3)
Excerpted from track 6 of the CD *Sri Lanka: Musiques rituelles et religieuses*
(Paris: Ocora Radio France, 1992). Courtesy of Ocora Radio France.

38 Tibet Mantra: Oṁ Maṇi Padme Hūṁ (ex 5)
Collected by the editor from recordings of Tibetan monks of the
Drepung Monastery made at Syracuse University, 1989.

39 Tibet Contour Chant (ex 6)
Collected by the editor from recordings of Tibetan monks of the
Drepung Monastery made at Syracuse University, 1989.

40 Japanese Heart Sūtra: Hannya-Shingyo (ex 7)
Chanted by women of the Jōdō sect in Kyoto, Japan.
Excerpted from track 2 of the CD *Buddhist Drums, Bell & Chants* (New
York: Lyrichord Discs, nd), LYRCO 7200. Courtesy of Lyrichord Records.

CONTRIBUTORS

Guy L. Beck has spent over six years in India studying and researching Indian music and religion, receiving support from both Fulbright and AIIS (American Institute of Indian Studies) research grants for his work. He holds an MA in musicology and a PhD in religion from Syracuse University, as well as degrees in Indian music from institutions in India. His book *Sonic Theology: Hinduism and Sacred Sound* (1993) won wide acclaim from scholars for its presentation of the theoretical dimensions of sacred sound and music in Hinduism. He also has published numerous articles on various aspects of Indian religion and music, as well as releasing a CD, *Sacred Raga* (1999), which demonstrates his performative expertise in Indian vocal music. As a result, he has received invitations from many universities, including Indiana and Princeton, to give lectures and demonstrations. In 2001, he was invited to be a Visiting Fellow by the Oxford Centre for Hindu Studies at Oxford University (UK), where he taught courses in Hinduism and music, and received additional support from the Infinity Foundation for research on the contributions of Indic traditions to world music. He has taught courses in religious studies and music at Tulane University, in New Orleans, and is currently teaching at the University of North Carolina-Wilmington.

Gerald Hobbs is vice-principal of the Vancouver School of Theology. He holds a BA (Hon.) from the University of Toronto, a BD from Emmanuel College in Toronto, and a Docteur ès Sciences Religieuses degree from the Faculté de Théologie Protestante in Strasbourg. His doctoral work focused on Martin Bucer's German and Latin commentaries on the Psalms, which he is editing and annotating for a critical edition of Bucer's work. Dr. Hobbs has also published extensively in Reformation studies, the history of biblical interpretation (particularly on the Psalms), and the music of the Christian church.

Before going to the Vancouver School of Theology, he taught at Huntington College in Sudbury and at the Université de Genève. He served as part-time chaplain with the Canadian Forces in Germany and Italy, and has also taught in Strasbourg, Paris, and Glasgow as a visiting professor.

Joseph A. Levine studied fine arts at the Cooper Union, and earned a BA in religious education at Yeshiva University and a PhD in sacred music at the Jewish Theological Seminary, where he taught modal chant. He lectures extensively on the aesthetic dimension of synagogue practice, and his text, *Synagogue Song in America* (1989), has been recognized as the most important study of Jewish music in the past fifty years. His articles have appeared in the *Encyclopedia of Jewish American History and Culture, the Gratz College Centennial, the Journal of Synagogue Music,* the *Maryland Jewish Historical Society Journal, Midstream, Musica Judaica,* and the *National Jewish Post.* He has also written monographs on the life and times of cantors David Kusevitsky, Josef Rosenblatt, and Abba Yosef Weisgal. An active cantor himself for thirty-five years, he is currently a faculty member at the Academy for Jewish Religion in New York. He serves on the editorial board of the Cantors Assembly, as well as on the Rabbinical Assembly Committee preparing a new High Holiday prayer book for the Conservative movement. His recently published *Rise and Be Seated: The Ups and Downs of Jewish Worship* (2000) deals with the ongoing creative process involved in the way Jews have approached God in prayer since biblical times.

Regula Qureshi is director of the Centre for Ethnomusicology at the University of Alberta. Her research focuses on music as a social and discursive process. A specialist in South Asian, Islamic, and Canadian musical practices, she is the author of *Sufi Music of India and Pakistan: Sound, Context, and Meaning in Qawwali* (1986), coeditor of *Voices of Women: Essays in Honour of Violet Archer* (1995), and a contributor to *Ethnomusicology, Asian Music, the Journal of Musicology,* and the *Journal of the American Musicological Society.* A cellist and *sārangī* player, her current book projects are *Hindustani Musicians Speak* and *Sārangī: Art Music and Political Economy in North India.*

Pashaura Singh is a professor in the Department of Religious Studies at the University of California, Riverside, where he teaches courses in Sikhism and religion. His dissertation topic (University of Toronto) was *The Text and Meaning of the Ādi Granth,* and his more recent research has focused on the life and teaching of Guru Arjan. He is the author of *Guru Granth Sāhib: Canon, Meaning and Authority* (2001) and *The Bhagats of the Guru Granth Sāhib: Sikh Self-Definition and the Bhagat Bānī* (2003). He also performs Sikh Kīrtan and specializes in Gurbānī Shabad hymns.

Sean Williams has a BA in music from the University of California at Berkeley, and an MA and PhD in ethnomusicology from the University of Washington. Her subject areas include ethnomusicology, Indonesian language and literature, Celtic languages and literature, and Southeast Asian studies. She is currently a faculty member at the Evergreen State College in Olympia, Washington. Her recent book, *The Sound of the Ancestral Ship: Highland Music of West Java* (2001) follows her work as co-editor of *Southeast Asia* (*Garland Encyclopedia of World Music*. Vol. 4. 1998). A recognized authority on Buddhist chant, she gives many lectures and demonstrations.

DISCOGRAPHY

Judaism

The Music of the Bible (Harmonia Mundi, 2000), based on a recently discovered ancient notation, contains reconstructed vocal and instrumental settings of the music of the Hebrew Bible as it may have sounded in ancient times, including seven psalms, and passages from Deuteronomy, Numbers, Exodus, Lamentations, and 2 Samuel. Modern Jewish liturgical music is finely represented in a trilogy of CD recordings by Cantor Adolphe Attia of Paris (Harmonia Mundi, 1994, 1996, 1998). *Jewish Liturgical Music*, vol. 1, contains the "Kol Nidre" and the Kaddish. *The Great Jewish Liturgical Feasts*, vol. 2 contains a rendition of the Shema, the Kaddish, and "Kol Nidre." *Synagogue Chants*, vol. 3, contains the Shema as well as other prayers. Early twentieth-century recordings of the "Golden Age of Cantors" can be heard on *Mysteries of the Sabbath: Classic Cantorial Recordings 1907–1947* (Yazoo/Shanachie, 1994), remastered from old 78-rpm recordings. Authentic renditions are also found on *Kol Nidre: Sacred Music of the Synagogue* (EMI Classics, 1995). *The Jewish Experience: Passover* and *The Jewish Experience: Chanukkah* (both from Delta Music, 1994), narrated by Theodore Bikel, present traditional and domestic songs of two Jewish festivals. In *Our Hope*, by the Male Choir of the Cantor Art Academy (MK/Olympia, 1993), there are splendid choral arrangements of "Shalom Aleychem," "Hava Nagila," and "Hatikva." An excellent example of a woman cantor is found in the recording of Cantor Rebecca Garfein of New York, entitled *Sacred Chants of the Contemporary Synagogue* (Bari Productions, 1998). The book and three-CD set entitled *Synagogue Song in America* (Jerusalem: Jason Aronson, 2000), by Cantor Joseph A. Levine, is an excellent compilation of essential synagogue chants and songs in musical notation in the text with accompanying recordings chanted by the author and other cantors.

Christianity

Christian religious music that is available to us begins with early Gregorian chant or plainchant. These are Latin settings from the Vulgate, mostly consisting of Psalms but also including canticles from the Old and New Testaments as well as hymns and other prayers. Richard L. Crocker's *An Introduction to Gregorian Chant* (New Haven, CT: Yale University Press, 2000) with accompanying CD provides a fine introduction to this tradition, with musical notation and accompanying examples chanted by the author and others. Prof. Crocker is also producing the entire Carolingian repertory of ninth-century chant, commonly known as Gregorian chant, as *A Gregorian Archive: Sound Recordings in a Study Edition*, sung by Richard L. Crocker (Berkeley, CA: Emeritus Press, 2001, 2004). Besides the best-selling CD *Chant* by the Benedictine Monks of Santo Domingo De Silos (Angel, 1994), there is *Gregorian Chant*, vols. 1 and 2, by Schola Cantorum (Sony Classics, 1995), which contains the five-part Mass and Mass for the Dead. The chant of Eastern Orthodoxy is well-presented on *Byzantine Liturgy of St. John Chrysostom*, sung by the Greek Byzantine Choir led by Lycourgos Angelopoulos (Paris: Opus 111, 2000), and on *The Liturgy of St. John Chrysostom* by Chorale Sofia (Harmonia Mundi, 2002). Russian Orthodox chant is found on *Russian Divine Liturgy*, sung by Novospassky Monastic Choir (Naxos, 2000). While the traditional Orthodox liturgy disallows instrumentation, several modern composers have attempted to set the Russian Orthodox liturgy in classical musical form, selections of which are found on *Sacred Treasures: Choral Masterworks of Russia* (Hearts of Space, 1998). The Protestant Reformation provided Calvinist psalmody, which is heard on *Psalms of the French Reformation* (Naxos, 1994). J.S. Bach's *St. John Passion* (Delta, 1993) and other works contain examples of Lutheran chorales. G.F. Handel's *Messiah* is the greatest religious work in English. There are innumerable polyphonic settings of the Roman Catholic Mass in Latin, from Machaut, Palestrina, Byrd, Tallis, Mozart, Haydn, Beethoven, Schubert, Gounod, Liszt, and Puccini, to Stravinsky. Beside settings of Marian antiphons and hymns, including the "Stabat Mater" and "Ave Maria," many classical composers have also set the Requiem Mass to music, from Ockeghem, Palestrina, Mozart, Cherubini, Berlioz, Gounod, Verdi, Von Suppe, Dvorak, Fauré, Duruffle, Rutter, and Britten, to Lloyd Webber. The Requiem masses illustrate how music has expressed the relationship of the living with the deceased in purgatory. Marian devotional music is found on *Ave Maria*, sung by The Benedictine Monks of Santo Domingo de Silos (Milan, 1995), *Salve Regina* (Naxos, 2000) by various artists, and *Ave Maris Stella: The Life of the Virgin Mary in Plainsong* (SONY, 1990) by Niederaltaicher Scholaren. Among the anthologies of favorite Christian hymns, there is *Hymns Triumphant* vols. 1 and 2, sung by the London Philharmonic Choir (Sparrow Records, 2002), and *100 Best Loved Hymns*. The latter is a three-CD set (Madacy Entertainment Group, 2001), that includes "Amazing Grace," "A Mighty Fortress," "Rock of Ages," "Holy, Holy, Holy," "Old Rugged Cross," and others. *The Rough Guide to Gospel* (World Music Network, 2002) includes key songs by various artists. *Best of New Orleans Gospel: Traditional Negro Spirituals*, sung by the Zion Harmonizers (Mardi Gras Records, 1992), contains many hymns of African

American experience. *Alleluia: An American Hymnal*, sung by the Kansas City Chorale (Nimbus, 1998) has Shaker hymns, sacred harp, and some Spirituals. For examples of the various Requiem Masses, there is *Requiem* (Naxos, 1999) by various artists. The series *Psalms from St. Paul's*, by St. Paul's Cathedral Choir (Hyperion, 2000), contains the complete Anglican psalmody.

Islam

There are very few commercial recordings of Qur'ānic chant available in the West. However, *Qur'ān Recitation*, vol. 10, in the series *The Music of Islam* (Celestial Harmonies, 1998), contains the Call to Prayer, the *al-Fātiḥa*, and several other sections of the Qur'ān chanted by accomplished reciters. The other volumes in this excellent seventeen-CD set, produced and recorded by David Parsons, contain various types of music representing the vast geographic expanse of Islam, including Egypt, Yemen, Turkey, Morocco, Tunisia, Iran, Pakistan, and Indonesia. Sufism as the mystical dimension of Islam has been the most conducive to the use of singing with music and instruments as means toward spiritual attainments. *The Rough Guide to Sufi Music* (World Music Network, 2001) contains a broad sampling of the diversity within Sufi music, covering Iran, Africa, Pakistan, Egypt, Morocco, Syria, and Turkey. *Music of the Whirling Dervishes* (Atlantic, 1987) presents authentic devotional music of the Mevlevi Sufis of Turkey. North African Islamic music is found in *The Rough Guide to the Music of North Africa* (World Music Network, 1997). For *qawwālī* music, there is *Pakistan: The Music of the Qawal* (UNESCO, 1990), as well as the superb recordings of Nusrat Fateh Ali Khan. *Hamza El Din: Music of Nubia* (Vanguard, 1964) presents Islamic-influenced songs of the Upper Nile region played with *ūd* accompaniment. The outstanding vocal renditions of Abida Parveen represent female *qawwālī* at its finest in *Songs of the Mystics* (Navras, 2000), and *The Best of Abida Parveen* (Shanachie, 1997).

Hinduism

Genuine Vedic chant is rarely available on modern recorded media. *Vedic Chanting* (New Delhi: T-Series, 1995), rendered by Sir Hariswami and Vedaparayanar, includes the famous "Purusha-Sūkta" hymn, as well as the Nārāyaṇa-Sūktam, Śrī-Sūktam, and Bhū-Sūktam prayers recited in traditional style. *Sengalipuram Anantharama Dikshithar* (Sanskrit Devotional) is an excellent CD of South Indian Hindu chants such as "Mahiṣāsura-Mardinī," "Ānanda-Lahirī," and "Āditya-Hridayam," originally recorded in the 1960s (HMV). A new series of chants is available from Music World International (based in Chennai, at www.musicworld 4u.com), including *Ganesh Sahasranam & Other Ganesh Stotras* (2001), *Shree Natraj Sahasranam & Other Natraj Stotras* (2001), and *Shree Sudarshan Stotranjali & Other Sudarshan Stotras* (2001). Also recommended from Music World is the *Vishnu Sahasranam and Bhaja Govindam* (n.d.) chanted by H.H. Kanchi Sankaracarya. *Ravi Shankar: Chants of India*, produced by George Harrison (Angel, 1997), has examples of traditional Vedic chant, the "Gāyatrī Mantra," *Bhagavad-Gītā* recitation, and other mantra chanting, but mixed with some modern instrumentation. There is also the CD *Religious Chants from India—Sikh, Buddhist, Hindu* (ARC Records, 1999), which has temple songs, *bhajans*, and a Baul song. The Kathakāli style (from Kerala) of musical dramatization of the great Hindu epics is found on *Le Mahābhārata: Musiques, chants et rythmes du Kathakāli* (Auvidis Ethnic, 1993), which has chanting of *Bhagavad-Gītā* verses, and *Le Rāmāyaṇa: Musiques, chants et rythmes du Kathakāli* (Auvidis Ethnic, 1993). *Ramnad Krishnan: Vidwan* (Elektra/Nonesuch Explorer Series, 1988) contains *kriti* devotional songs from the Carnatic (South) tradition. Another great Carnatic vocalist is heard on *The Mellifluous Maharajapuram Santhanam* (New Delhi, T-Series, 1992). For traditional Hindu *dhrupad*, there is *Dhrupad of Darbhanga: The Mallik Family* (VDE-Gallo, 2000), sung by Bidur Mallik and members of the Mallik family. An authentic recording of *Havelī Saṅgīt*, devotional music of the North Indian Puṣṭimārg or Vallabha Sampradāya, is found on the two-cassette *Krishna Leela Keertan* (HMV, 1993), sung by Pt. Askaran Sharma. There is also the more accessible *Praising Krishna: Ashtachap Poets*, by Purshotamdas Jalota (Audiorec, 1993), with full notes including texts and translations by literary scholar Rupert Snell. *Sacred Rāga* (STR Digital Records, 1999) by Guy Beck contains classical compositions and *bhajans* of the Hindustani (North) tradition. Devotional prayers from ISKCON (Hare Krishna Movement), including the famous "Hare Krishna" chant, are heard on *Hare Krishna Classics and Originals* by His Divine Grace A.C. Bhaktivedanta Swami Prabhupada (Bhaktivedanta Book Trust, 1994). For commercial religious songs and *bhajans*, there is *Aarties & Bhajans from Films* (New Delhi, T-Series, 1997), containing "Oṁ Jaya Jagadīsha Hari" and "Raghupati Rāghava Rāja Rām." Many of these and other famous *bhajans* sung by D.V. Paluskar, Omkarnath Thakur, M.S. Subbulakshmi, Hari Om Sharan, Lata Mangeshkar, and Asha Bhosle are found on *Bhakti Geet—The Golden Collection* (London: The Gramophone Company of India, 1997)

Sikhism

There are some excellent recordings of Guru Nānak's songs or *shabads* as well as other verses from the Sikh Ādi Granth or sacred scripture set to music. The famous *Japjī* and other prayers are found on *Japjī Sāhib* (New Delhi, T-Series, 1995), recited by Ragi Tirlochan Singh Ji, and the two-CD *Āsā Di Wār* (New Delhi, T-Series, 1997), contains morning prayers from the Ādi Granth sung by Bhai Ravinder Singh Ji from the Golden Temple in Amritsar. For good traditional Sikh *kīrtan* and *shabads*, there is *Har Kīrtan Sune Har Kīrtan Gaavai* (New Delhi, T-Series, 1999), sung by Bhai Nirmal Singh Ji, and *Sat Gur Bachan Tumhare*, sung by Bahi Harjinder Singh Ji (New Delhi, T-Series, 1998).

Buddhism

Chants and Music from Buddhist Temples (ARC Records, 2000) contains the Theravādin *Mangalacharanam, Trisaranam*, and "Recollection of the Three Treasures," as well as Buddhist music from Taiwan, China, India, Thailand, and Tibet. *Religious Chants from India—Sikh, Buddhist, Hindu* (ARC Records, 1999) contains the Theravādin "Jayamaṅgala Aṣṭagāthā," eight verses of benediction in Pali. *Sri Lanka: Musiques rituelles et religieuses* (Ocora Radio France, 1992) contains Theravāda chant from the Pali Canon, including *paritta* chant ("Set Pirit," "Mahā Pirita," *Mahā Mangal Sutta*) and the *Dhamma Chakka Sutta*, as well as Theravāda Buddhist temple music. The audiotape *Mahā Piritha* (Nugegoda, Sri Lanka: Ransilu Enterprises, n.d.) contains authentic renditions of the Theravādin *Mangalacharanam, Trisaranam*, the Five Precepts, "Recollection of the Three Treasures," and the "Mahā Piritha" chants. The audiotape *Santi Pirit*, produced by the Mahābodhi Society of Kolkata and the Jinaratana Memorial Trust, contains *Tisarana Vandana, Jayamaṅgala Gāthā, Ratana Sūtra*, and other Pirit texts. For Tibetan ritual music of the Gelugpa tradition, there is the three-part series recorded by David Parsons at the Dip Tse Chok Ling Monastery in Dharamsala: *Sacred Ceremonies: Ritual Music of Tibetan Buddhism*, vol. 1 (Fortuna Records, 1990), *Sacred Ceremonies 2: Tantric Hymns and Music of Tibetan Buddhism*, vol. 2 (Fortuna Records, 1992), and *Sacred Ceremonies*, vol. 3 (Celestial Harmonies, 1996). Vol. 2 of this series contains separate examples of the Tibetan ritual instruments with explanatory notes. For Nyingmapa traditional music, there is *Sacred Ritual Music of the Tibetan Monks* (Inner World, 2000), which includes chant and music for the Vajrasattva and Green Tāra rituals. A Tibetan ritual for the dead, chanted by fifty monks of Namgyal Monastery in Dharamsala, is heard on *Buddhist Chant 1: Buddhist Ceremony of the Goddess Palden Llamo* (JVC, 1996). *Buddhist Music of Tianjin* (Nimbus, 1994), contains Chinese Buddhist ensemble music, which is similar in style to older forms of imperial court music (Confucian and Taoist). *Buddhist Drums, Bell & Chants* (Lyrichord, 1994) contains two songs of *shōmyō* chanting and music from Pure Land, Zen, and Shingon rituals recorded at actual services in the temples of Kyoto, Japan. For the music of *Noh* drama and Japanese temple music, there is *Japanese Noh Music* (Lyrichord, 1993) and *Japanese Temple Music: Zen, Nembutsu, and Yamabushi Chants* (Lyrichord, 1980).

Website Resources

ARC Records (www.arcmusic.co.uk)
Elektra/Nonesuch Explorer Series (www.warner.com/nonesuch)
EMI Hemisphere (www.hemisphere-records.com)
Lyrichord (www.lyrichord.com)
Music of the Earth Collection from Multicultural Media (www.multicultural media.com)
Putumayo World Music (www.putumayo.com).

Rough Guide to World Music (www.worldmusic.net)
Rounder Records (www.rounder.com)
Shanachie/Yazoo (www.shanachie.com)
Smithsonian/Folkways (www.si.edu/folkways)
UNESCO Collection (www.unesco.org/culture/cdmusic)

INDEX

Page numbers in italics refer to illustrations.

SACRED SOUND

Experiencing music in world religions

CD track playlist

Judaism
TRACK

1 1st Question of Passover (ex 1)—*Sung by Joseph A. Levine*
2 High Holiday Prayer (ex 4)—*Sung by Joseph A. Levine*
3 Shema (ex 5)—*Sung by Joseph A. Levine*
4 Torah (ex 6)—*Sung by Joseph A. Levine*
5 Passover Haggadah (ex 7)—*Sung by Joseph A. Levine*
6 Night Prayer (ex 8)—*Sung by Joseph A. Levine*
7 Priestly Blessing (ex 9)—*Sung by Joseph A. Levine*

Christianity

8 Kyrie, Sanctus, Agnus Dei (ex 1)—*Sung by Richard L. Crocker*
9 A Mighty Fortress (ex 2)
10 Salve Regina (ex 3)—*Sung by Richard Crocker*
11 I'll Praise My Maker (ex 4)—*Sung by Gerald Hobbs*
12 Holy Holy Holy (ex 5)
13 All Things Bright and Beautiful (ex 6)—*Sung by Gerald Hobbs*
14 Amazing Grace (ex 7)

Islam

15 Call to Prayer: Adhān (ex 1)
16 Qur'ān: Al-Fātiha (ex 2)—*Recited by Hafiz Kani Karaca*
17 Ai Nasim e-ku-e (ex 3)—*Sung by Regula Qureshi*
18 Allāh Allāh Allāhu (ex 4)—*Sung by Regula Qureshi*
19 Mujrayi Shah (ex 5)—*Sung by Regula Qureshi*
20 Ai wa-e-nahr-e alquaman (ex 6)—*Sung by Regula Qureshi*

Hinduism

21 Gāyatrī Mantra (ex 1)—*Chanted by Guy L. Beck*
22 Rig Veda: Purusha Sūktam (ex 2)—*Chanted by Sri Hariswamy and Vedaparayanar*

Hinduism, *continued*
TRACK

23 Bhagavad Gītā 18.65–66 (ex 3)—*Chanted by Guy L. Beck*
24 Dhrupad: Dekho Sakhī Vrindābana (ex 4)—*Sung by Pandit Bidur Mallik and Family*
25 Padāvali Kīrtan: Śrī Nanda Nandana (ex 5)—*Sung by Guy L. Beck*
26 Bhajan of Sūr Dās: Aba Merī Rākho Lāja Hari (ex 6)—*Sung by Guy L. Beck*
27 Raghupati Rāghava (ex 8)—*Sung by Sonu Nigam*

Sikhism

28 Japjī Prayer (ex 1)—*Chanted by Ragi Bhai Tirlochan Singh Ji*
29 Shabad of Guru Arjan: Har Kirtan Sune (ex 2)—*Sung by Bhai Nirmal Singh Ji*
30 Shabad of Kabīr Har Kā Bilovanā (ex 3)—*Sung by Bhai Harjinder Singh Ji*
31 Kaisī Āratī Hoye (ex 4)—*Sung by Bhai Harbans Singh Ji*
32 So Dar (ex 5)—*Sung by Pashaura Singh*
33 Anand (ex 6)—*Sung by Pashaura Singh*

Buddhism

34 Drum Invocation
35 Invocation: Mangalacharanam, Three Gems: Trisaraṇam (ex 1)—*Chanted by Theravāda monks*
36 Five Precepts: Pañchaśīlā (ex 2)—*Chanted by Theravāda monks*
37 Four Noble Truths: Dhamma Chakka Sutta (ex 3)
38 Tibet Mantra: Oṁ Maṇi Padme Hūṁ (ex 5)—*Chanted by Tibetan monks of the Drepung Monastery*
39 Tibet Contour Chant (ex 6)—*Chanted by Tibetan monks of the Drepung Monastery*
40 Japanese Heart Sūtra: Hannya-Shingyo (ex 7)—*Chanted by women of the Jādá sect in Kyoto, Japan*

Please see pages 195–99 for details on each recording.